TAKING

THE BLINDSIDE

TAKING IT UP

THE BLINDSIDE

by
Jon Prichard

DCO BOOKS

Taking it up the Blindside
Copyright Jon Prichard, 2019
First Published 2019
DCO Books

This edition published 2019
by Proglen Trading Co., Ltd.
Bangkok Thailand
http://www.dco.co.th

ISBN 978-1-7940-2031-3

Cover design front and back by Ian Baker

Illustrations by Brian Rutherford

Dedication

This book is dedicated to the loving memory of our dear and sadly deceased buddy Andy Skelly and his surviving lovely wife Sue and their daughter Laura.

Andy Skelly RIP

"And there, in those words and in that silence, is the thing history does when you meet it halfway. It bends in on itself and folds away the run of years to touch the present, not with a cold hand but with the warm breath of a moment ago."

AA Gill. Towton

READERS COMMENTS

"I read it cos I was told it all about spreading seed and I was interested in any new crop rotation system...but it ain't...it's about fat perverts in Asia...don't buy it ...it's complete manure!" *Gardener's Apparel Weekly.*

"This book is not for everyone. Only a very small select group would be interested and of those a high percentage would be deranged, incarcerated, alone, divorced or in the hospital for Incurable Tropical Diseases." *HD Surgical Gloves Inc.*

"Fabulous, hilarious, a constant companion throughout Asia leading you to places never covered by the supposedly Five Star Tour operators." *Dr. Lars Hope Groin Clinic. Luzon.*

"Clearly a collection of short stories based firmly on the premise of... 'why let facts stand in the way of a good story !'" *Anonymous....that's also not me on page 208...lies !*

"As a work of fiction, it's right up there with the best...however, if it isn't and some of it may even be true then the writer and his filthy mates need to see a F$@&ing Doctor! " *Star Trekkie Club UK.*

"This expose is the first of its kind and I feel I stand on reasonably firm ground by saying...when his team mates get hold of this back-stabbing F#@&er there will be another volume but in the style of a posthumous autobiography! " *Proprietor: The Itchy Cat Inn. Manila.*

"I was particularly enthralled with the tale of the lady of the night with a bad cold administering 'relief' with her mouth and apparently breathing through her ears. Are there any further medical papers on this topic? " *Dr.Nyguen. ENT Dept. Saigon General.*

CONTENTS

Acknowledgements

There are numerous old rugby players, spectators, mates, fans and even whistle blowing officials who have stood in the bars these past months and kindly chipped in with their recollections on the events being discussed about each chapter. Well blow-me-off but their memories are so clouded and self-preserving that I have, for your benefit, ignored any facts that could possibly ruin a good rendition of what I recall.

I want to thank all of those mates who have really clarified events that I have only misty recall or indeed no recollection of at all other than I was there in body, because I've got the scars and the T shirt.

Guy Hollis has the memory of a herd of elephants and can recite dates, times, tour attendees, locations and heaps of mischief throughout the '90's like it was yesterday. Bruce Hill, the greatest Asian rugby tour organiser ever - was responsible for dragging me out of my mental-nadir-divorce-doldrums and back into the Bangkok rugby fraternity in the mid 1990's only to get me married and divorced again – cheers mate. Without Bruce, many of the tours would simply not have been affordable and thereby engaged so many players to come…repeatedly.

Bob Merrigan, again a chum with an enduring memory bank has offered stories from a non-playing-on-the-pitch perspective and acting as a sounding board, has given the thumbs up to some of the more-bawdy tales. He did suggest that I removed his real name from any of the stories…just in case.

On the production front, I must award a Gold Merit Star to Danny Speight my publisher, for his forbearance and teaching skills on the vagaries and generally unknown dark arts of publishing. A special mention must go to my hard-working editor Duncan Stearn down in Pattaya as he is suffering from not only my shocking syntax and spelling but also from cancer and he has battled both at the same time – a duty rarely inflicted on anyone!

Other chums in Bangkok who had offered extended boozy lunchtime advice, direction, spurious names and even some professional help would be; Colin Hastings, Roger Crutchley and Patrick Gauvain aka *Shrimp* – of calendar fame.

The embedded cartoons are supplied from my lifelong buddy Brian Rutherford, an accomplished graphic artist who gave it all up to get a proper job for his family and has now retired. We wiled away many hours in The Royal Oak in Wooton Rivers Wiltshire arguing over cartoon content and whether to get yet more KP nuts or have a proper meal. His thatched house is right next door to the thatched pub but the KP nuts won every time…oh and maybe the delightful barmaid pulling the pints.

The cover images come from Ian Baker a super cartoonist up in Sheffield, England and I thank him for turning my sketchy e-mailed ideas into delightful amusement. Whilst thanking those in England, I am forever grateful to all my old mates at Windsor RFC in particular: Rob MacDonald, Lindsay & Leslie Small, Tony O'Brien, Andy Skelly (RIP), Alan Davies (RIP), John Emmett (RIP), Bill Emmett, Ian Sams, Phil Meltzer, Judo-Jack, Martin Unsworth, *Chalky* White, Uncle Robin Platt and Jon & Andy Blythe and their lovely wives; Liz and Zhanna and all the others of course.

Thanks generally to all my playing and drinking mates whether they actually suggested ideas or were just there and who made all the mischief which contributed to me losing yet another house.

Cheers to the British Club mob throughout the years; Bruce Hill, Roddy Kerr, Vinno, Andy Talling, *Uncle Fester* Russ Coad, Julian Olds, Peter *Stitch* Hutton, Joe & Bea Grunwell, Pat Cotter, *Ratcatcher* Jimmy Howard, Dickie Barton, Ben and Gilli Knowles, Dickie's mate and Dickie's mate's wife, Paul Meggison, Ramsey McPhearson, Paul Gill, Sam Hagag, Taff, Nigel Wixey, Porky Parsons, Alex Stewart, Marco Belonje, Gille Bonadventure, Matt Minich, Mike Lamb, Peter Young, Alan Lovell, Andy Davies, Huw Butler, Eddie Evans, Gordon Ellard, Stephen Reece, Nick Moore, Alan Black, Simon Dakers, Keith

Acknowledgements

Rowley, Minkey, Trevor Day, Rusty Challon, Khun Prote, Khun Dakorn, Khun Yai, Dominic Whiting, Mike Pincock, Semi and Bulla Tui, Angus McKernan, Paul Smiddy in HK, Bevan Morrison, Roger and Judy Fitzgerald and all those I have forgotten.

And from the Rhino's RFC: Les Bird, Andy McRobbie, Giles Russel, Rick Fields, Paul Hoban (RIP), Vinno again, Billy Monkey, Andrew *G&T* McDowell, Chris *Hornibloke*, *The General* John Edwards and little Robbie Williams married to the Inky-Chinky (wife of many tattoos) and all the rest.

Our games and tours and tournaments would not have been possible without those wretched blokes in the middle with the whistle and a very heartfelt and warm thanks to them all at every match and tournament but most especially: David Viccars and John Kelly (UK), Grant Signal, Matt Oakley and all the Thai officials.

My loving thanks to my beautiful Lao wife Nang and our two new offspring Jessie and Nicky for their unbridled patience putting up with my disruptive in-the-mood-gotta-type-this-now behaviour. Late meals, disturbed sleep, no holidays and my tedious blank moments for about ...the whole of 2018.

Cheers,
Jon Prichard.
Bangkok. 2019

Escape Clause

As with all true tales of this nature, real names have been changed to protect the guilty and if I have inadvertently left in real names then I must put that down to forgetfulness, Alzheimer's or the fact that some grudges never die.

Seriously, these memories would be a shallow and worthless collection of pathetic scribblings without the spark of inspiration gained from the fabulous characters I have met and enjoyed playing with, sparring with, getting royally pished with and in many cases waking up with in the same bed...pillow in between!

If by some freak of coincidence or long term memory jogging, a suspicious wife eventually puts two and three together, makes seventeen and that spirals into a ghastly case of acrimonious divorce then for that I am sorry...highly unlikely I suspect as almost all these characters are already divorced by their own error or they are unfortunately dead and past that concern.

Club names, companies, hotels etc to which the tales are about have also in many cases been morphed into an option that would be less legally actionable, without I feel detracting too much from the valour the players exhibited in the name of those institutions.

So with as much sworn secrecy as MI5, the acquired twenty year prescribed limit on release and with the principles of Kim Philby, I lay down before you what I hope are short tales for reading on the bog, in the airport or in bed. I seek forgiveness only for the poor writing style and not the repetitious nature of much of the action, I for one giggle with every passing, fleeting memory...if you weren't ...you should have been there.

Jon Prichard.

GLOSSARY OF TERMS
(Helpfully, not in alphabetical order.)

Yes I know The Glossary should be at the back of the book after the Appendix IF one were following the normal protocols of publishing structure…but we ain't and on the basis that many people may not be fully familiar with some of the phases or rugby terms in this book the listing will give some insight…or possibly not?

Arsehole	Prop's greeting at first scrum.
The Referee	The bloke the Props are talking about.
The Whistle	Controlling equipment used incessantly by megalomaniacal small men. David Viccars excepted: He's a nice bloke.
The Scrum	Official linked body of men, bent almost double, with an opposing thrust motion, mandatory eye-bulging and gradual release of compressed air. Can result in exploding hooker.
Hooker	Bloke in the middle of the scrum with a greater density than Plutonium. Not to be confused with purchasable Beaver, usually in dollars.
Pished, Pished-up:	Friendly translation for *'pissed'* so the Yanks don't think there's a fight in the offing. There may be but this generally refers to excessive alcohol intake.
Pissed	Standard UK term for being drunk. Sometimes may involve damp trousers.
Drinking Piss	An unfortunate term, really meaning *drinking alcoholic beverages*. Apparently, some initiation ceremonies do demand

the real thing.

Trousered	Also meaning pissed or pished depending on which side of the Pond you are from.
Naked	Without clothes.
Naked again	Caught out again by rugby bar game: Mirror Man.
Whores	A derogatory and unacceptable terms for 'working girls, Ladies, OAP's in the trade.' If found in this book please score through.
Shag	Tabaco for Pipes.
A shag	Sexual intercourse. Sometimes followed by a pipe in bed. Affectionally known as a Brace of Shags.
Tits.	Complicated but usually the context will assist, ie: 'Gosh she's got big tits', 'He's just a stupid old tit', 'Marge have you fed the Tits the weather's closing- in don't yer know.'
Fanny	For Yanks it's only a woman's bum. Elsewhere on the planet it's a lot more involved.
Beaver	Most schools teach about this semi-aquatic, hard-working, industrious, hydro-engineering mammal - but for Yanks it's a lot more involved.
Tea, Cha, Cuppa	Hot beverage drunk by the World in various forms. Vietnamese morning tea with-bits-in is to be avoided at all costs.

Glossary

T Shirt	Yankee invention. Sleeved vest.
On the Toot	Out with yer mates guzzling booze.
Booze	Anything that helps make you dizzy by drinking it. *Stella* is in another category and normally involves sleeping overnight in The Grey Bar Hotel.
Mates	Blokes you go drinking with. Guys on the same team. After full time: The Opposition.
Mating	Not done with your Mates. See A shag.
Puke, Vomit	Natural gastric reaction to make room for more booze.
Pavement Pizza	Colourful street art. Can be slippery if walked on.
Bugga	Aussie expression used mostly in the form of a disappointment: 'Bugga...the Roo's are through the fence again!' and more recently: 'We've lost again to the Welsh...Bugga!'
Bugger	A term for a chum one hasn't seen for ages: 'Wilkins, you old bugger, where have you been?'
A Bugger	Chap who has no interest in Beaver and chases the chocolate star-fish.
Buggering	Colloquial expression used publicly in times of stress: 'Useless car jack! The buggering nuts just wont budge, bugger it!' (Now that's enough of that!)
A Corker!	Very pretty girl indeed. Unfortunately, inevitably above your pay grade.

Shite	A term slightly adjusted to reduce offense in the use of the actual word intended.
Shit-fight	Not actually using the implied material. An activity generally involving the two teams on the pitch in a *bit of biffo*.
Arm wrestle	Needs an opponent.
Mrs Palmer	Euphemism for one's hand (Mrs Palmer and her five sisters). Generally, a male pastime.
Strumming	A gesture and contact with the strings of a guitar…sometimes a girl's favourite when lonely.
G Spot	The optimum and central point on the tennis racket strings…or…the never-to-be-found-Grail.
Orgasm	A moment in time when every muscle in the body is tensed in unison. May involve some shouting, shrieking and scratches on one's back. If not experienced with the wife: wear pajamas for two weeks.
Multiple orgasms	Fiction.
White Line Fever	Not an illegal substance habit but usually exhibited by greedy, selfish backs with no chance to score. I blame the scrum half for giving them the ball in the first place.
Trouser snake	Unreliable appendage. Can cause pregnancy if used properly.
Fat Boy	A true mate and a member of the

Glossary

Scrum. During a game Fat Boys can become Backs in an emergency - the reverse use of players is a complete waste of time, laughable.

The Backs — A group of individuals with distinct aims and ambitions usually focused on self-gain and publicity. Fat Boys take them along to make up the numbers.

The Bench — As used in this book: refers to *compact* players not impact players.

The Sofa — Natural habitat of the trouser snake.

A Fridge — Chilling device for beer.

A frigid bird — Girl who works in an Aussie Bottle Store…apparently.

'Taking it up the blind-side' A ruse used by highly talented forwards and a compliant half-back, to take the ball as far away from one's own Backs as possible and at the same time confusing the opposition by running stupidly close to the touchline. Normally results in a Line-out. Not to be muddled with chasing the chocolate star-fish!

Line-out — Device for getting the ball back in play. Creators obviously never had to lift those fat bastard Locks themselves. Diabolical number of Laws surrounding this set piece.

A Punt — A bet on a nag.

The Punt — A ball hoofed up in the air with little regard for its destination or purpose. Backs use this to escape being tackled.

A drop kick	A useless individual.
The Drop Kick	The almost impossible human trick of dropping an oval ball on its end in muddy or stony ground and co-ordinating a running kicking motion at the same time. The purpose is to score three points in open play. Only attempted by selfish, glory seeking fly halves…oh and Zinzan Brooke. (He's a Fat Boy and therefore excused.)
The Post	Bangkok's best English-speaking newspaper.
The Posts	The things that Zinzan was aiming at. Also used by Forwards to re-orientate after a particularly long scrum or a hoof to the head.
Assistant Referees	No known adjectives can succinctly cover the use, purpose and promotion of these individuals.
The Sponge	The miraculous simple sea-squirt fabric used with water from The Bucket on tuckered-out Fat Boys.
The Final whistle	Sadly the end of the game but the joyful signal that 90% of the reason for playing rugby has just started.

*****

Preface

I think it is useful for me to explain the premise of this book so the various chapters make sense and characters tie-in to the time warp. There are various tales spanning the last thirty odd years that I have been resident in the Orient as well as a few old rugger tales from my playing years at Windsor RFC in the 1970s and '80s.

Not so complicated, you might say. But I have not *narrated* the stories in any planned or chronological order and so they jump about in time. Maybe that is confusing but really each chapter does stand alone on its own content.

The stories are generally about my time with the various rugby sides I have played with and the mischief they have encountered or been the architects thereof. There are a few stories that are the memories of other people's adventures, like my ex-wife's trek to Everest Base Camp – included for its energy, unlikely lifestyle achievement and the ghastly end.

I always wanted to work overseas, had travelled a lot as a youngster and my building qualifications generally allowed me to go anywhere. I accepted a two-year contract with a Hong Kong based company to become the number two to the MD, assisting him with their work in the-then colony. I was almost immediately posted to manage a large development in Phuket, Thailand. Despite having a Geography 'A' level under my belt, I was concerned that Thailand may still be building in bamboo as I reflected upon the *Tenko* series on UK TV.

That two-year contract has extended to this day as I fell deeply in love with Thailand and the Asian way of life. I cannot suggest my life has been a bed of roses and bliss, I have had some shocking times and very personal upsets but, and here's the real part, despite never winning lotteries or raffles, I have been, and continue to be, extremely lucky in life. With no personal regime of care and attention to my body, I have treated the old machine with total disrespect and ignorance and yet here it is still just chugging along…for a bit longer I hope.

The luck has come from the people I have met along the way: the colour, fun, mischief, love, friendship and memories of those times. Some of them are recorded herein so you can have a smirk and think 'wow, did that really happen? it sounds so very unlikely.' In other cases you may think, 'oh I did that too…and got away with it.'

The principal institutions of which I relate are generally based around my time and membership and captaincy of The British Club of Bangkok and being a minion in the Rhino's RFC.

There are various British Clubs dotted around the world and are all affiliated as well as being connected with other clubs in most countries. If you travel with the right prepared paperwork, your country of residence membership allows you entry to enjoy their inevitable sanctuary in the very centre of big cities.

These cities would be old Empire locations and also obvious ancient trading places. The Clubs have lots of ideal family and young and old sporting facilities, plus bars and restaurants offering subsidised food and beverages and of course a tranquil space in today's hectic lifestyle.

All transactions in the Club were by the member simply signing a chit for whatsoever was being consumed or used or booked and the filthy idea of money was never mentioned until the end of the month when the bill arrived. Hence no guest could ever pay for whatever was on offer and was truly a guest of the member. Some will brand that Imperialist nonsense but I loved it then, and I love it now.

At the BC in Bangkok there were, in 1991, sports sections covering soccer, tennis, squash, cricket, bridge and rugby. There were other non-team sports activities such as amateur dramatics, book clubs, video watching as well as kids activities.

On my arrival in 1991 the rugby section could have been likened to the Carlsberg Complaints Department, all dust, cobwebs and skeleton staff. I met up with Joe Grunwell, who was the big tool, in more ways than one, in resurrecting the rugby Phoenix from the dust.

All of our players were corporate managers and in the early 1990s there were few international schools and therefore few young, fit, skilled games masters on offer. This eased in the late '90s when work permits were not as rare as unicorns, but by then new clubs emerged with their preferred ethnic roots. The French and some Aussie lads formed the Corsaires RFC and not long after the Aussies and New Zealanders split again and formed The Southerners. So our team was composed of aging chaps from accountancy, stock markets, construction, insurance, financial services (very few of these bums) and even newspapers.

Joe was a quantity surveyor by training but working at that time as the Contracts Manager for a large oil and gas corporation on the Eastern Seaboard, and so in fact had lots of time on his hands. He fell headlong into training regimes, team formations, membership subscriptions, kit design, fixture cards and general committee works. A lot for one man you think, but no, Joe is from Yorkshire and so control, self-fame and clipboards were right up his alley.

Joe was 5'7" tall, stocky, balding but for a halo of still-dark locks around the shiny pate, aka *Slap Head* or just: Slap. He commanded respect for being the-guy-that-does-everything and this enabled him to always select himself as fly-half. More of that despotic democracy in the tales to come but it was Joe who drew myself and a selection of other old guys out of rugby retirement and formed a great playing side from 1991-1993.

With Joe's initial enthusiasm and then later taken on by Bruce Hill in the late '90s and first decade of 2000s, the BC toured throughout Asia and fought valiantly in the local Thai leagues and it is those tales I record in this book.

Many stories also relate to the Rhino's RFC which is a sort of reincarnation of an old and defunct side called the *Gentlemen of the East*. The Rhino's RFC is an invitational club that does require you to be proposed and vetted and then admitted to their hallowed halls.

Principally you needed to meet certain criteria: you should have played a high-to-representative standard of rugby, be over thirty-five years old, adequately funded and most importantly a good fellow who does not deteriorate into a rabid, fighting idiot after a few beers. Apart from age, how I got in, remains a mystery.

The Rhino's *modus operandi* was actually only to play twice a year. Once would be against the Hong Kong Police team at their Kowloon sports centre at the time of the Hong Kong 7's in late March and then a four to five-day tour in Asia at the beginning of June.

The players had probably originally been recruited from Hong Kong, many being ex-coppers; in fact an inordinate number of them are/were coppers. The rest were found from stray entrepreneurs, men who had married money, rugby clubs in the Colony and from the main Asian cities, Jakarta, Bangkok, Manila, Singapore and KL. These diverse locations then proposed key players from those cities and the Rhinos grew and did become a truly Asian club.

Various tales then provide more colour to characters cited and many key figures recur throughout the book with mild memory-jogging information to assist your enjoyment.

I provide no excuse or apology, for my style of writing which has brought grey hairs to my editor, but I hope I have told the stories in the same 'voice' I have recited in many a pub with wild arm gesticulations, rolling eyeballs and wholly incorrect accents. I have also pressed the boundaries of PC with some aged terms on nationalities, and stereotypes but I hope I have treated any religious issues with respect. I have enjoyed my life in Asia and have no racist corpuscles in my body so I hope again my allusions to coloured, black or Asian or white folk are taken in the spirit of mutual fun that they are meant.

I hope many of you see parallels with 'activities' you have also undertaken in your sports career...but could never mention.

Jon P

RUSSIA.

Japan

Ulaanbaatar

MONGOLIA.

Beijing

S.korea

CHINA

Shanghai

Tibet

NEPAL

Taiwan.

Hong Kong

Boracay Is.

Hanoi

INDIA.

BURMA

Lao

THAILAND

Manila

Bangkok

Saigon.

Samui

Phuket

MALAYSIA

Kuala Lumpur

SOUTH EAST ASIA.

INDONESIA

Jakarta

Bali.

----> FLight route from Phuket to Mongolia.

AUSTRALIA

16

FROMMELLING

"To the man who only has a hammer, everything he encounters begins to look like a nail." Abraham Maslow

The Rhino's RFC hidden committee had done it again and we were off to Ulaanbaatar in Mongolia, the primitive and completely undeveloped grasslands of Genghis Khan to play rugby against the local tribesmen. They had gone as far as picking a team that surely had never played rugby before, these guys should be a cinch.

We were a team with players based from cities and towns around Asia but over the seasons some in their careers had been forced further away, to Africa, the UK and, the really unlucky ones, to Australia. Wherever we were based, Ulaanbaatar was bloody miles from anywhere and as I looked at a copy of the world map my finger moved north from the verdant green pages of Bangkok into China's brownish green, moved north-east and across the vast expanse of the Sino provinces and on and on north through the yellow Gobi desert areas and there tucked in the very armpit of the semi-frozen Russian tundra was purple Mongolia.

I was living in Phuket at the time building extortionately expensive and outlandishly extravagant villas for wealthy blokes. One client, a multi-millionaire Swede, visited his recently purchased and completed villa designed to another person's specifications and decided he must change it all and instructed me to demolish just about everything except the RC frame, the roofs and outside patio with pool.

Now the villas on this development were easily the most profligate on Phuket's west coast, perched amongst mature trees and coconut palms on granite headlands, miles above the turquoise sea which would break on the rocks with a romantic, expensive sounding crashing far below. The villa was in fact designed as a sort of mini-village of beautiful timber and white rendered walls with intricate Thai-style roofed buildings, carved stone Naga statues grinning out through the foliage, with gardens between wings and hidden stepping-stone paths through luscious tropical greenery.

Numerous en-suites, fabulously furnished guest rooms, many I am sure forgotten in the undergrowth, and open patios that were more like Venetian piazzas were clustered around the jewel of a sunken pool with integral bar and Jacuzzi all set about with enough sun-bed loungers for the entire Horse Guards annual binge.

Just to give you a taste of the things money can do, one day, midway through the renovations, Bullion-Bjorn whilst visiting the site from Smorgersborge-ville, looked at me through the dust and cocked his head outside as an invitation for some clandestine chat. Imagine that lilting Scando-speak from the Muppet's Swedish Chef, he said, "I am now looking for a new pool, for me. I want a pool for my exercise, a laps pool you call them. I must swim every day and this pool here is no use. I want the new one… there."

We were standing on the edge of his cliff and I had my back to the drop and he had pointed over my shoulder and jabbed in the direction of the setting sun. I whirled round and sure enough he was pointing with the Macbeth witches' knuckled old hand at empty space.

"What?" was all I could manage. "Where?"

He didn't suffer fools easily, truly amazingly I was still employed, must remember to put that in my CV.

"There. Not so bad and hey there are no trees to cut down. Oh and it's gotta be at least twenty-five meters long, and no ugly columns eh."

"Sven," I panicked, always good to get the client's name right. "That's thin air and I would have to cantilever the whole bloody thing over the cliff, that's tonnes of concrete and water hanging in the air." I wailed.

One pale eyebrow was raised, which obviously was multi-millionaire speak for. "So?"

"Hahaha next you'll be wanting a spa massage bed underneath the pool with glass windows in the bottom of the pool itself?" I quipped and shivered.

"Oooh good idea Johann ...make it all happen eh."

And with that impossible task now set in thin air, he swept off to the land of Krona, Sweden. Well we did it in the end and there, suspended in the jungle, is a magnificently engineered hanging pool set about by broad leaved trees and tiled with hand-cut and crafted green marble from Indonesia, complete with weirdly perverse windows.

Mongolia beckoned half way thru and off I went for a five-day trip.

*

My flight alone was a nightmare and entailed driving my car to the airport and leaving it in the long-stay carpark at \$5.0M per minute and then flights: Phuket to Bangkok, a three-hour wait for a connection from Bangkok to Hong Kong to meet the team and thence to Beijing and a six-hour wait there and then over the Gobi desert to Ulaanbaatar.

My Quebecoise Canadian buddy Joel Gauderault, who in 2016 visited Ulaanbaatar for meetings to establish mining opportunities, assured me Ulaanbaatar was no longer the old Bolshevik-style grey, cobble-stoned square, ancient and backward city we had been to in 2001 I had described to him. Today Ulaanbaatar is a fabulous example of how much money China's Politburo can pour into a country to ensure future business and extremely profitable unique access to the massively rich and varied natural minerals and gas reserves in the wastelands populated only by tribesmen, their Yurts and ponies.

The city when we went there was, as I mentioned to Joel, a collection of grey buildings in stucco grey, with ornamental official buildings in grey, grey roads, huddled locals in grey shawls and the only colour in the whole urban drab came from the solitary set of traffic lights in the grey town square. Our hotel even had grey sheets on the bed.

On the Saturday, our coach dropped us at the sports ground, which was an assemblage of numerous facilities, tennis courts, track and field and discus nets all clustered around a peeling white-painted club house of fusion stock not knowing if it's skinny Corinthian columns and Vatican glazed domes really matched the modern cheap aluminium sliding doors and windows.

It was then revealed to us, that far from playing some small people without their ponies, we were to play the national team and their Olympic Selection Committee were to arrive and watch the match and attend upon us in the evening for a post-match dinner.

We changed and took to the field without any sight of the opposition and we were led out under an overcast sky but calm day to the rugby pitch. This proved to be a small, to very small-sized pitch of artificial grass surrounded by a high boundary of tennis chain-link fencing and very little space between the pitch edge and that fence line.

Artificial pitch in Ulaanbaatar you ask? They didn't even have this at the Hong Kong Football Club. Well the reason was that this was obviously the first, very first ever Russian-fabricated prototype of artificial grass and we suspected it must have been used only for sporting events like chess or backgammon because to even roll over and lie down on it generally took off a few inches of skin.....oooh this match was going to hurt.

The national team took the field and we inspected each one to see which was our opposite number, or at least tried to distinguish forwards from backs, a difficult task even for a qualified anthropologist. Including the subs standing on the sidelines they were all, to a man, about 5'7" tall, hugely muscled in the shoulder, bulging thighs and with those characteristic Mongol expressionless faces, their eyes like slits against either blazing sun or blinding snow and they walked with a threatening gait and hands opening and closing like carpenter's workbench vices.

Someone kicked-off and that's about it in terms of rugby, because it was like a bar fight from the moment the whistle's pea stopped spinning until half time. What became apparent was that we had wildly underestimated the local team's store of testosterone and chauvinistic intent as to which of their XV on the pitch was the *Alpha male*, bugger, they were all vying for the title.

In the scrums and mauls and rucks and lineouts those grasping powerful hands were a menace to deal with, but ball we did win and quickly spun it out to our backs where we figured our long-legged giraffes would outpace those genetically modified turkeys on the wide outside. Again our homework was sadly prepared because they evidently had no intention of chasing the ball all day on the wide outside…they would bring the ball to them by a ruthless scheme of systematic elimination. Even elementary investigation by our committee would have uncovered that THE Mongol national sport was …wrestling.

Not that wrestling crap on TV, but wrestling with a capital 'W'. When each of our backs passed the ball, Genghis didn't watch its flight even with his peripheral vision, he simply grabbed the last passing player, bear-hugged the air out of him and then in a death-throw clinch he would arch his back and pile drive our player's head into the unforgiving plastic carpet. Well thank fuck I was a slow-moving forward was all I could muster, as yet another three or four of our backs lay, well, on their backs, with the odd one still embedded in the shagpile. This went on for the requisite 40 minutes and then the whistle blew for half time.

The wind had picked up during the first half and there was now quite a stiff cold evening breeze blowing as we tucked into water and traditional orange slices. Then the Governor, or Mayor or the President arrived and an array of gilded, high backed, armchairs were placed in line on the side of their 22 and the dignitaries took their places and there proceeded the most bizarre parade of Circus folk, local cultural figures and costumes and two girls in leotards who could and did, tie themselves in knots…backwards.

This halftime televised show took another thirty-five minutes and then five more minutes to clear the Vatican's furniture and we were off again in the wrestling ring of neck-breaking tackles. Suffice to say that, by guile, use of those surviving long legs and a continuous stream of penalties and successful kicks we did win the day. Roddy Kerr, our heroic scrum half and corner-of-the-field tackler, only weighed about 79kgs when he went on but he must have left 4kgs of epidermis on that ghastly plastic field. We all came off with stinging *grass* burns, broken fingers, sore or bent necks but we had beaten the national squad and that was a first for our club.

Manly but pathetic yelps of pain in the showers ensued as we were advised by our travelling (unqualified) medic that we must wash and scrub those grazes with soap. So, wishing we had brought our shorts, which we had not, we staggered, open-legged like a file of Egyptian Mummies from the changing rooms to the dining area with those weeping sores already sticking firmly to the inside of our trousers.

A youthful Roddy Kerr before elbow and knee skin loss

The dining space was a well-lit white room with those delightful aluminium patio doors allowing in the last rays of tundra sunlight. Trestle tables, seating ten, were set about the room with a long, slightly elevated podium for top table and seats for about twenty, which was to be for their Olympic officials, that Mayor/President bloke and our Club toffs. The room was a polygon of faceted sides, another remarkable fusion of ghastly interior design with half-sunken Greek columns, floor-to-ceiling mirrors and hidden doorways.

Our opposition were already in their places which allowed for a clear mix of us and them on each table. We looked distinctly shabby compared to the extremely well-dressed Mongolian players – again to a man: they had shiny, black leather trousers, belt buckles any Hell's Angel would have given his gearbox for, immaculately pressed and open-chested, brilliant white shirts and gold medallions any respectable 'A' Team would have envied.

They nodded, dutifully and respectfully shook hands and passed around beer cans to all of us and a few could speak some words in English, mostly based around, "DRINK NOW...WE DRINK NOW!"

And so the dinner got underway with various fabulous Mongolian stews and meats, flat breads and more meats, mashed swede or some form of squash and beer. Andy McRubble, our multi-purpose Scottish flanker, had coincidentally recently opened a Mongolian Restaurant in Glasgow, which, in the nature of wild and incredibly stupid ideas, had turned into an amazing success story and beloved by all in that recently-crowned City of Culture.

Every toast, and they were legion, was bookended with clasping male bonding hugs and sometimes a wet slobbery kiss on the cheek. Top Table were slightly more refined but after the TV cameras were expelled from the room, they too got into hugs and snogging.

Beer was clearly their staple and they were great hosts. From our midst, however, stepped forth our tour hero. An unlikely beast, a South African prop named Ronny Rutland. This was not an ancient wing-forward who had gradually gravitated to the front row, no this was a twenty-seven year-old boy who had come out of the womb as a prop. Balding, but for some short golden curls around where his ears would have been if he had been normal, stocky, thickset and whilst schizophrenic on the pitch, he was the softest, nicest, grinning bloke after any game.

Ron had been to Stellenbosch University and there he had either invented or championed all comers in *Frommelling*.

What is Frommelling?

Well, we Rhinos had all undertaken numerous courses and tour tests and become tolerably proficient in this 'sport' for a few years now and figured we, as a team were good at it, good enough to challenge the Mongol horde.

Despite being from the Cape coastal regions, Ronny preferred to think he had been on the Great Trek himself and spoke English with the gravest and hardest Afrikaans' accent he could muster.

Ron explained to a two-tiered circle of avid, smoking, slurping, burping and farting Mongols thusly:

"Fuurm unto grrupps oh feir, naar teams you warts, every mhann fuur heeself and the last baaarstard standing is a Doos !"......which roughly translated meant: "Form into groups of four, there are no teams as such old boy, so it's every man for himself and it's just the last one left in is the *loser.*"

We all dutifully shuffled into groups of four, equally divided with Rhinos and elegantly clad Tribesmen.

"Earveywaan then graab a bheer and holding thunn like this .....you smash it zo!....You buuurst the can, you wuun and leaf the game."

Grab a can of unopened beer, hold it sideways to your face and smash it into your forehead. You only get one smash at a time as the game goes round the circle of four. It should burst on say the third hit and you can sit down licking the dribble off your face, proud in the knowledge that you had achieved a manly game of Frommell. One round of course followed another, which followed another.

In all the excitement of meeting our new chums and hosing beer none of us had noticed two things: Firstly, any all-male sport that requires an immense store of profound stupidity and courage was bread and butter to our leather-trousered mates and secondly, the local brewery had not yet heard of aluminium light-weight cans and we were drinking out of traditional seam-welded, steel-capped tins. This had the very undesirable habit, if you were slightly off-aim with the rapidly advancing can, of catching that uncrushable steel rim and opening up your tightly-bound scalp. The cans were actually almost indestructible and would take about 10,000 smashes to win.

There followed the most expansive game of thoroughly competitive Frommelling ever conducted with bursting cans and split foreheads gushing fizzy claret about the table like some Inca sacrificial event. There were whelps and screams of joy from anyone 'going out' and more hugs from those still in, despite horrific facial damage.

Then an official from the Olympic Committee stood up and, calling for quiet as he had something to say, which despite his high status in Mongolian society, took some time to achieve.

With a grave face and a rumbling growl he pointed at two blood-stained and still-seeping locals who had been brought forward by their comrades and he admonished them in perfect English.

"**YOU have brought Mongolia shame and dishonour. You have been caught cheating!**"

"Eeerr…how ??" was the collective but silent thought passing through all bruised Rhino heads.

"You have been practicing Frommeling in the Ladies Toilet on your own, DISCRACEFUL!..now go and stand in the corner."

And with that bewildering command in the almost circular room, the two miscreants shuffled with bowed heads and stood by the wall. They stayed there all evening.

"**CONTINUE MY FRIENDS !!**" and with that Kublai Khan sat.

The next day, after a continuing late-night beer festival and a long stay in the Marco Polo Night Club, we all arrived at breakfast at the agreed time. A pre-requisite of any Rugby Club's touring is that whatever you have done or not done, pissed, no sleep or suffering from dementia, breakfast was a Holy writ and must be attended.

Sunday was AGM time and Rhino tradition held that it needed to be organised over water and was always a fabulous event of tour courtroom fines and drinking and a totally spurious involvement of the players in choosing where we would tour next year. Options on destinations were always offered by the invisible committee and we would all gleefully vote democratically. In true despotic Mugabe-style any such findings would be tossed out of the window and the committee would decide what they wanted for next year, but we felt we had been involved. (Note to Ed. *Dr.Robert has been deposed, should I change the reference to a tyrant still standing?*)

Sadly I was not to partake. Your mobile phone may not work even between rooms in a First World nation but mine rang bright and clear across the vast expanse of China's rice belt and the Gobi desert without a glitch and on the end was Bloody-Bjorn demanding I return to Phuket immediately.

Well, I didn't get to see the Yurts or the unending sea of grasslands, or McRubble getting an arrow embedded in his back from a Mongol bow fired not-accidentally-on-purpose by our

Chancellor, nor too the AGM but we had beaten the national side and survived a serious frommelling with only minor scars to tell our grandchildren.

*****

Post Script:
My good intentions to return by Monday morning were in fact thwarted and I transcribe the e-mail I sent to the Team when I finally reached home:

"Glad to hear that you all survived and I was sorry to leave when I did (Sunday morning) cos:

Apart from not leaving UB until midnight that Sunday evening (flight delayed by 15 hours) we landed in Beijing and went to an hotel at 02.00hrs for a 4 hour kip and then to airport only for my flight to BKK to be delayed until 20.35hrs that Monday night and so…missed the flight from BKK to Phuket which arrived at the island but couldn't land cos of winds. Returned to BKK with 2 hrs on the ground and then took off again and landed in Phuket at 2.30pm TUESDAY to find that my car had a flat tyre and a flat battery IN THE POURING RAIN!!

Got home at 3.30pm…that's more time than I had on fcuking tour!!"

AFRICA.

D.P. CONGO.

UGANDA.

KENYA.

SOMALIA.

Lake Vio.

TANZANIA.

ANGOLA.

MOSAMBIQUE.

ZAMBIA.

MADAGASCAR.

NAMIBIA.

ZIMBABWE.

BOTSWANA.

ATLANTIC OCEAN.

Johannesburg

SOUTH AFRICA.

Durban

INDIAN OCEAN

Cape Town

RHINO'S RFC 2000 TOUR.

28

MILLENNIUM TOUR

"Do not look where you fell, but where you slipped." African proverb

Now, you may recall from the earlier story the strictly invitational nature of the membership to the Asian Rhino's RFC. The original concept of the Rhino's RFC had an embryonic genesis as *The Gentlemen of the East* but I am advised the base principles waned or were abused and it fizzled out only to rise again as The Rhino's we know today.

It was conceived and nominally based in Hong Kong. Now however, it has a new wider, broader base of players who had either migrated from Honkers or indeed were selected from far-flung regions of the Orient. This was a boon to healthy population growth but of course such procreation must strictly adhere to *membership proposal procedures*, meaning that there were checks and balances on the players introduced, such that there were no lunatics or pathological murderers who popped out of the woodwork after a few beers in foreign climes.

Players had to have played 'representative rugby' (this originally meant a *standard* equivalent to playing for the Hong Kong Colony in the 1980's and early 1990's). Many, and certainly I, had no such qualifications, but one would be admitted on some other quality to bolster any flagging rugby expertise. Mine were incessant talking, law enforcement and prosecution in the tour court.

Anyway, as with all rugby clubs there are normally some 98% of the club membership who have no drive, wish, ability or actually any knowledge of the club's administration or the gears and cogs that organise the functioning and annual budgets, planning and the like, to the extent that many even came on tour with no kit at all - the dopey, useless tossers.

This clueless and ignorant mass are so well represented by George Orwell as the general farm animals and then there is the Politburo, clearly and cleverly represented by the pigs on the farm. You will have heard or read somewhere *"all pigs are created equal...but some pigs are more equal than others."*

And herein lies the enigma wrapped in a paradox of the truly expressed democracy of the Rhino's RFC, that in fact the remaining 2% makes up the 'Invisible Committee' (IC) (herein read; Pigs) and it is they who hold all the cards and pull all the strings and twist and manipulate the wishes of the great unwashed (quite literally in the case of some players), and thank God for that or we wouldn't go anywhere.

The committee has not, you understand, been 'elected' *per se* but formed by the 2% themselves and to prevent any accusations or possible recriminations, they prefer to remain as an unknown and unnamed cabal. Hence the term 'invisible' best suits these clandestine, self-serving commanders.

Anyway one of the items on every year's AGM held (always over water, so generally on a boat or remote island) on the Sunday of every June tour would be, Item 17. b) iii. *Where shall we tour next year?*

As you can imagine, this serious decision cannot be left to the great mass of moronic beefcake thugs that actually play the game but they do need to appear to have been consulted and take comfort in the due process of putting their hands in the air when a vote for each destination is called out. Even raising a hand can cause some serious work anxiety with some players.

The committee will have done some research (as we know from past experience this is normally undertaken by the Insp. Cousteau of the group and it will be flawed and bungled and fudged from incorrect data leading to misleading advice to the Politburo).

Three or four or even five alternative destinations for next year's tour will be offered to the Floor of the Chamber (ie: top deck of rickety, cheaply-hired, Vietnamese-made tugboat) and votes will be called and counted. As you all know the assembled congregation will have been instructed that they can only ever have ONE vote per destination and only raise ONE hand when they do decide.

These rules are clearly and intentionally, or more likely unintentionally, flaunted by the shear stupidity of the members and as such the statistics produced can be confusing. Out of a total AGM attendance of say forty members we could have:

Tour Destinations	Votes
Hanoi, Vietnam	10
Brisbane, NT.	Where? OZ.. fffaaak off.
Manila, Philippines	78
Goa, India	Ffffaaaak right off you twats.
Phuket, Thailand.	78.5

And so, the data will be welcomed by the Committee Secretary who then assures the Chairman all is accounted for, the Chairman announces that the fair and democratic tools of the Club have once again prevailed and The Destination for next year will be announced shortly after a final double-check-count-back has been undertaken by the reliable and honest figure of the Club Secretary.

The voting results are of course immediately binned and the Committee decide where they want us to go next year.

Now in 1999 at the AGM, a wholly new and seriously worrying thread appeared and that was that the IC, having considered just in time that next year was a new Millennium, we should tour somewhere special, somewhere we had never been before but we imagined with the same basic principles of wholly inept and incapable opposition, cheap beers and comely, cheap hookers. But for 2000 it had to be super special and a memorable place and also a coloured feather in the cap of Club historical annals. That was the worrying thread.

And so as options were presented on 4th June 1999, the hands waved unsteadily up and quickly down *like gypsies in the Job Centre* (Honey-badger expression), until the final destination was read out for the vote.

"The final tour destination is, and here we can confirm enquires have been made with a local club and they have responded enthusiastically…is…Cape Town, South Africa."

Well fuck!!!...there was complete stunned and unmoving silence from the mass of sunburnt faces staring at the Top Table. No one moved at all for many seconds and then chaos ensued with Loki running amok amongst the barely working synapses of every fizzing player's brain.

The one key tenet that they had held so dear when joining the Rhino's, was that the opposition HAD to be pathetically bad and useless and beatable but now Tour 2000 was presented as being, not the Springboks themselves, but all the nasty, dangerous, huge-to-massive, eye gouging, expert South African army trained, thugs that **didn't** make selection!

Uproar and genuine girly screaming ensued, food would have been tossed if it weren't for the fact that Rhino's never have any spare and it took many minutes before the tumult could be quenched to such a degree that a vote could be counted.

Not one hand even quivered from where they were all being sat upon by their owners when SA was put for the vote.

*

It came to pass on that Thursday afternoon, as the Malaysian Airways Flight MH 213 touched down in Johannesburg, this first group of arriving tourists from Bangkok and Singapore stumbled unbelieving up the air bridge to stand quaking on Terra-Africa. Never in their wildest dreams at thirty-eight to forty-five and more years old, did they even vaguely believe they would be playing rugby, full contact rugby, in South Africa. Many player's wives had copies of their dear husband's Last Will and Testament already held firmly in the grasp of the family lawyer as they said goodbye.

We then flew on a domestic airline to Cape Town and caught the pre-arranged coach to the ultra-modern hotel nestled lovingly in the bosom of the Victoria & Alfred waterfront area. Actually, the coach was a hired vehicle with a driver and tour guide and belonged to the Western Stormers and had their name and logos splashed all along the flanks.

It was planned that Thursday was the main influx of mates and one last early morning flight arriving on Friday would see all of the tourists assembled in one place and able to bond and enjoy their last days alive together before the match on Saturday.

One of my other almost self-appointed duties was to design, gain approval and then have made, some three thousand small 4" circular stickers with the Rhino head logo and tour date and destination. These were a creation that most Asian rugby sides make to advertise their club by sticking to bar toilet walls, chrome poles and dancing girl's tits and bums.

I had succeeded in my mission and the stickers looked great and we discovered early on that the sticky backed goo to adhere them to whichever surface was chosen was almost Araldite in its ability to 'once-stuck-will-never-come-off'. This was proven by the massive array of stickers throughout KLIA (Kuala Lumpur) airport that stayed stuck from 2000 until about 2005. There is still one today on the high-cab roof of the glass lift near Burger King.

Cape Town airport is a clone of all new modern airports with steel and aluminium glass panels everywhere except that, probably due to the short-sighted and bovine nature of the average Afrikaaner, the authorities had decided to put bright yellow circular stickers on any glass panels at hip height so that no-one could walk into these hazards. Amazingly they were exactly 4" and matched our predominantly yellow Rhino badges. So it was that our group had multi-handedly adhered stickers to all the official yellow dots from air-bridge to the taxi ranks, even including the automatic-opening double doors (the timing and activation of which were bloody tricky to co-ordinate and could not be attempted by any member of the front row).

On Friday morning, it was with some joy and barely stifled giggling, that we were dropped by the famously decorated coach at the Cape Town Airport Arrivals area and stood watching a platoon of khaki clad, crew cut airport employees vigorously scrubbing and scratching our stickers from the entry doors and surrounding glazing.

We were there to collect, not some last-minute hangers-on tourists, but our actual chief Club Toffs who had chosen to fly together and ignore the presidential OP on never having all senior officials on the same flight.

These distinguished figures were none other than:

Les Bird; Club President and Ex-Chief Inspector of the Royal Hong Kong Police, 'ex' on account of the colony being handed over on 1st July 1997 and he was offered early retirement and with the speed of Fagin, he grabbed his gold watch and scarpered to his clifftop home 'The Eyrie' in Phuket. (note; Bird....home = Eyrie). Les joins absolutely all Rhino tours. His ashes will attend all tours after he has snuffed it. Not a member of the IC...maybe.

Giles Russell: Aide-de-Camp to Chris Patten, the 28th and last Governor of Hong Kong (and by coincidence MP to my home town constituency of Weybridge in Surrey) and he too had been discharged on a healthy whack after doing fuck-all for many years in the post. Giles's 5'6" frame promptly donned the mantle of entrepreneur with his winnings and opened a 'T' shirt and sundry garment factory in SA which, owing to a complete lack of commercial acumen, rapidly and sadly spiraled into decay and financial administration. His confidence, rigid British spine and sense of fair play have allowed Giles to maintain his wit and repartee even as Rome burns around him.

Vincent Swift: A master entrepreneur of considerable wisdom and training, educated at Oxford from a humble Gaelic background, a self-made millionaire and rugby-club-philanthropist (one who spends his cash on worthwhile rugby celebrity dinners at his own highly successful restaurant in Soi Thania Plaza near

Patpong, and annual Rhino tours). Known for his Martian stare and rather abstract wit. Absolutely not a member of the Invisible Committee...maybe.

Andrew Mc Dowell: Of New Zealand descent apparently. Now ex-senior manager of a German pharmaceuticals corp, a leading drugs, sorry medicine manufacturer and self-taught home-clinic using those very drugs for any 'extra-curricular' afflictions or those odd rashes in the groinal area. A trusted and respected member of the Club's medical team (pax 1) for any of the young lads who may be so afflicted with 'jungle itch'. Mc.D, was and is, also partial to the odd G&T.

It was with pride and much cheer that we welcomed our venerable elders as they staggered, arm-in-arm for mutual support more than comradeship, through the last Indiana Jones-like challenge of the auto-doors. These captains of industry and commanders of legions were all dressed in suitably smart lightweight cotton cream and pale blue shirts with matching pale or tropical white trousers with polished brown belts.

The effect was only slightly spoilt by the fact that each and every one of the first three were splattered and soaked in spilt Claret from chin to lower groin. Apparently, a bad case of turbulence just as the 11th, 15th, 18th and 19th refills were being obligingly provided in business class. Al Capone's worst enemies' bullet ridden bodies lying in the Chicago gutters did not look so thoroughly blooded.

And so, with much handshaking and arms-length embracing we gathered up our toffs and their baggage from the helpful local bag operative and headed for the bus.

Our progress was only halted when a tall, blond trooper burst through the final doors and shouted, "Oye!...I think thuus Doos is also with you!"

The automatic doors opened once again and four huge, beefy clones of the Aryan staggered through, each holding a leg or an arm between them. With head lolling backwards and bouncing uncared for on the airport tiled floor, was a giant, recently shot, game trophy Impala in the form of Andrew McDowell. The lads, with true military precision, let go of their offending limb at the same time and gravity delivered Andrew the last rather violent 8" onto African soil. It would seem that Gordon's Gin was also served on that flight.

Once aboard the team coach it was announced that we would visit the Victoria & Alfred Waterfront and could browse and buy trinkets from the local arts and crafts stalls throughout the refurbished East India Company's old warehouses. Before the back-of-the-bus wail of expletives announced some reluctance to this idea, the MC noted there were numerous well-stocked bars and fish'n chip shops there too.

The MC was one Dai Lewis, a scrum-half of redoubtable fame from one of the Rugby Clubs of Cardiff, Llanelli or Cearphilly Cheese who had played alongside the celebrated Gareth Edwards, but mostly sat warming the great man's bench. He had come to Cape Town some time it seemed after the Second Boer War and now sadly had galloping arthritis in both hands, which were gnarled and crumpled appendages, but could still grasp a pint.

Jimmy Howard and I sat near Dai at the front of the bus and in a short time became mates as amazing tales were exchanged between those ancient warriors. Dai insisted that after the lunch break wander around V&A, we must go to his personal watering hole, The Olympic Club. It was the only remaining Men Only bar still surviving the feminist scourge of *equal access* on the whole of the African continent. Soon, he said sadly, it would be no more, as a club resolution had already been debated that would see this venerable space open to all.

It was clear that most married or players with partners were on a promise to bring back something from Africa as a present and so we did positively wander the stalls of beads, impala skin rugs, drums, silver jewelry and multi-coloured garments which filled the huge warehouses, with the lads soon burgeoned with plastic bags of local tat.

The trip continued to be blue skies and blazing sunshine all day, most unusual apparently for this was mid-winter for the city in the southern Hemisphere.

Dai led us to a famous fish'n chip restaurant right on the marina edge, a modern Sydney-harbouresque venue with fully opened folding, glazed doors on a timber boardwalk, picnic-style tables and first-rate prompt service. We guzzled Castle beers and burped through the battered seafood until about 4.00pm.

The coach took the main troop of baboons back to the hotel or further sightseeing but without Dai. Dai, *Ratcatcher* Howard and I caught a taxi to the Olympic Club.

In a cool suburb and down a tree-lined avenue of long-established acacias we turned through the green-painted, wrought-iron gates of the club and there before us was a series of single-storey buildings with surrounding squash courts, open sunny swimming pools for adults and kids alike and tennis courts stretching away to Kenya.

We were dropped at the main building and stepped from the bright heat of the day into the musky entrance hall with its two-hundred-year-old polished quarry tile floors, walls festooned with sepia team photographs of long-dead mates and dim five-watt ceiling lights poking through a quaint nicotine-like-stained ceiling.

We walked passed shadowy uninhabited function rooms, toilets and back of house doorways and eventually Dai waved us ceremoniously into the Men Only Bar.

This too was equally dimly-lit with exposed red-brick walls and white-aged pointing. Persian rugs and green leather-topped bar stools aligned the hundred foot long bar on the right-hand side. The bar was facing a fabulous Inglenook fireplace some ten feet wide set about with 1940's RAF deep-bedded, pitted and slightly-torn, leather armchairs and magazine racks all enclosed within a charming two-foot high white-painted picket fence.

The bar was a joy to behold and the pristine mirrored rear wall shelves were full of every alcoholic beverage made before and since the Zulu Wars. There were three uniformed, white, lady bar staff and a range of hand-pulled beer taps and others beaded with perspiration. Freezing Castle on tap.

There were only two or three old guys there in the bar sipping quietly on their brandies or pink gins. Three pints of cold Castle appeared by magic and Dai waved away our cash and signed a chit. *FREE ice cold Castle*…Rats and I were loving the Olympic Club more with every heartbeat.

The ancient customary basis of the Men Only status, was just so that the men of the club could, after work or at weekends, relax in their manners and language without any rude expletives upsetting the fairer sex or the kids. So, as I discretely nodded to the ladies behind the bar, my silent enquiry was answered by Dai.

"Don't worry about these daft old birds, they have heard and used worse language than you have even known and have forgotten more."

"Yeah, don't mind us Sir, nuffin' could shock us." said Doris #1, seemingly from Wapping.

All this whilst cleaning a pint glass with a clean bar cloth in her hand and I really was waiting for her to spit in it and hold it up to the dim bulb over the bar with a wistful 'faak it' on her lips.

The beers flowed and Dai came out with endless fabulous old tales of Welsh mischief and Cape Town histories and games at Hamilton's, not one was boring and all leaving us wet eyed and cramped with laughter. His old bar mates crowded around and joining our laager (ho ho), offered even more yarns.

There was a lull in the laughter and Dai and Rats waddled off to the gents and I glanced about and wandered over to the Inglenook fireplace, leaning on the mantle piece like some old fighter pilot with his pipe. I grabbed a magazine and disappeared into the depths of one of the cavernous leather armchairs, wallowing in hippo delight at the sensation, musty smells and provocative memories such a haven exhibited.

I was awoken from my reverie by an urgent, speechless and very worried returning Dai who, with mangled hands, hauled me from the seat and propelled me back to the bar.

"Fookin' fook Jonny Boyo don't ever go in there, see!" he squealed and indeed the other old blokes had startled and worried looks on their faces.

"I am so sorry, have I broken any rules of the club?" I pleaded, all contrite and apologetic.

"No, no, no, no," mumbled Dai, "Nothing like that boyo but I'm afraid that whole area is known as the Departure Lounge, see" he muttered in a mystical manner.

"Urrgh?" I offered.

Dai leaned in towards Rats and I and whispered in almost forgotten valley-speak, "That's whurr the old boys go, see…and if they go in there and sit down for a rest, weeeell…they're all dead see…in about 24 hours…isn't it. Aye, doomed they are…always…without fail…they diiiiie."

Well, there were two opposing sides to my immediate reflections. On the one side 'That doesn't affect me because I am young' but the other nagging doubt was we _were_ playing a ghastly, violent, old boys South African team within that allotted timespan.

Jimmy and I returned to our hotel replete and merry, staggered to our shared room and slept the sleep of the Departure Lounge, on a temporary basis.

THE DAY was upon us and the whole group were at breakfast promptly at 08.00 and even though it was a buffet spread fit for a king with trays and trays of beans, beef bacon, piggy bacon, scrambled eggs, pancakes and a small mountain of pastries and croissants, almost all playing players were sitting with a small plate of warm toast and jam, unable to eat anything for the fear of bringing it all up in apprehension of the match.

Who were our opposition: The Hamilton RFC anyway?

Well they were established in March 1875 and claim to be the oldest club in SA, playing its first match at Newlands stadium on 31st May 1890. Mr W. Nightingale gathered some local enthusiasts at a meeting in the offices of Hamilton Ross Co Ltd and they took the name from the Hamilton Football Club in Scotland where Nightingale had been a member.

The Club merged with Sea Point RFC in 1910 and adopted their current jersey of hooped red, black and yellow in 1914. Unchanged to this day.

They have a formidable pedigree and between 1883 and 2011 they have won the Western Province Grand Challenge Cup some fifteen times, mostly in the early 1900's but more recently in 2009. Many more cups and awards adorn the clubhouse.

Hamilton RFC have also been responsible (coincidentally working with our own SA Rhino, Ronny Rutland, of Frommelling fame) along with Bobby Skinstad and I think Robbie Fleck, in establishing the Cape Town Rugby 10's in 2008 and they continue this tournament annually.

They have enjoyed a number of Springbok players from within their ranks over the decades but of far more concern to us was that they were and are renowned as having a thoroughly 'decent Old Boys side'. *Decent* in this instance meaning successful, not necessarily upstanding and sporting chaps. Many players having been born from the dregs of violent past Afrikaans rugby, many apparently with serving or suspended manslaughter charges. Obviously an illusion put about by their marketing gurus…or was it?

Well we had our own superstars, in the form of:

Chris Hornabrook - 'The Horn'– speedy, powerful, young, handsome second row with great hands and a penchance for scoring…on and off the field. The actor Chris Hemsworth modelled his skinny frame on our Chris.

Paul Featherstone – poisonous hooker and CEO of a major credit card company. A vicious nuisance in the tight rucks and mauls and a cited ankle biter in the open.

Andy McRobbie – weight-training fitness tool, strong flanker with an enormous dynamo. Often been seen still doing laps of the pitch in the twilight until our team bus is ready to go home. Comes with a surprisingly friendly Scottish attitude.

Dughall Aitken – side stepping, high prancing 6'2" fly-half who, whilst sporting a coiffe of poncy Singaporean Estate Agent hair, is a fearless and resolute tackler. Can hoof a pill as well.

Russell Chalon 'Rusty' – our converted basketball player and who at 6'5" may be able to look their No8 in the nipple. Our principle lineout jumper except, as a complete contradiction to his earlier chosen sport, cannot catch a ball for toffee. This cheery fellow never stops smiling.

Roddy Kerr – Scottish-Aussie scrum half, renowned for leaving most of his skin on the field of play during last ditch, fearless and violent try-saving tackles. From the Rusty School-of-Rugby, can catch, cannot pass to save his…skin.

Bevan Morrison – Young, fit, good-looking, daft, NZ centre, the hardest running, fastest centre on the planet, wherein by running at a distinctly forward leaning angle, he gains an even greater image of speed with the only draw-back being that he normally makes first contact with his snout. Claret ignored, he will win the game for us.

There are many more stars and *also-rans* who, like me, needed to make up the cannon fodder to place before the enemy. We were a confident if slightly apprehensive group of lads, that is, until we arrived at the splendid open turf of Hamilton's RFC and saw our opponents.

Even their wives and children had broken noses. These players were wildebeest in clothes, huge, rangy, knuckle-dragging thugs. The No8 was actually so big he had to go through clubhouse doors stooped and sideways. Well as the old adage goes, *'the bigger they are, the harder they fall'*. And the dopey public-school officer who thought that line up must have been a flaming back who never tackled anyone in his puff. The truth being the bigger they are the more bones you yourself are going to break.

Wise old Les and mumbling, non-playing Giles led us away from these sights on the basis that should we dwell further on our prospects there could be mutiny and anyway we needed to get into our kit.

We took to the field in a rush and tossed a ball about until the Potsdam Giants arrived. Dughall Aitken won the toss standing in the shade of their Captain No5, a tranquil spot also enjoyed by the Welsh referee.

Aitkin opted for the wind, the sun, the slope and whispered a healthy tip for the referee at the end. When all was said and done, a Scotsman knows the Welsh are partial to some extra change and maybe, just maybe, it would strike home.

The ball was hoofed into the air by Erasmus van de Waldt von Kepple and not one South African eye paid any attention to it's parabola but focused on being first to offer the most crushing, bone jarring tackle of our man shouting 'mine'. Luckily this was proudly and fearlessly shouted in parade ground fashion by Robert Bulloch, our ex-Gurkha officer. If any of the Yarpies had missed locating the recipient in the charge, this clear shout allowed for pinpoint targeting. Bulloch went down like a sack of poo in a welter of armless shoulder charges and raised knees.

Well this proved to be a complete eighty-minute shitfight with blows and kicks raining down on anything vaguely human by both teams and we can only thank the Gods that whilst their No8 had a ginormous upper body, his legs had not maintained their prize bull dimensions and his running was slow and predictable.

Wales was responding nicely with a profusion of penalties, all justly applied of course, allowing Dughall to kick us down their end for a lineout. In the blink of an eye we were momentarily stunned that Rusty actually caught a lineout ball but not

Hornybloke, he grabbed the ball and sped off and scored just outside their posts.

This continued all day in fact and as I recall, The Horn finally ended up with six tries and the Yarpies lost to a bunch of pished-up Rhinos. Obviously, any tries against the locals generally created more friction and a touring casualty was dragged every fifteen minutes from the field bleeding or deflated from the bottom of a ruck.

The highlight of the game was deep in the second half when Phil Crotty, an aged Rhino and I mean well past his sell-by-date, skinny old bag of bones, demanded his turn on the wing. He too was a New Zealander and could, we assumed, spy an honourable Maori death on the field. This was not a good idea at all and with many shaking heads and at least two screams of *"get off you stupid twat"* by Featherson, Crotty did finally get the sacrificial nod from Giles and on he came.

No sooner was the hallowed turf of the halfway line below his feet than he looked up and saw the most humungous monster of a seven foot tall, 120 kgs winger heading his way with the ball under his arm.

Give him his due Crotty assumed the position ready to tackle this juggernaut and with no pity in the eyes of this predator, the winger actually increased speed and lowered his frame into a veritable wrecking ball shape.

Timing is everything in rugby, and at the very last, the very, very last moment Crotty turned and fled down the touchline.

Not over the touchline to safety but straight back down the pitch to our end. His decrepit old legs eventually gave out on the 22 and again in an ironic twist of serendipitous fate, his flailing body was caught up in the locomotive stride of the monster winger and he felled the brute in the greatest tackle ever perpetrated by a Rhino.

Bugger the six tries, Crotty was unanimously elected Man of the Match…mainly I have to submit, because Hornybloke was a penniless student and Crotty was loaded and could afford the massive bar bill.

*****

EYES OPENED

"He has all of the virtues I dislike and none of the vices I admire."
Winston Churchill.

I tramped off the pitch at the Royal Bangkok Sports Club in about 1995 with haemoglobin spurting profusely from my split eyebrow, the result from my own hooker's inept second strike for the ball, which he missed…again, but in his enthusiasm, he simply kneed me in the face. I searched about for a medic to get me back on the pitch.

Whilst gazing in vain at the spectator's stand I heard a voice behind me ask in perfect English with only a hint of a local inflection, "Hello young man can I help you with that injury?"

I turned around to see who had made such a kind offer but there was no one there, only a lonely old Thai hobo (heaven knows how he had got through security) covered in grass cuttings and adorned with what can only have been manure smudges on his dear old cheeks. I cast about, but there was no one else there. He raised an arm, "It's me….do you want me to stitch that up?"

"Good Lord NO….I need a proper medic you silly old cabbage,' I said nicely, without scorn or intended discourtesy.

"The offer is closing fast young man and I happen to be the King's own surgeon," he replied, straightening and fixing me with a steady and above-average, patient glare.

It just goes to show that even with the heat of battle still coursing through my veins, one cannot judge other people too quickly and especially not in the hallowed grounds of the Royal Bangkok Sports Club.

Gulping air and wai'ing profusely through the curtain of claret, I apologised and begged for his help, whereupon he directed me around the stand and into the first aid room, sat me on a chair, washed his green fingers and proceeded to stitch away.

As I sat there, I reflected on how on Earth had I ever got myself into this fabulous game and then the swirling, soft focus kaleidoscope of memory took over…

*

I was back in England, aged nineteen, fresh out of my public school 'The Oratory' in Berkshire and had met up with my rambunctious Uncle Robin who had just finished playing for Saracens and 'retired' to an easier game at Windsor RFC. He insisted I join up a.s.a.p and, amazingly, after I played one game for the second team was immediately put into the first XV for the match against Newbury the following Saturday. I was naive and assumed that by such rapid promotion I was *that* good and they had snapped me up, but the fact was the current wing-forward knew only too well that this local derby was always a bloodbath of mortal combat proportions and had gone down with overnight flu…cheers Dave Middleton.

Now Robin Platt was about 5'9" tall, barrel chested with powerful shoulders and a hugely merry exterior, always laughing and taking the piss: the epitome of a front row forward. But no, those powerful thighs were not for anything as mundane as pushing and shoving, those legs were there for speed and almost beyond belief Robin …was a winger.

Mr.Lomu, Bannahan, Fanni'alatatooeepoopoo and others of that ilk are two-a-penny today charging like mad bulls at high speed and barely distinguishable from fast moving pan-technican trucks. Except that these trucks could swerve, sidestep, fend-off and wore studs, but in *those* days, well…wingers were wingers and there was generally more meat on a budgie. So Robin was really that first proto-munt on the wing.

To further explain how dysfunctional our wingers actually were at our level of the game is to say, giving them a fair crack of the whip, *if* they ever saw the ball once it had survived the very unreliable hands of our back line from jittery fly-half, through our crash-ball merchants in the centre and thence to the supposed gazelle on the wing.

We all knew they first had to catch the bloody thing. UK Premier league rugby skills, Currie Cup speed, natural-born Aussie thirty metre passes and the innate New Zealand sleight of hand were so far from our level of skill sets as to be almost cosmically foreign.

If KPI's ('key performance indicators'- business staff gauges) had been invented in those dark mediaeval days then Robin's end of season report may have read something like this:

• Fitness :	Good. Non smoker.
• Reliability : available.	Annoying prompt. Always
• Presentation :	Cuts a fine, clean figure in Club colours. (White)
• Speed : powerful.	Extraordinarily fast and Very hard to stop.
• Passing : hand.	No need – if ball was actually in
• Catching : medically	Abysmal to point of being defective.
• Tackling : low	Robin sets himself exceedingly standards and regularly fails to achieve them.

One must forgive him some minor failures, he was one of the cheeriest, loveliest blokes in all of Christendom…and my uncle.

But I digress. Thursday morning came along with a postcard, yes a *postcard* through the Royal Mail from the Windsor RFC committee and selection panel, confirming I had been selected for the first team and should appear at the club at 11.30am ready to travel together in convoy to Newbury.

It all moved so fast and after arriving at the Club at the appointed hour, I shook hands with four of my new playing mates and was bundled and crammed into an estate car.

Obviously, the proud owner and driver was a farmer, evidenced by the hay stalks blowing through the dashboard vents and the floor mat essence of chicken shit.

I had never played with these guys before and so in the car they taught me the lineout calls, easy enough for even my cat to decipher, but it made us seem like we were covert beings fooling the enemy. They also gave me a briefing about the other members of our team. This mainly consisted of a character assassination of all of their missing skills: their non-existent but always attempted sidestep to the left under pressure, spinning in the tackle and then running the wrong way, calling for the ball and then looking the other way. All of these being *backs* of course; we forwards were a solid set of professional – well all except me as an unknown entity.

We arrived on a dreary, desolate, drab shallow hillside adorned only with a single-storey club house and the outlying sentinels of goal posts prodding the grey, overcast sky. Bleak House eat your heart out I thought, this was truly a depressing ground.

Speed forward to the changing room and the pre-match pep talk by our captain, Ian Sams. He didn't have a nickname, no one dared to even suggest one. He was our lock and at 6'5" tall, bearded, Hagrid hair and a snarling face with corner of-the-mouth white dribble and spitting froth he laid about himself with screaming venom about what we were gonna' do to the opposition today.

"These trumped up, no good, inbred, retard farming twats," He roared with more flying spittle.

"YOU ARE GOING TO KICK THE LIVING SHIT OUT OF......Oi!?....who the fuck are you ??" This last directed at me sitting on the bench fumbling fingers and thumbs.

'Prichard Sir I am….'.

His reply sped through space at 120dB.

"I don't give a flying-fuck who you are you snivelling little shite…here wait a minute… you don't look properly warmed up?!"

And with that he smashed his huge Neanderthal fist straight in my face and as you can imagine my head went backwards faster than a speeding bullet and caught by surprise, all the blood in my cranium and nose went the other way…outside my body.

Content with his new boy warm-up routine, Sams returned to his vitriolic tirade and detailed surgical analysis of what we were to do to our Newbury chums across the passage way.

And here, as I staunched the flow of nasal claret, I had a further moment of inner reflection on the wise council of Robin about wholesome sports with chums and what I would gain from playmates and the spirit of rugby.

Well we took to the sloping meadow of a pitch and after the referee blew his whistle there commenced the most awful sporting event since the Roman arena gladiators massacred the Christians, except there weren't any Christians. These were just two sets of demented twats smashing into each other gouging, biting, punching, kneeing and elbowing. The ball was completely irrelevant.

These weren't our sworn enemy who had invaded our shores from foreign parts with conquest high on their agenda – these were kindly rural folk from the lower reaches of the same county as ours. I hadn't got the intrinsic fundamentals of club rugby, had I?

This sporting carnage, you must understand, was as remote from the game of public-school rugger I had just left as the Milky Way would allow. Yes, we had played hard and fast and were encouraged on by our teachers invoking pleasant, and they thought helpful, comments in the Queen's English from the side-lines.

'Jolly good Rupert... yes go on man keep going…look to your left Cuthbertson #3…Up in the air Hastings-Brown kick it up old chap….'.

So you see whilst I was seeking and scampering after the ball as my innocent quarry, my fellow Windsor players were seeking to open-cast the opposition's spine with specially long studs which were reserved and installed only for local Derby Days like this one, oh and of course the Maidenhead match mid-season.

In a haze of atomised blood and spittle I was at the rear of a ruck about to join when I was barged out of the way by our prop running in at his top speed approximating five mph towards the scrummage. It was only then that I spied his target: the trapped, bald head of his opposing prop sticking out of the base of the human pile…on *our* side.

With the sickening, earthy thud of a pile-driver, his monstrous size ten leather dubbin-coated toecap smashed into the top of baldy's bonce and there erupted a fountain of blood.

Imagine a Hollywood set where a speeding but injured driver leaves the road and crashes into one of those Yankee fire hydrants. Yeah that bursting, whooshing geyser of liquid spraying in the air and covering the street and local pedestrians.

Well that was what was coming out of Baldy's head, but it was blood, lots and lots of it. He lay there shaking and quivering and spurting until the whistle went, bodies extricating themselves from the pile. With no one remotely trained in first aid, other than their farming expertise at delivering baby cows, piglets and puppies – most of which is, of course, done by the mummy. They stood wondering what was to be done, absentmindedly wiping the blood off their boots.

The referee attempted to take charge but he was clearly a librarian or council committee member in his day job, and he turned away and threw up on the pitch.

Kojak was carefully picked-up by his comrades; none of us moved a muscle on the basic premise that we could be construed as tampering with a murder scene. He was carried to the side-line and left there shaking, still leaking blood and staring blankly into space. I don't remember seeing him in the bar after the game, nor too at the next year's fixture. Probably retired and living a happy life on his farm.

Well I looked about for our guilty man-slaughtering prop and spied him sauntering nonchalantly out on the far wing pointing at a flock of passing geese.

If nothing else I had my eyes well and truly opened to the world of men's *club rugby* and the possibilities it offered. With that memory fading fast and the taste of dried blood, I returned to the present day in 1995 to the RBSC's attendant, helpful old medic.

I thanked him profusely for his kind and professional manner and nodding sagely at his strict words to '*not play again for at least three weeks and keep that wound clean*', I sprinted back to the field and joining the fray, I definitely made sure I walloped my hooker at the next available maul.

*****

COUNT THE TRAPS

"In hotel rooms I worry. I can't be the only guy who sits on the furniture naked." Jonathan Katz.

Circa 1979 at my beloved Windsor RFC, the whole club, and not just the First XV were all on a massive saving campaign to put money in our bank accounts ready to pay instalments for our planned three-week tour to California at Easter in 1980.

I was trying to save cash but, as a newly-started construction employee on a salary slightly less than a low-caste punkawalla in the Punjab and almost crippling house mortgage payments, as well as vital beer purchases every Saturday, I knew pretty early on that these goals were poles apart and very unlikely to succeed but maybe I could save better during the summer tennis playing months.

My closest buddies at the time were all going to be on this tour and so it's worth introducing them here as they do crop up in further stories in my life.

Andy Skelly: (RIP) Our ginger-haired, highly-skilled and capable fullback. Andy had one of those huge sidesteps like the sprinting David Duckham or the slippery Phil Bennett. Today that skill has morphed into the wonderous lightning-fast footwork of Sinoti Sinoti the Samoan playing at Newcastle Falcons that even keeps David Flatman speechless...for a second or two. Except Andy's skill was not to do the deed at speed but to catch the high kick and then annoyingly just wait deep in the 22 until the leading opposition player had his grasping hands outstretched to grab shirt, shorts or flesh and then a feint to the left and a massive spasm of power to the right and then with the acceleration of a high-performance car he'd, be off jinking and weaving and then kicking us to safety. This truly was **The Outrageous Dummy** of all time. Only a flanker at Maidenhead RFC and another bloke in Ireland ever figured out and remembered which way the real sidestep went and then Andy was fucked.

Andy was of Irish decent. Dad was a huge, imposing gruff-voiced Paddy and a practicing surgeon, but Andy wasn't built that way, he was svelte and graceful, almost a dancer but his heritage gave him native courage in the tackle. He was our tried, tested and trusted fullback.

Andy also had a modern brain and worked at Honeywell's *doing computers.* Nobody really knew what that meant because in the late '70's even my college central computer was the size of a mobile home and it could only do simple arithmetic. But Honeywell paid him well and he was never short of a quid. Very sadly Andy passed away years ago after a frightful car accident. One of his old sayings I imported to the Spoofing Fraternity here in Bangkok was: when having to communal chug a chosen mixed potion of shorts it was customary to shout "Bosch the Bitch" and then guzzle the concoction. A fond memory still alive.

I don't remember ever seeing Andy eat anything solid, he was a drinking man and that probably explains his lithe figure, penchance for mischief and an innate skill at starting fights with strangers. Unendurable.

*

Bob McDonald: our 5'7" scrum half of Scottish heritage but brought up in Buckinghamshire, so there was no Gaelic twang at all. He was the archetypal No 9, small, agile, bandy-legged, overly-talkative, skilful and uncatchable even in a fight. An accurate picture of Bob in civilian clothes, and upon whom he modelled himself for years was: *The Fonz.*

Bob, at that time, worked for Leverton's selling forklifts in Slough trading estate but as with Austin Healy's verbal skills, he could actually sell sand to the Arabs, so his job was a cinch and paid him enough.

Within a further six months Bob went to work for his Dad selling drill bits and grinding tools to the construction industry and the workshops of Slough. To a man, we vowed this was not a proper job and not worthy of his schooling and abilities. Well how wrong were we in the real world. Within a further six months he was driving a Porsche and in the next quarter a Ferrari. A haughty halfback with cash, fast car and abounding wit. Insufferable.

*

Lindsay Small: my partner in crime in the back row. He was an open side flanker, schooled and trained and imparted with great skills at Loughborough Grammer then honed those skills playing for Keynsham RFC somewhere between Bath and Bristol. Lindsay was about 82.5kgs, good-looking and a blond-haired young executive and as you know there is always one like this in any team: the girls young, old, single, committed or married all just swooned over him.

He was already playing at Windsor when I arrived and we 'ham and egged' it brilliantly, Lindsay tackled like a Trojan and here I mean anything that moved, big, small, huge, fast, even those sneaky and twitching backs were all mown down tirelessly. I was super strong in those days from rowing, using a *Bullworker* and wanking for England and so I simply arrived at the scene of the devastation and effortlessly ripped the ball off whomsoever thought they could hold on to it, and gave it to our people who knew what to do with it. Lindsay had worked at some boring old accountancy firm but had recently acquired, in our opinion - *The Job of all Jobs* – he was the investment manager for the newly-opened and highly successful Windsor Safari Park. Inequitable.

So, it came to pass that we would frequently find Lindsay, before a home game, in a corner of the club house, head in hand and twiddling a pencil with a page of scribblings for a complex algorithm he was stumbling through which was whether to buy another tiger or a silverback gorilla, or maybe a rhino. Oh, but they eat a lot and the last one got sick and the insurance premium is higher; so maybe a dodecahedron…nope they spit and carry ghastly desert diseases. His life was one long fun assessment of animal life options and their potential appeal to Joe Public and their costs to keep - still bean counting of sorts, so he was very happy immersed in figures and it kept us intrigued as to what next exotica may be arriving in Berkshire.

Anyway, I was between girlfriends at the time and generally after mid-week training or Saturday matches I would be camped over at Lindsay and his lovely wife Leslie's house in Ascot. Yes, after years of swooning, crooning birds Lindsay had finally been nailed to the floor by Leslie. In fact, I was such a bloody leech that their end of the street, semi-tiled and pebble-dashed house had a master bedroom, a spare bedroom and then a sign on the third bedroom door saying "Jon's Room". Poor suffering couple.

On a pretty average Saturday in March we were at home for a match at our grounds under the Castle, we drank gallons of beer and here old guys I ask you to dredge your memories: those were the days of draught beer from the Club tap at 22p per pint – that's five pints for a quid. Now its more like five quid a pint!

At last knockings, we tidied up the bar and then farted our way from the clubhouse toilets, found the car park and drove home in my company-owned red Ford Fiesta. It had been an awful day of incessant rain throughout the match and the evening and now it had morphed into Noah's Downpour. We tinkered through the woods from Deer Park to Ascot almost blind, peering through the thoroughly inadequate wipers' efforts and going around those thousands of mini-roundabouts that some imbecilic tool in the highways local authority office with an overly generous annual budget thought were, well were what…an improvement?

All the time Lindsay was moaning and bitching about a gut

ache and not sitting straight in the car. Got him home and more moaning, watched TV, more moaning, bed time, more moaning. This was very unlike my buddy, but who really cared as McGarrett and Danno got their man in *Hawaii 50*, so at least I could sleep peacefully.

At 02.45am Leslie came and woke me and said we must drive Lindsay to the hospital. Taking one look at the grey-faced, shrunken, embryo on the bed I agreed and we started to gather his stuff and escort him down the stairs. Well you've guessed it, it was appendicitis and he was very feeble and sore and I had to really lean on his head to get his unbending body into the back of my three-door Fiesta. Getting a small child into the back of a Fiesta is a challenge that Clarkson better describes, but an unbending flanker with attitude made for some very un-Christian remarks in the driveway. The rain was unrelenting and so with three miserably wet, tired, complaining but warm adults in the car, the windows immediately misted up before we were out of their Close.

The trip to Ascot hospital was over relatively quickly despite not being able to drive faster than an ambling donkey because we would bounce over gravel or twigs or even oxygen molecules that would make the car vibrate and be savagely denounced by Lindsay's appendix as complete bastards, with his poor wife branded with the same invective.

The hospital appeared through the deluge and windscreen mist with huge A&E signs and flashing lights and we heaved a sigh of relief. We dragged the soaking victim in his Jim-Jams, writhing and screaming *"that-Ford-shitheap-of-a-fucking-midget-car-get-another-one-Prichard-you-cheap-twat!"* into the medic on duty.

After a very cursory but professional check the medic called me over and whispered, "Listen very carefully, I shall say this only once." (*'Allo 'Allo'* I would have thought to myself but I didn't, because it wasn't on TV yet). "Your mate's problem is not now appendicitis. I strongly believe this is already a very serious case and on the cusp of peritonitis and your buddy has maybe only minutes before it does burst and then he dies."

He went on whispering more loudly, "We have no operating

facility open here and you must go and I mean GO FAST to Windsor hospital and do not stop for the cops or anyone just get him there or he dies!"

"What about an ambulance?" I wailed.

"If I had a fucking ambulance then why have I been wasting my breath talking to you, you retarded ape?!"

Well he must have said something like that because I remember thinking: that's twice someone has been nasty and spiteful to me and I'm only trying to help…whimper-whimper. Hey it was 03.00am and I was wet through and really still trying to remember if 'The Cusp of Peritonitis' was an old boarding school play or a holiday resort in Greece? Late nights and no sleep can cause such confusion in a crisis I was told.

Back in the back of the Fiesta now with the hysterical accountant, we sped off in the direction of Her Majesty's pad and a scalpel. Well with the 95% obscured misty windscreen, screaming patient and horse-pissing-rain I made the mistake of thinking, 'this cannot get any worse.'

I looked down at the dashboard and there was a solid red lit petrol pump icon. Completely out of fuel. I knew from that night's earlier driving experience that there were no petrol stations between Ascot and Windsor, only dark woodland, millions of mini-roundabouts, a ghastly and unfriendly pub called the 'Horse and Manure' and open deer park and I imagined the horrific scenario of the Fiesta spluttering to a halt and me cutting open my buddy with the spoke from the spare tyre jack, in the rain.

Very gratefully the Almighty allowed our chariot, gasping on fumes, to reach our destination and our sweating, agonised friend was transferred to the people who know how to chop out bad bits. Leslie and I retired back into the gloom and downpour, amazingly found a petrol station open and drove home to their house.

Sunday morning was a slow start but the telephone told us that Lindsay was stable in bed in an open ward and we could visit about 11.30am. We duly arrived at the appointed hour and found Lindsay half way down a long ward and in ok spirits, visibly in pain but relieved because the surgeon had said it very close call indeed. Obviously oblivious to the mental aı verbal scars inflicted by those hurtful remarks the night before, he did not apologise but that good-looking, disarming, lopsided grin of his won us over and of course we instantly forgave him.

In hindsight we had to forgive really because there was an early Easter BBQ planned at the rugby club that afternoon and we had already bought the tickets a month ago. So, in the true, honest and backstabbing nature of a best mate, I took Leslie off and guzzled burnt meats and cheap vino whilst Lindsay lay aching in his hospital bed.

I visited again on Monday evening after work and as I sat by the bed Lindsay, holding his lower belly, sniggered and recounted the early morning activities.

Apparently, five of the guys in that ward had all had operations and appendices removed and everyone was very sore and slow to move. The pretty ward nurse had come around and, starting with Lindsay, closed the privacy curtain and administered a suppository 'pill' to assist with post operation constipation or less strenuous pushing come poo time.

Well he lay there in his NHS cot reflecting on life and pretty nurses having to administer such things and then realised that after about twenty minutes there was an urge that was building rapidly and unreservedly and unstoppably.

Moving slowly and painfully he sat up, bum-swiveled, slid off the bed and then looked up. There in front of him were the other four guys all doing the same thing in varying stages of desperation and agility. Thank fuck he was an accountant because he was able to remember from last night that he had counted only four loos and a couple of urinals so there was a very real sense of urgency to his movement. As quick as a crippled, aged, really slow sloth, he slithered into his slippers and then hobbled to the central toilet area and bumping aside any other desperate crapper, he lunged into a cubicle, locked the door and sat exploding violently on the throne.

Amongst the various noises in those few seconds, he did hear the other three bog doors being slammed shut and urgently

the unappetising sound of liquid bowels
ploding load. Then came the sorrowful wailing

**please help…. please help…someone open
up …, en up…aaarrrgh"**

And then his fingers were over the top of Lindsay's door and
wrenching to get in, shaking, fist thumping, nail scratching and
then he stopped. Silence.

"Oh nooooooooo" he howled.

And with that and a slight delay as the slippery contents of
the poor man's entrails maneuvered down the trouser legs of
his pajamas, the floor outside Lindsay's safe, but whiffy little
haven was awash with a very liquid and fetid pool of expanding
filth.

As with most things, there are positives to take from this
sorry tale and with barely a twinkling synapsis, Lindsay was able
to make up his mind for the Safari Park and buy a very large
South American Boa-constrictor that ate only rarely and
defecated twice a year.

The Catcher's Joy

"We are happier in many ways when we are old than when we were young. The young sow wild oats, The old grow sage." Winston Churchill.

By 1993 the British Club of Bangkok had been appearing in the Hong Kong 10's for many years on an almost perpetual annual invite from the affiliated Hong Kong Football Club. This was the *world wide* club rugby 10's competition which was a prelude earlier in the week leading up to the ever-improving, super spectacle of the now much-vaunted Hong Kong 7's weekend, at the old HKFC grounds. The current HK 7's are held at the Hong Kong Stadium at San Po Kong.

In fact the Rugby Tens were always played, in those days, on the Wednesday and the Thursday and then there was an invitational Northern Hemisphere versus Southern Hemisphere match on the Friday between combined teams from each hemisphere. The Sevens tournament was then, in 1993, only a two-day event over the weekend.

There was massive wealth in those days in the *Jockey Club* who owned and ran many a sporting and commercial business and it wasn't long before someone in the accounts department realised that they had far too much money in their coffers and that despite their massive capability for spending, in reality, they could never spend that much cash before the fateful handover back to mainland China, planned for 1997. This on the correct and rightful premise that leaving the larder full of goodies, was a recipe for misappropriation and waste.

And so, with the confidence and rather ugly-to-vulgar nature of folks with loads of dosh, they decided that they wanted to extend their race course to enable a wider variety of distance races. So it was agreed that the old club and pitch facilities would be demolished. They would then extend the track and the new clubhouse would be incorporated on the inside of the racecourse (well the pitch and Sportsman bar). They spared no expenses and the new facilities and quality are five-star at least.

The Clubhouse was refurbished just recently, to add more gold taps and unobtainable-marble finishes.

So for this story, the Club 10's were held at the old HK Football Club and there were adequate facilities of concrete bleachers for the spectators and players between games. The pitch was a cramped muddy space with as much grass as that which would be expected in a horticultural Bobby Charlton comb-over.

This was a two-day event with the various Pool matches from Day One eventually filtering out the dross.

It must be remembered that Rugby 10's was a new genre in rugger and this was only an invitational tournament used to gather the expatriates and local players from around the Asian region and so the actual quality and capabilities of the teams were limited to the city's playing population of mainly expat-led folk and the fact that everyone was amateur and held a proper job. So yeah, generally we were not a feast of open running and expansive rugger – we were all quite shite.

This tournament, and some other fledgling non-descript, unstart tourney in Dubai, had also started the fad for further 'celebrity sides' from around the globe. It was quite exiting actually when you were pitted against them…well it was for the first five minutes and a mounting deficit of forty odd points.

Celebrity sides were like the *White Hart Marauders*, a group of players mixed with a liberal smattering of current or recently-retired actual England First XV players. Names such as Gareth Chilcott (a long-term visitor I had met many times in Bangkok with his partner and buddy 'in crime' Dewi Morris) and this year, unfortunately for our team's draw, a coming-back-from-injury Rory Underwood.

So the format would be that on Day Two the better teams were to play in the Cup with *the others* sharing the ever-decreasing and wretched spoils in the Plate, Bowl, Dish and Spoon, depending on the variously inept levels of skillsets or indeed how much piss they consumed, that took any team from the high echelons of the Cup to the sad crockery on offer for the losers.

Tournament organisers the world over have a seriously spiteful and vindictive culture which states that: '*all those who won their matches or the majority of them on Day 1, would only be asked to take to the field later in the morning, whilst the hairy-arsed losers were always expected to rise with the dawn, don boots and try and insert gum shields without retching and start the mad bashing before the poncy teams had even considered brekkie*'.

Eminently sensible you say, but we at the BC and the Manila Napkins RFC were actually always filtered to appear early, and so whilst it was demanding and frankly demeaning, we stoically stuck to our known level of play and knew we'd be trudging out early.

If the BC were not renowned for their rugby 7's skills there was no doubt about Asia at the time that their true vocation for hoovering beers and other short glass pots of anything from revolting Vietnamese snake wine to the lowest grade of Filipino cactus hooch, was legend.

After everyone had enjoyed their first or second night in Wanchai the realisation dawned that they were actually there to play rugger and tackle men not Filipino maids.

*

On Day 1 the tournament announcer burbled out the names of the teams to next take the field when the current game in progress was over. This was sensible management to keep the matches on schedule and also allowed any team that wanted to plenty of time for putting on boots and taking to the dead-ball area and having a stretch and even familiarising their players with that elliptical ball. A shape and catching object easily forgotten in a haze of burped Tequila from the night before.

So it was with some surprise that I heard, "*The Hanoi Hamsters versus the White Hart Marauders next up on pitch one,*" the last part a little redundant as, there was only one pitch. My surprise because I had not yet seen any of the Marauders at the ground.

The nearest pile of kit bags farted and without mouth parts somehow said, "Ooh you can'art be zeriuz?!" And with that Roy Downton, a spitting image of our much-esteemed Mr.Chilcott, emerged from his impersonation of an Adidas warehouse and, looking about himself, said in his west country Bath inflection, through a cloud of distilled alcohol, "Ok boeys cum on then…get'z ready…we're on in faive…arzes up…come on you'z twaaats."

And like an ancient horror movie, various shapes now appeared out of the mists of the disturbed baggage and very slowly donning kit, they then staggered past us and took the steps gingerly to the pitch, many clutching their heads and moaning in true *The Mummy-like* realism.

This remember, was one of the first of the pool matches, winners progressing to the main competition knock-out Cup matches. The opposition were already out there and doing press-ups and high-knee running on the spot shit, in readiness for what appeared to be a swift and easy victory over these ancient and truly buggered Marauders.

There were only five broken and hands on hips, back-arching figures at the White Hart end, which was obviously their strict regime for a warm up.

"Ok Captains, over here and take the toss."

With the guile of all ancient front-row players before and after him, Dowton knew his remaining team mates would be arriving in dribs and drabs and he needed to buy some time. So, with the speed and intent of a glacier, he wandered in super slow-mo mode towards the pitch centre and then absentmindedly fumbling the coin 4,000 times, he won and pointed even less enthusiastically in the direction of his depleted team of four other mates and said to the ref, "We'll playz *with* th'a wind, Zuur."

It being a completely calm and zephyr-less day this statement immediately creased the referee's brow. "Wot?"

"With th'a wind, Zuur," he repeated, gaining another twenty seconds and one more player onto the pitch. Brilliant, just brilliant time wasting.

"Which end would that be Harts Captain?...I am a referee, not a weather desk!" ...more seconds ticked by.

"CAN THE MATCH ON PITCH ONE PLEASE KICK-OFF!"

With that the ref turned and waved a frustrated but disguised rude hand signal at the announcer in the commentary booth and again asked, "Which end please."

Seeming like he had exhausted his opportunity for more time, Roy turned and ambled, as only West Country folk can do when they have all day to open the gate, back to his team mates ready to receive the kick.

"Hold on there Marauders, there's only six of you...Cannot be doing that, I need the whole team out here or the match will be abandoned and you will forfeit."

"Wot?" said the selectively deaf Captain, "Sorry...whatz waz that Zuur?"

"You heard me Harts, where are the rest of your ten-man team?"

Now again, the Rules and Laws of the Ten Man game were in their infancy and the Hong Kong set may have missed some of the regimental and all-embracing nature of a *British Standard* type handbook. None of this was lost on the old, mostly bald captain, who had avidly read the tournament rules, presumably whilst sipping a pink gin on a tropical balcony. See, professionalism is active and thriving in a thin and duplicitous sort of way.

"Where'z it sayz that then Zuur in the rulz?" innocently raising his enormous single eyebrow.

"CAN THE MATCH ON PITCH ONE PLEASE BLOODY WELL KICK-OFF!"

The referee sent a laser beam of hate to the announcer and with a huff of indignation, blew the whistle and ten keen and happy Hanoi Hamsters dashed towards the depleted, scratching and farting celebrities.

And here we have a true example of that tried and tested eulogy to unsuspecting losers; *'Age and experience will always overcome youth and enthusiasm'.*

One of Roy's fellow four props plucked the ball out of the air and with all the Marauders suddenly adopting that Roman Legion tortoise-shell-protective-shield thing, they marched inexorably up the field and scored under the posts.

This went on for the whole of the first half, somehow either receiving or kicking the ball away, the old bastards eventually wrestled the ball from a squealing Hamster and the tortoise set off again and again. It was a sad and deflating period of Hanoi rugby history and I am pretty sure many returned to the capital, gave up rugger and made do with only their wheel as exercise.

At half time, two more White Harts took to the field and it became a riot. Needless to say, they won and would move on through to the Cup draw.

We played our various matches on Day One and unfortunately also drew the Marauders in our group for their final game. Luckily the forwards were all completely knackered and so we too took the field with some confidence, only to notice that with much leg-strapping and tape, bloody Rory Underwood was on the wing. Well all they had to do was ship the ball to that Exocet and it was a try and nothing we could do about it. Serious wheels with BMW-assisted braking and cornering allowed Rory to remain un-tackled all day despite numerous late efforts.

So as Day Two did dawn, it transpired with little shock, that we were drawn earlier than most but luckily, we had also not been encumbered with anything so trivial as sleeping the night before. So after staggering from Popeye 2 bar (still massively populated with Filipino maids even at that late hour) we ducked in for a greasy Full English Breakfast at the Old China Hand and one last beverage. At about eight-ish our ten good men and true lurched out onto the area of mud that was apparently the playing surface, took up our various positions and prepared for the worst.

The opposition was an un-remembered team, or maybe the Manila Napkins RFC, for the sake of this snippet but pick any one of the Asian nations and extract the fattest, ugliest, spottiest, meanest-looking expats from that capital and you have a good idea of the team image we faced. They, equally fortified from the night before, were farting and belching in a quasi-Haka to enliven their spirts and prepare for the battle ahead.

Our young and chisel chinned fly-half Stephen Reece, as all bloody fly-half's on the planet, was in his playing kit from the day before, which had been a rugged and desperate twelve hours of intense physical contact involving both humans and Mother Earth for most of us. He on the other hand, was, apart from a few sprinkles of mud splashed up the rear of his shorts, from where he had evaded any need to tackle the day before, as pristine as if he had come straight from the laundry.

That's Reecey on the far left ignoring the pre-match pep-talk and trying to spy naked Chinese birds on the 50th floor of the surrounding condos. A tough challenge normally when he was wearing his glasses!

Anyway, Stephen, in all his Persil splendour, stood centerfield with the referee and used his heel to create the traditional muddy kicking tee on the spot. He then looked about himself as some ancient Greek general might have done surveying the lay of the land before the battle of Heydudeopolous, nodded to the referee as if they were old mates and bent down to place the ball on the mound.

Then in a display of almost unparalleled *Omen-like* zeal, Stephen proceeded to vomit massively over the ball. He didn't flinch or move or redirect the flow, nor too did his involuntary reflex decide to retain any of the semi-solids or liquids he had consumed until the entire contents of the Old China Hand breakfast with whiskey chaser, had been deposited in all it's glory onto the still erect hallowed elliptical ball.

Reece was mortified…well he was also faaked and out of breath from his exertions but in a truly repentant and begging manner turned to referee and sputtered, "Oh my God, I am so sorry, really so sorry Sir."

To which the referee looked down his aquiline nose with an air of disgust for mere players, and with a slight smirk and in the manner of Colour Sergeant-Major Bourne in *Zulu*, boomed, **"Never mind son, never you mind …you're not receiving!!"**

*****

LUZON.

PHILIPPINES.

SOUTH
CHINA
SEA

FLIGHT IN FROM BANGKOK.

Manila

SULU SEA

MINDORO

SAMAR

BORACAY

Airstrip

PANAY.

Palawan Islands

CEBU

NEGROS.

70

BORACAY

"The only thing worse in the world than being talked about, is not being talked about." Oscar Wilde.

'Poor kids' I thought as we boarded the Tagalog Airlines plane for Manila in the Philippines. Both Jane and I were leaving our three-year old twin daughters and year-old mud-puppy son with the *two-and-a half maids* in our house in Bangkok to attend a mate's wedding in Boracay. Truth be known, they were in very good caring hands and we left them with no illnesses and a promised return Sunday night.

We were flying with Simon and Susan Dakers, dear friends in Bangkok for the past three years, who had also been invited to the wedding. In fact it was through Simon that I had got to know the groom, Rick Fields. Both played for the Rhino's RFC, a club to which I had not yet been invited. Actually I had been invited *twice* by Vince Swift - but both times on the very night they were actually leaving on tour, and to save both my marriage and my job, I had declined…twice.

Now Simon we may have met before in these tales and at 6'2" he was an imposing figure, but dear Susan topped him by at least another inch (and her brother by another seven inches) and in my opinion was definitely the one wearing the trousers in the Daker's household. No offense Simon, but sometimes you just have to submit and cower, apparently.

Anyway, Susan was a bundle of Scottish fun and cheer with a shock of blond hair and a permanent sweet smile and could probably drink more *pish* than five or six regiments of skirt-wearing squaddies in one sitting, *and* get up at 06.00hrs to do the ironing without burning herself.

Come Calcutta Cup time, however, it was best to wear a spit resistant smock and sit on the other side of the TV room. Her contribution to 'Flower of Scotland' was the *'and send the baarrrstard home again!'* She was and is, lovely.

Manila airport is, well it was in 1993, an awful place to arrive with expectations of sunny fun in paradise. It was massively crowded with current and delayed passengers both arriving and departing, and immigration was a seething press of humanity more like a refugee camp with people almost camping out in the queues. Baggage reclaim was a joke and pot luck if you ever got your bag. If you were one of the lucky ones, then it generally came through 'tampered with' and thoroughly licked by Pedro, the donkey doubling as the baggage tractor.

Once through the official Customs post and spewed out into the Arrivals hall, you had to pass the gauntlet of happy or wailing relatives either greeting or waving off their kin, all the while surrounded by teams of cherubic, dusty child pick-pockets and fight off taxi and bike-boy offers all at 95 degrees F and a matching humidity level, joy.

The plan was to get to the booth marked "In-island flights – Boracay" and they would provide us our boarding passes and give directions to the small island-hopping light aircraft hangar.

The booth was probably titled more like *Paradise Pilots* or *Best Beetch Airways,* I really cannot remember. Whatever it was, it was a bugger to find but we finally plonked our baggage down at the stall with Susan and Jane on guard to fend off the urchin army. Amazingly, Miss Thelma in front of me was all pre-stamped paper and tags and efficiency, a complete contradiction to the seething hordes behind me, excluding Jane and Susan of course.

"Mr Juan, Suur, thank you so much for waiting Suur, and here are your papers and please go out of those doors at the end of the concourse, turn right, through the fence gate and there is a big green hangar ahead of you where the pilot is waiting Suur. You are the only passengers today so have a nice day Suur."

You may have gathered that it is a feminine trait of politeness throughout the islands and when they travel and work in Wanchai, Hong Kong, they always address you as *Sir*...but through Talalog lip-search it is released in a long exhaling happy wheeze of 'Suuuur'. Delightful.

Despite the fact that this island wedding was to be held on the beach it was to be a formal Morning Suit affair with the girls in summer frocks and broad brimmed hats and the only concession to limited wardrobe baggage was that we men didn't need any black shoes and socks. Despite the need for four days and nights of clean clothes, we all made sure our baggage was in handy soft-sided carry-all's and not rigid-framed G4 suitcases.

We picked-up our bags, smacked a few inquisitive, dusty groping small hands and made it to the end of the concourse, out through the doors and turned right. There was the fence and there was the gate.

This led directly *airside* of the airport and out over the very concrete aprons the arriving and departing planes were maneuvering about on. There was no lock. There was not even a provision for a lock on this gate, just a handle and some hinges.

We walked through and made it to the corner of the main airport building and waited as a dark ambling shadow approached. Pedro the donkey and his master appeared and I asked politely where was the green hangar for the Boracay plane.

The joy of the Philippines is that they all speak English and have a brain, many of them thoroughly pickled with Tequila, but still functional and operating happily above the level of a sea squirt.

"Hello Suur, yeees eet is over there'a, see?" he said pointing across the runways. (Obviously with his Suur - there were a lot of girls in his family too)

"What?...where?" I peered about with a flat hand shading my eyes.

"Suur...over there, see...green building...hangar Boracay...ok?"

And with that he loped-off as fast as Pedro could lope.

We all squinted and sure enough on the very edge of the horizon was a green blob shimmering through the heat haze off the concrete and tarmac.

"Whoa there man," I hailed our slowly retreating guide. "How on earth do we get there?"

"Ah Suur, you have to walk."

"What across the bloody airport runways…what just walk with bags right across the…the traffic?"

"Seee Suur," was his closing confirmation and shake of his head, as if directing me across the complexities of a Zebra crossing, you stupid Whitee.

And so, we did. We just walked across an operating airport with no one to stop us. We picked up bags, slung them over our shoulders and marched purposefully and with little or no confidence of survival, across acres and acres of open apron, taxiways and the two runways in that quadrant, all in the joyful blazing sunshine looking left and right for large active flying machines.

We arrived breathless and sweaty and frankly relieved at the green shed and there indeed was our proud chariot of the air, a single-winged, propeller-driven, eight-seater Victorian looking machine and a corporate green boiler-suited Senor Fangio leaning against the raked fuselage, smoking a fag.

After a delightfully expansive arm waving greeting, which was mostly directed at his fine flying machine, a cursory, almost absent-minded glance at our proffered official papers, he announced 'all aboard' and so from the scalding desert of the tarmac we plunged voluntarily into the cauldron-like heat of the oven-baked interior.

Well without dwelling on the cigarette smoking pre-flight procedures and the coughing and farting of the single engine start-up, we were crammed into our seats, which were luxurious as we had two each, strapped in with WWII webbing, and took to the sky in a cloud of fumes and jinking air maneuvers normally used in a dogfight.

These small light aircraft are a joy to ride in. They offer none of the comforts of the commercial airliner, none of the innate life-protected feeling you get from a well-designed and proven flying taxi, they are a small box scurrying about in the blue and thrown about by any minor air turbulence even a passing seagull fart.

We left the main Manila island of Luzon, turned south over the neighbouring green jungle covered blob of Mindoro, glanced down at the Straits of Panay with the last Western-most island of Palawan off to starboard and sped on to the island of Panay.

As we approached Panay we peered down over the beautiful shallow waters of the Sulu Sea and there lay the fabulously romantic vista of turquoise pale water lapping at the milky shores of thousands of tiny islands and coconut trees in a tangle of shapes and mini-bird's nest abandon.

We had to land on the island of Panay and then somehow make our way to the longish thin island of Boracay.

As we circled over the grandly-named 'North West Panay Peninsula National Park' I spied the runway. Now clearly the Philippines do like their titles and liberally apply them to almost anything. Undoubtedly the *Paliparang Godofredo P.Ramos Airport* must be the grandest ever name given to a recently mowed field.

With the gut swooping and wing tip gyrating approach we finally touched down and taxied our way to a shed set amongst some trees.

Fangio cut the engine, raised his fighter pilot goggles, turned his baseball cap to the front and leapt from the cockpit announcing our arrival on Panay. This really was an adventure with real live heroes and unpronounceable names.

There were no formal paper arrival procedures, in fact there were no arrival people. Fangio directed us to the island taxi service to take us to the Caticlan jetty port for transfer to Boracay. He kissed the girls and waved goodbye, striding away while lighting another fag and tossing the still-flaming match into the tinder dry scrub at his feet.

To give the two motor-bikes with side-cars parked in the shade with reclined sleeping drivers the title of *taxi rank* was a stretch but again, who cares - there was romance in the air.

We awoke the sweaty, much-stained, vest-wearing chaps and after a good scratch and itch of parts usually only approached in the privacy of the toilet, they gesticulated that we should climb aboard the two seater side-cars and hold bags on laps and in a cloud of two-stroke smoke, we left P.Ramos and headed into the jungle.

It was a short ride to the 'port' and after a US$3.00 fleecing, we bade farewell to the sweaty vests and turned to the ferry ticket office. This bureau of business actually doubled as the local open-air store selling coconuts (probably from the tree above) under an aged large umbrella with Thelma's Mum brandishing a well-fingered batch of purple raffle tickets.

After a short period of negotiation with Mum, who incidentally was the only Filipino out of 66.65 million to not speak a word of English, we surrendered more small denomination Yankee dollars and with the comfort of our formal shipping passes, we turned and looked out over the short gap between the islands to see if the ferry was approaching.

With a series of grunts and much puffing, Mum raised her bum two inches off the stall seller's stool and reaching up, she tapped me on the hip and pointed furiously at two dug-out canoes with outriggers, pulled up alongside the jetty.

"Jumpy inee boatee quik quik"…not bad directions compared to any help you may get from a Frenchman in their native land.

By magic, two almost identical twin sweaty-vested blokes appeared from under the shaved-tree boardwalk pier and happily waved us to our designated vessels and with giggles and much hands-on-bums assistance, the ladies were seated and baggage piled aboard and the paddlers took station at the rear and we headed off into those turquoise blue-green waters lapping inches below the thwart.

Fabulous, a simply fabulous means of primitive travel and I basked in the regal nature of our carriage as we sped past other boat travelers, red-faced and grimacing with their huge rigid Samsonite steel-reinforced cases.

After crossing the straits between the two islands, which were unusually benign in my humble opinion, we paddled up the underside of Boracay with mangrove aligned to our right until we came to the landing jetty. Again, jetty implies but misleads what was actually there. Let's go with four saplings cut from the bush and stuck temporarily in the mini cove mud recently cleared from the swamp. More primitive magic and none of this was in the brochure, a heaven-sent bonus.

We waved goodbye again to the happy smiling faces of our paddlers. Happy really because, as a parting traditional Filipino gesture there is a hand out combined with a wave, they had earned themselves a crumpled Washington note. This constant tipping and smiling was never a problem and why not, they were, as a nation, poor but honestly respectful, smiling and kind.

Again, we found more genetically-identical bike boys snoozing under the wonderfully large canopy of a local tree, produced the hotel name and with a glimmer of recognition from the bloodshot eyes, Fangio's cousins loaded us into their sidecars. We burped our way up the two-and-a-half miles of sandy path (there was actually a sign advertising this hippo track as "The Boracay Highway") northwards to our hotel.

The happy couple had booked us all into the romantic 'Sniper's Inn' (a type of indigenous wading bird I should add, not a brush-covered bloke with a high-powered rifle) and in a cloud of now almost habitual abuse, we coughed out the bike fumes, waved goodbye again and took stock of our 'hotel'.

If we were expecting a modern clean four-star international hotel, then we had been dropped at the wrong place. We had actually booked into a rectangular single-storey, rusty, corrugated roof of a beachside shack, with an earthen covered eroded brick floor. Even *rustic* was a further huge stretch of one's imagination. There was a central bar area with stools and an eye-catching set of bar-to-ceiling shelves heavily burdened with every conceivable alcoholic beverage ever distilled on God's green Earth.

The bar area, some twenty feet wide, had a small low brick perimeter wall aligned with old rattan and local weave chairs and settees but sumptuously decorated with clean and brightly covered cushions and pillows. There was a sports area designated to the north with a recently re-baized blue cloth pool table and a dartboard with darts. It was perfect.

Peering through the bar and it's primly, potted palms and broadleaf cheese plants, there, right there, not fifty paces from the AA shelving was the most fabulously bright, beaming-white sands of the beach and that shimmering water.

"Heeello Suur," Said an equally bright set of teeth appearing from the interior gloom as my eyes readjusted from the intense sunlight outside. A beautiful dusky maiden clad in a bright flowery sarong and petals in her silky, plaited trestles, met us all with a handshake and more smiles. Knowing we were part of the wedding party, surprise *not* I suggest, as Rick had actually booked the whole hotel for their nuptials and our use, she quickly dispensed our room keys and signed-us-in.

We were then shown to our quarters along more rural brick paths all set about with tended flowering shrubbery, which proved to be equally humble corrugated-roof, brick, terrace-style structures.

The rooms were simple, clean, functional and fresh. We unpacked and washed briefly knowing that the Sulu Sea was gonna' get a pasting. Then donning our swimmies, we gathered towels, sun-cream and headed East back to the beach shack and the start of the booziest three days ever experienced until the infamous ten-day Manila-Hong Kong Tour of 1997.

This was now mid to late afternoon on Thursday and we had the place to ourselves until gradually, and in the patient David Attenborough documentary style, we witnessed the natural history and partially-nocturnal arrival of the original "Walking Dead".

Staggering, scratching, farting and mumbling the chums and chumesses of Rick and Jane emerged from the shadows and stumbled into the bar to order any ambrosia that would bring back life from the night before. Some of these wrecks had been there for days (and nights) of revelry and there was some doubt in my mind if they would last the weekend.

The happy couple also appeared and there was much hugging and kissing from the boys while the girls demurely shook hands. This was a mixed bag of friends but heavily weighing in favour of the Rhino's RFC. I had my suspicions and was introduced to them all with many names ringing bells, if not alarms, from past stories recounted in Soi Cowboy bars.

The evening went very well in a surprisingly civilized and controlled drinking manner with excellent local Filipino foods served at tables near the sports arena. New friends were growing closer and there seemed a very real kinship with them all. Well they were all of the same genus really, rugby mates…and their long-suffering spouses.

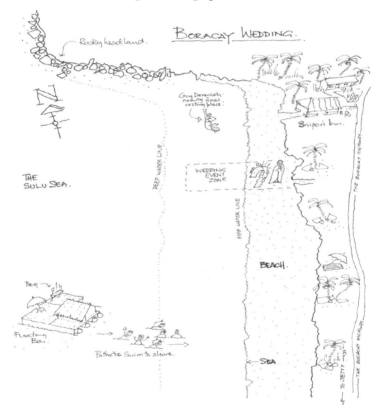

As twilight turned to dusk and then darkness, it was a delight to note that because Boracay was about the same size in ground area as a large W.H.Smith's store, there were few puddles or stagnant water areas and as a consequence NO mosquitos. A most unusual and well-received Asian bonus.

Moths and other minor non-stinging or biting bugs flitted and gathered around exposed light bulbs much as the friends bumped around the well-endowed bar and gradually couples burped good-byes for the last time that day and headed for bed.

*

The next day, Friday, saw a new crew emerge from their overnight chrysalises (that magical thing butterflies do from hungry grub to the colourful wonders they become). Everyone attended breakfast either pink from the last rays of yesterday's sun or many of the lads burnt to a crisp from collapsing in the midday blaze.

Everyone took to the beach, laying out towels, smearing sun cream and the lads tossed the ubiquitous holiday mini-rugby ball in the shallows.

In fact the beach was exceptionally shallow and shelved barely inches for the first forty metres and only then took on a sea-like profile in which you could swim on out to darker, deeper blue waters. During low tide, this shallow three to four inches of lagoon-like water was pearly pink and shimmering on the silver sand below with a fine ribbon-like, almost invisible pea-green seaweed adding further colour and substance to the sheen on the beach. Magical.

We were right at the very top, north-end of the long western beach near the Yapak district and home to Mount Luho. This western side of the island was really reserved for tranquil swimming and sun bathing, whilst the eastern Bulabos beach side of the island was slightly more choppy and dedicated to the noisy sea sports and jet skis.

Nominally bored of receiving a hard, flat pass of the rugby ball to the face, we lads spied the super large floating pontoons anchored some hundred yards off the beach and about midway down the two mile long sandy stretch.

"We'll swim there!" the athletes shouted and plunged off into the dark blue waters in a froth of foam and kicking legs. Well it wasn't long before the peloton was gasping for breath, treading water and waiting for the non-swimmers to catch up.

The hundred yard swim felt like a mile and turned from a happy amateur sporting idea into a struggle for survival and at last, ten semi-drowned pathetic shapes heaved themselves onto the pontoons and lay there as beached whales gasping and flapping for at least three years. The pitiful pile of heaving flesh eventually realized that on the pontoon there were the recognizable sounds of the cheery "Heeello Suur" and the chink of glasses. Faaak there was even a bar on board.

Well we all loved our wives or girlfriends dearly, but this was all a man could ever dream about in life - a floating tropical bar, served by smiling nubile nymphs, cheap beers and cocktails and cooling tranquil waters in which a dip could be taken without expending any more energy than simply falling over.

Needless to say, that whilst our girls lazed and tanned on the beach and then later assisted the bride-to-be and the priest's assistants in erecting the beach archway frame and flowery garlands ready for the morrow, the boys stayed all day firmly, if unsteadily, committed to drinking the bar dry.

Now you would be wondering how we paid all day for our beverages and the burgers bbq'd on the rear platform. Well we cobbled together whatever wet Yankee dollars were in our swim shorts and then when that was exhausted at about 11.00am, we asked if we could have credit at the bar and we named our hotel and promised we'd be back tomorrow to settle up.

"Yes certainly Suur," was the happy and confident reply. Wow credit. The impossible dream was getting better...if that was ever possible.

As the sun approached the western horizon and the bloated whales realized there was still at least a one-hundred yard swim to terra-firma, it was reluctantly agreed we should probably stop drinking and head home. And so, with promises to repay in gold and jewels the next day, we waved goodbye to the waitresses and bar staff and flopped into the sea and pathetically doggy-paddled to shore followed only by a mystical trail of sea creature-effervescence and a less than mysterious cloud of underwater gas.

We were greeted upon arrival at the hotel with kind and sympathetic delicate hugs from our beloveds. Delicate hugs because only as we staggered along the beach northwards did we realise that we had applied absolutely no protective sunscreen and had all been exposed to the full 180 degree reflection of the sun from the sea surface all day as we wandered the pontoons and were, to a man, burnt scarlet or even, provocatively, burgundy.

And so, as the sun set romantically over the western horizon and bathed our outside bar patio in a primrose tint, the girls sipped tropical fruit cocktails with extremely suggestive names and the boys, having showered and shaved, cringed in a swelter of post-burn Aloe Vera green goo until it was time to stick to the bedsheets.

*

THE DAY had arrived and it was agreed in the itinerary that with the tide coincidently out and the sun low over the coconut trees, the ceremony would be in the early morning to prevent over-heating. With ushers buzzing and faffing about doing nowt, the girls attended the bride-to-be, and once dressed in our prim, if slightly crumpled, full dress morning suits with trouser legs rolled up to mid-calf, very Monty-Pythonesque, we set about some light ales for breakfast.

The priest arrived and we were all shuffled into areas of tented shade at the back of the beach and then led forward to form a file of guests down which came a most beautiful Jane with attendant bridesmaids. The groom was fidgeting and shaking in a most unlike Rick manner. It was a big day, a brother lost and sister gained…or whatever.

Standing under the arched flowers for a part of the service and surrounded by chums, the couple were then led into the sea and we all stood in the shallow warm water as the final words and eventual permit to snog was announced.

The ceremony over, we all headed indoors to ply Father O'Giddy with sweet sherry and get on the lash. Everyone kissed the bride, lightly on the cheek as Rick had now morphed into that elephant seal master for the Beach role - jealously guarding what was now definitely His.

In a momentary lull of the party festivities I approached Rick and Jane and her gaggle of maids and the odd bloke and said, "Amazingly eh, it's quite unique, you guys could combine and have your fun surnames hyphenated?"

Both Rick and Jane turned to each other with a quizzical look and with raised eyebrows always evident in that WTF moment replied, "What Fields-Cow?"

"No," I blurted, "the other way around."

A stunned silence and then a gathering of brows beckoned the dawn of understanding…both Jane and Rick babbled, **"Oh my Gosh…** *Cow-Fields***!"** they exclaimed clapping and smiling.

"That, we can say, has never, ever, ever occurred on us!"

With a brief glance around the assembled throng, who had known the couple for decades, the co-operative shaking of heads also endorsed this lack of imagination and what I thought was a rather evident *game-for-a-laugh* idea.

"Naar we'll just stick with mister and missus Fields." An opportunity missed in my opinion and with that rejection, I shuffled off and got pished.

Heavy morning suits were exchanged for Hawaiian shirts and shorts and ceremony frocks for the girls were reduced to bikinis and diaphanous silky sarongs. All the while Father O'Giddy got more so, as he demolished Harvey's entire annual production and the bar staff excelled themselves silently and insidiously topping up glasses with fizzy-pop and beers and those sexily-titled cocktails.

Now with time, and inactive brain status, it was possible to look about and even crane one's neck backwards and be amazed. Across the entire ceiling and around a slight wooden down stand to the ceiling perimeter and the upper reaches of the bar, there were carefully and lovingly screwed hundreds and hundreds of little polished and aged brass plaques all with individual names on.

Vince Swift, aka Vinno, sidled up to me late in the afternoon evidently having taken the free bar at its word and said, "Yeah I've zeen vose too and Hodges'es and me arr' gonna' do it."

"Do what?"

Leaning across the bar and grabbing a laminated drinks-menu slip he said, "You jist have toe dwink twinnee'un of the cocktails lizzded here and you get's a plagg up there…wiv yernameonit."

It was at this time that Ted Devereaux hiccupped his way past us, pissed as a very pissed thing, exclaiming he too would be doing the 21 Shooter Challenge.

And so, with practiced ease, the bar staff lined up eleven tall shot glasses in three rows and started mixing the most lethal looking concoctions with the intent of the refilling them as the mess was consumed. Probably also to reduce glass breakages as the gladiators became ever more unsteady...bless 'em.

Well the proverbial starter's gun went off and the intrepid lunatics downed their cups with casual and nonchalant ease, sipping and admiring and waving glasses with a welter of mates egging them on.

It looked like the easiest of challenges from where we sat but it became evident that Ted was simply not going to make it the whole way. One last time he lent on the bar at an angle which increased rapidly until he accelerated the last two feet and ended lying horizontal with the bar's foot-rest as company. He was heaved up and, despite loving care and attention, forgot whatever challenge he had been in and wandered to a corner table near the beach patio and slumped into Morpheus's gentle arms.

By now, even the experienced liver of our professional expat photographer Dave Hodges was wavering, but resolute and half-way through the second row of cocktails Vinno exclaimed, "Oooh vat one was nize ...can I 'ave No 18 again pleaze?"

The proprietor had firm rules on this challenge which, if you completed it was half-price together with the plaque, but if not, then you needed a bloody mortgage to pay for the cocktails and so the rules were strictly adhered to.

"Sorry mate you cannot chose which cocktails you want, you have to have them as they come."

That seemed fair but Vinno scrupled up that little endearing face of his and with some force, articulated, "Naar yoous stupid twat, I just wannna annuffa' one of vose before I finiissh ver last few pots...it wazza nice 'un and I'll pay," Adding, as an after-thought, "you bastard."

Jon Prichard

Cheers and singing all around of '*Vinno's a stupid old bugger...oh yeah Vinno's a...*' and the barman, equally cheerily, mixed an extra No 18 and as these things go, continued with extras for No 19 and No 20.

Photographer Hodges had, I think, expired or over-exposed himself during the negotiation and there only remained one surviving, bald, burnt, buggered and merry gladiator with fist raised at the end. Vinno's plaque adorns the ceiling even to this day if the Sniper's Inn still exists.

Anyway, at this stage many of the girls had retired to a corner and were sipping "Cool shags against the wall" by the dozen and it was only after Maximus's final guzzle that someone asked, "Where's Devereaux?"

Blank looks and almost nonchalant shrugs implied 'Ted...who cares', but the inquisitor continued a slurred, "I sawz 'im headin' off for ver beach 'bout an hour ago mumblin' abaart a zwim.....jew reck'n he's alright?"

Now even though every man jack was as pished as a pirate, there was a collective moment when all realized that Ted was stupid enough to go for a night swim and, whilst the beach was shallow, the tide must be coming in.

As one, we leapt like electrocuted frogs in the physics lab and scrabbled out of the bar and hurtled like an accelerated cast of bump-a-car zombies to the beach. It was dark but there was a large bright gibbon moon by which we could see a dark unmoving shape lying in the shallow lagoon mid-way back to dry land.

We arrived beside the unconscious, almost naked figure of Ted who had managed to collapse in a crescent shape, parallel with the beach so that he had a small mini-lagoon of water trapped in his belly area. As the waves passed him, for the tide was indeed coming-in, so upon the wavelets' return, they each deposited more and more of that delightful green wispy seaweed.

We could see from the bright moonlight that Ted was fast asleep and actually snoring but amazingly with his mouth open and half-filled with seawater and seaweed actually moving in and out of his gaping maw with every snort. Amazingly I think we had caught the tide not minutes too soon and this was a very sobering experience for us all.

And so, hauled to his feet, not an easy task as we were all again lathered with aloe vera after-sun goo, he was unceremoniously dragged back to the shack and room keys found in his upper beach discarded clothes, he was placed caringly on his bed and covered with a sheet with all his loving mates hoping that the sea-salt and after-sun cream would itch like hell by morning.

And so not twelve hours later and after two exciting ceremonies on the same beach, we ALL had to once again bid farewell, but this time to a united Mr. & Mrs. Fields who were staying put, as this was *their* honeymoon destination, and for once all the guests drove away leaving the happy couple smiling in their wake.

Any movie of this event must surely have been dubbed: "One Wedding and a bloody near miss Funeral." Catchy eh?

*****

THREE PINTS

"Don't ever wrestle with a pig. You'll both get dirty, but the pig will enjoy it." Cale Yarborough

It was the summer of 1998 and the Rhino's Rugby Team found themselves bound for Shanghai and a match against the Shanghai Hairy Crabs. The Rhino's modus opperandi, as you may recall from an earlier chapter, was to gather together annually in June as a tribe of old, keen, capable and reasonably well-heeled gents and gallivant off to some obscure location in the hinterland of the South East Asian nations searching for some opposition. That opposition needed to be one that, in the best case, had never ever played rugger before or at worst, maybe had fifteen semi-able bodied scrotes to front up and get bashed.

If the opponents pitch had only recently been hacked from the native vegetation or had been cast upon the side of a mountain with a distinct propensity to have the ball roll independently straight to the wing, well that just added to the fun.

There was only one real proviso and that was the opponents generally had to provide the referee. It was simply not done to have a fellow Rhino castigate or punish another simply because he had the very unenviable task of blowing the whistle. It also mistakenly gave most of our adversaries a glimmer of hope that their man could sway the day's outcome.

Many of our number had been to Shanghai on several occasions before as most of the host had been drawn from Hong Kong's finest and had popped over for spurious business activities and some cheap R&R. For others this was a first into the much-famed Chinese underworld and was surely a city of mystique, ancient heritage, dubious beverages and loads of cheap tarts.

Shanghai today is a far cry from the undeveloped and steamy city surrounding the grand Victorian stone banking structures we encountered on our first walk from our hotel. The Strand

Hotel on Kung Fu Street in itself was a microcosm of the ancient trading post and clearly had not received any commendable or recognisable upgrades or refurbishment since the Boxer Rebellion. As an example of summer-comfort the aged, irritable cast-iron heating system seemed to be jammed on *swelter n' die mode* at all hours of the day and night and the engineering department could not assist because the boiler room could not be found.

We walked the fabulously famous Bund Wall on the outer meander of the Huangfu river with all those huge Gothic-style stone or stucco edifices to banking, commerce, opium and the flesh trade sneering down at us from above. The Bund was also the Oxford Street of the city without the shops, as thousands and thousands of Chinese and the odd American paraded the banks (pun slipped in) in the misguided but evidently best wardrobe selection for that day. Bizarre hats perched on white painted faces with knee length diaphanous pink blouses hugged-in by woollen Scottish Tartan tank tops and loons the Beatles would have been envious of, all atop leopard-skin super high heels…and that was only the Yank.

Glancing across the yellowish river in the cool respite of the first day's arrival, one would spy The Pudong, the land trapped inside the huge snake-like meander that had selected the city's location all those millennia ago. Apart from the imposing and immediately recognisable shape of the three diminishing balls of the Scrotum Tower and a couple of pathetic mid-rise unremarkable buildings there was nothing else out there. Today of course it is an immense, heaving, sun-reflecting, tower block, glass porcupine of a place boasting two of the tallest buildings on the planet: the Werrwerryhi Tower and Hoogivesafaak Convention Centre.

The Pudong, in 1998 and it's flat, green horizon-to-horizon paddy fields, was to be the setting for probably the very first ever confrontation between the irritable and irrational Rhino battling against the local, scuttling, hairy Crab, something not even David Attenborough could ever have conceived.

But first I return to the mysterious workings of the invisible Rhino Committee and its unerring ability to select shite opposition from anything remotely resembling a team that could actually play rugby. Well obviously the committee's Inspector Cousteau of fixture research had clearly had a bad day at work and decided there could not be fifteen good men and true in that remote outpost of any merit and simply booked the match, rubbed his hands, reported all was tickecty-boo and that was that.

It transpires, after meeting a local connection in the city, the Hairy Crabs had at the start of the season received an influx of experienced, aged, but very fit New Zealanders, Australians and semi-pro English union players with added attitude not normally found in an Old Boys side and they had smashed, bashed and annihilated any team at home or on tour that year and were apparently, absolutely, definitely unbeatable.

Armed with this information, reluctantly revealed by the Committee's spokesman - who was invisible of course- the Rhinos set about the important business of their usual pre-match psychological build-up with some extra trepidation. This exertion started initially with lying prone on the pleasant sloping grassy banks surrounding the gladiatorial area, farting, chatting and smoking Chinese manure fags (Rhinos may be well-heeled but scratch the surface and they are cheap cunts).

Peter Hutton, aka *Stitch*, our eighteen going on twenty-six stone second-row power house, sorry typo, powder horse, sat on the edge of the slope and bent forward to don his socks collecting our group's attention as he regaled us all with some massively untrue story about his younger days and playing prowess. Whereupon, by some freak but not unscientific gravitational equation, he slowly toppled forward and in a graceful belching and farting movement, tumbled and rolled like some massive Alpine boulder down the slope to end up amongst the pitch-side plastic water bottles. Upon coming to rest his wits and wit returned, shouting *"aha my new Rhino warm-up revealed!"*.

Anyway, as you can imagine whilst the Rhinos were busy nursing hangovers and applying medical creams to areas not normally associated with daytime sports, the Hairy Ones arrived, trooped silently and ungreetingly into their portacabin clubhouse and changing rooms and did whatever all good Kiwis and Aussies do before battle. This was the least hospitable team we had ever encountered as rugby players. Maybe this was their aloof and arrogant manner because they had won all their matches for the year so far – a curious paradox in the rugby fraternity.

Whilst the Pudong was a desert of development, the rugby club had struck gold with their temporary use of the pitch area. A fabulous open area of bright-green, fertile, succulent grass and in the middle and the best part, was their pitch. Impressive by Rhino standards where for our pre-warm-ups, we normally spent twenty minutes collecting stones and broken glass from the hard dusty playing area.

This missive is not a record of play by play rugger for keen tossers but more a glazed, myopic memory of the dour and frankly unhappy conflagration one gets when one team is massively motivated to kill and win. The other team has at least 95% of its mind and brain receptors considering how much the tart was going to cost that night and would she really do all those things that the guys promised they did do in these parts.

Amongst the biffing, bashing, yelling and stumbling of the game the Rhino's rather unexpected hero appeared: the languid frame of the retired maths teacher Micky da Monkey running with ball in hand, swerving past crumpled crabs and scoring outlandish tries in the name of all that is holy. He was ably assisted in his demented line running with American football style blocking by Rick Fields and with their evident leadership in the truly unusual underdog-over-comes-Goliath tale, we beat the unfriendly bastard Crabs 22-7.

Well there was a happy coming together for a group photograph of spent and exhausted bodies in which all players were present, except Roddy Kerr who had to dash off for a poo. But after that oh-so-brief an embrace, the Crabs reverted to type, snubbed any offer of shared pitch-side warm beer, offered nothing from their own clubhouse and sulked off into the late evening gloom.

Well *fuck you Losers* was the ungentlemanly, unvoiced but unanimous sentiment amongst the visitors. Such trivial behaviour was not going to diminish the joys and spoils of victory so unusually acquired by the Club and after such a surprisingly strife filled pre-match build up, we all drank long and hard as the Eastern sun set in the West and we all took it in turns to take a fresh can to Roddy in the bog.

*

After returning to the oven-like heat of the Strand hotel, we washed, sprinkled ourselves liberally with Old Spice, donned out best fig and climbed aboard the decrepit timber-framed tour bus (another example of Rhino thrift). The aged vehicle took us about the city and surprisingly, without the aid of smart phones and Google Maps, we managed to find our quarry: Murphy's Pub. This sat amongst the suburban scrub and we all piled in for libations at the cold and remarkably well-maintained Guinness tap.

Murphy's was a delightfully melancholy, poorly-lit, large, open-style, dark-stained, timber-framed and lined pub in the usual panache of any Mick's drinking establishment. It had the time-honoured trappings of Irish farming servitude to their Protestant English lords with plough heads, shovels, horse harnesses and the odd chastity belt, all nailed to the walls and beams.

There were a few expats and locals lining the long side bar or skulking in the shadowy recesses but many thanks to the fine management and planning of the committee (no thanks to that Cousteau twat) there were also gaggles of lithe, tall Chinese tarts strewn about in giggling groups. Well in truth that was what we were hoping but maybe those Rhino rose-tinted spectacles had not been polished enough to allow a true visionary inspection and understanding of the ladies' virtues.

I joined a quartet centre floor with our on-pitch hero speaking in broken Cantonese-cum-Mandarin-cum-Geordie to two enraptured local beauties who only had eyes for Micky's mischievous, articulating face. I briefly glanced about at the other groups but in doing so, all was cut short with a piercing screech from behind me. One of the hopefully erstwhile virgins had lowered her vision and spied the front of Micky's trousers. For there, for all to see, was his exposed meat and two veg.

Now as we all know, such accoutrements can come in all shapes and sizes but this hanging garden was a veritable World Gala collection of vegetables. Micky's willy was probably an average-sized shriveled weapon but dangling behind the leathery, flannel-like pipe was the most enormous ball bag of a scrotum ever carried by a human being. This knapsack could, in times of emergency, easily have been slung over his shoulder.

The ladies fled the scene and Micky, oblivious to the normal dress codes in public places, simply turned and engaged another group, now consisting only of Rhinos…not surprisingly.

Anyway, tales of the Micky da Monkey's kit were retold in ever unlikely glory until some arse from the defunct Royal HK police force shouted.

"Do the beer glass thing Micky, go on show 'em all".

It is also an unwritten law and clearly high on the list of 'not to be undertaken ever' rules of man-to-man chumminess (unless you are one of those bloody Aussie Mardis Gras mob) that one does not generally ever voluntarily grasp another man's appendage (off the field of play)…nope…not ever…even to assist in life and death medical emergencies.

So it came to pass that Micky announced that an amphitheatre of Rhinos should be created about his person and two volunteers were needed. In a moment of sheer forgetfulness, being as I was also a virgin on tour, I found myself in a ringside seat and was pushed forward as one of the volunteers and Rick Fields stepped up with a knowing grin.

Three full pints of cold lager were ordered and ready for placement but first we needed to have a table. After brief instructions and howls of derision from the laager (shocking pun), Rick and I reached forward and plucked a proverbial corner of the hanging ball-bag and with other assistants grasping Micky by his belt as a restraint, we proceeded to reverse and with an encouraging demand to grab on firmly, the full magnitude of this flappy bag of skin unfolded like a gigantic bin liner.

Pulled taut like the spinnaker sail of the leader in the Fastnet race, the Micky scrotum took on the very lines of a Louis XIV triangular walnut coffee table, except the ancient timber grains were now living, pulsing, pink flesh.

With the dexterity of an eye surgeon, Micky proceeded to balance all three full pints of lager on the quivering blushing surface and hold them there for a period of not less than thirty seconds. A huge roar of approval and genuine joy at having witnessed such an impressive and unrecorded Guinness Records feat, was shrieked by all.

The un-spilt beers were then handed to the two bag-pullers and the ball-bag owner to enjoy at their leisure, as some sort of reward. In a fit of sudden tour hygiene mania everyone then went to the loo and washed their hands.

*****

.

GREY HAIR

"In this world there are only two tragedies; one is not getting what one wants, the other is getting it." Oscar Wilde.

I was summoned to my Thai Joint Venture Partner's hallowed Chinese-style office, with super heavy rosewood furniture littering the massive hangar of his edifice to power, late on a Friday evening on Rama IV road, offered a seat and he spake thusly in quasi-English:

"Jron, on Mrunday ten o'crok we have werry big boss of company come here for meet me. He want all reports on your dewission. You no come meeting cos too young, no grey hair, baby not come werry big boss meet."

At that time all foreign companies working in the Land of Smiles had to have a 51% local stakeholder(s) as part of the corporate licence regulations and so my JV Partner was my boss. I didn't know it at the time but I was to learn a lot from this old son of China, a myriad of ancient Eastern ways and rude Western presumptions that were taboo in the Orient. Generally, such advice was not in a calm, kindly, mentoring manner but more akin to bamboo water torture, or a blistering tirade of barely comprehensible Thinglish. Shocking when you consider he went to a very posh English public school, but then so did I so we should have a lot in common-ish.

I protested profusely that I was the only one able to deliver the reports in person on all the activities of my department's two-year long struggle, but it fell on stony ground and I was ushered out with a mumbling of 'no grey hairs' ringing in my ears.

I was youngish and impetuous and massively forgetful and the incident left my mind like a passing wasp, there was a niggle of worry but hey… it's Friday.

Saturday dawned and after a morning's work on our construction site I hurriedly rushed to the ascribed pitch where our rugger chaps were gathering and already deep in their pre-match warm up regimes - lying in the sun smoking Malboros, farting and regaling preposterous tales of their sexual prowess from the night before.

If nothing else, our team had gone large on wardrobe and we were resplendent in pink and black shirts, black shorts covered in sponsor's logos and matching hooped socks. Who gave a toss about playing ability when you looked *that* good.

The Japanese opposition arrived and leapt from their air-conditioned coach like epileptic impala all carrying matching team bags, adorned in hooped royal blue and white Sumitomo shirts and all wearing the staple Japanese Sony Walkman headsets. Faaak they looked athletic.

Well whatever happened on the pitch remains a mystery really - but like all bad things that happen the brilliant human psych erased the bad stuff and kept the good. It would have been frantic, breathless and battering; they were clearly much fitter than us and even the props were turbo-charged.

I think they were victorious on the field and that's annoying because whilst I feel I, and many of our team were good-spirited losers, we certainly didn't *enjoy* losing, in fact we would mentally vow to win the next one. Then in the blink of a black eye and a ruptured lung everything changed as their coach challenged, "Now we beat you guys at drinking."

There are some things not done within the hearing arena of a Brit (and all the other proud Caucasian chaps in our team) with our mixed psychopathic Viking-Hun-Saxon-even-Gaulish heritage and that was to even suggest or bring a smidgeon of doubt as to our drinking attributes.

The modern day sporting medical knowledge and insistence on re-hydration had not existed at that time in the early '90s, well certainly not at the lower levels of UK club rugby where we had been weaned, where a slice of orange at half time was considered a veritable fruit feast. So with the blazing tropical sun of Thailand we were utterly clueless – despite having two doctors in the team – and had only brought a large stainless steel water pot with those bloody porous disposable paper cone cups for forty big blokes, three sips per head and we were feeling like demented troops in the Arakan!

The benefit from this self-imposed, rehydrating ignorance was that we were always amazed at how much beer we could drink after every match and the Marketing and Accounting managers of the British Club always came over and congratulated us on the ever improving club coffers.

Some thirty minutes later through Bangkok traffic we arrived at the BC for a shower and change of clothes and a dash of pong-juice, whilst the Japanese lads returned to their hotel nearby and then came on to meet us for the dinner and beer reception we always held for visiting foreign teams. These were always paid for by the Club itself and not as contributions from our own pockets. Tally Ho - here we go again.

The Churchill Bar, a normal haunt for most of the old club members, was generally regarded as a no-go zone on a Saturday after a rugby match. We were reasonably well-behaved but certainly the library-like tranquility could not be guaranteed.

Robin Eyers, Minkey and Ramsey McPherson
our medic, preparing to take-on Sumitomo.

The room and chairs and tables were all rearranged to allow for the curry buffet-style offering, we adopted and made the centre of the room our own. We were brash and rash and pleasantly rude, noisy, and petulant after a loss. After the food, we became ever more so with beer drinking boat race challenges and singing. Tuneless awful screeching's (that would have been my contribution) amongst some of our talented Welsh throats booming out old Celtic numbers.

So, with that animated scene in mind we set about utterly demolishing the entire Sumitomo RFC Team and management staff in our usual orgy of beer games, boat-races and personal sparring with dangerous concoctions of spirits in short glasses. They were good to start with, in that Japanese Samurai sort of proud manner but Anglo-Saxon drinking really did make a serious mess of them. But from the unwatched blind-side, our efforts were to be surpassed in elegance and stage stealing.

There was a Banzai-like cry from their tour director as he stood up at the bar and, brandishing a full frosted pint glass of Carlsberg, he gulped that final glass of freezing lager and promptly fell dead.

I picked up the lifeless bag of bones from the floor, considering whether the Club had insurance for this sort of 'incident' and in which nearby alley I should dump the evidence, when there was a spasm and the recently consumed lager revisited the bar in a fountain of extraordinary violence. Chairs, tables, recumbent occupants, wall hangings, carpet, hundred-year-old plaques were all either drenched or at least covered by a patina of the semi-digested brew.

With the wit and brainpower of a demented rabbit, I gathered up the still-leaking Jap and half carried, half dragged the daft fucker down the everlasting corridor to the Men's Room all the while leaving a trail of filthy, stinking puke that even Kipling would have been proud about when concocting his great, grey, green, greasy, Limpopo river title.

How one small Asian body can hold that much liquid inside without the decency to look even a little bloated beggar's belief but Kano-san continued to exhaust in the basin, urinal and on the recently and proudly renovated white marble flooring turning my predicament into a ghastly ballet on ice to eventually wipe him down and wash his face and clothes into something resembling his old living self.

The Sumitomo team had left when we returned to the Bar – maybe something to do with forgetting embarrassing senior management at a time of National Drinking Pride or they were simply so pished they had forgotten their general in the heat of defeat. So, with the aid of my driver Khun Songwuth, we bundled Kano-san into my car and drove him to his hotel, staggered through the lobby and took him to his room where I carefully removed most of his puked-upon clothes, put them in a bath of cold water, lay him in the 'recovery position', sang him a lullaby and, tip-toeing my way out, carefully closed the door.

Sunday was a write-off and all too quickly Monday arrived and the disastrous memory of the wasp returned and no report (other than a vacuous verbal one) was available. I started to sweat, not perspire but as Honey Badger would say: sweat like a gypsy with a mortgage.

All divisions of the JV's Empire were summoned and arranged in an ever-degrading two columns of managers lining the long corridor to the equally overdesigned Board Room and I was fitted in somewhere between the manager in charge of a low-quality paint company and the stand-in avatar for a sick papermill technician. So about half way in the line-up, not bad.

In marched the squadrons of Samurai flunkies and henchmen as a vanguard to the approaching god. All filed past in solemn black suits wearing grave but blank Oriental faces. I cast a glance at my diminutive JV Partner some fifteen yards away wringing his hands in anticipation and as the Main Man appeared and JV's wee eyes lit up, I turned to see the quarry of his vision. It was non-other than Kano-san and as his probing glaze wandered the downcast faces of the great unwashed it eventually alighted on mine.

With a shriek of joy and obviously broken imperial protocol, Kano-san leapt forward, grabbed me in his bony grasp and shouted, **"Jhon-san my Bruvver"** and then clasping me to his lightweight frame he skipped past the JV Partner with a disparaging wave and into the Boardroom all the time exalting *his big Blittish Bruvver.*

Report worries, balance sheets and future proposals for increased commercial success would be forgotten for another day. The JV took it with good grace but was still smouldering all day and glancing at my lack of experience clearly manifest with the lack of grey hair at my temples.

Possibly time for that old adage: 'It's not what you know..........'

*****

BISHOP TO PORN 3

"The English country gentleman galloping after a fox...the unspeakable in pursuit of the inedible" Oscar Wilde.

Our far-sighted but *invisible* committee had the healthy and genuine goal to lead the club to new exotic lands whenever they could. They were also aware of the need to ensure that their players enjoyed some of the more easily acquired low-hanging fruit once in a while. Nowhere were such quality goods on better display or more freely and economically acquired than in Thailand and the Philippines.

This year we were scheduled to play the Cebu Dragons and this was to be seen as a new era in tour management in that we were to play against what was essentially the whole of the Philippines national side. As a result of the lure of such Babylonian garden produce we had the largest tour group ever - amounting to some twenty-two Rhinos, sadly that's more Rhinos than are left alive in Lesotho.

We also sported Bevan Morrison as El Capitaine. And in his inimitable words of address 'the adopted Motto was "Back to Basics" and for many this will also be a back to our roots tour...so to speak.'

Bevan is a New Zealander and worked somewhere in the oil and gas industry – not I suggest at the actual drill head humping pipes but somewhere his education would help. Beven was a strong running, massively skilled centre with Olympic side-stepping at pace and an ability to pass a ball like a bullet right into the guts of his fellow centre or winger. Except he didn't.

He knew only too well what would happen if he passed to a puffing Rhino on the outside. So, Bevan's MO was to hold the ball on two hands and sprint at speed in that slightly leant-forward-almost-falling-over position and take on the opposition with his face.

Despite personally witnessing Bevan using his face as a fend on three different continents he still sports an unblemished complexion and a pointy wee nose to this day. Annoyingly he still has all his teeth too.

Bevan could actually win the game for us almost single-handedly, always assuming we fat boys upfront got him the pill. But Cebu was not to see Captain Morrison on the park because as a first for the Rhino's (I assume?) our Captain was a non-playing Captain. Bevan had come on tour despite being on crutches after his third ACL reconstruction.

So, it was agreed that with Bevan enjoying the hallowed status of Captain, his duly appointed understudy for the match would be Luceri. Pronounced: 'Loo-cheery'.

Luceri was 5' 11 and 7/8th inches tall, with a cropped mass of black curly hair, a face like a bulldog with Kirk Douglas's chin and only slightly less slobber. He had that thick-set hard torso of all wing-forwards and everywhere else there was firm concrete - Canadian muscles which came with attitude. No bad vibes at all and a most likeable and soft-to-middling-spoken chap off the paddock, but Canada imparts a certain robust desire in its male offspring to overcome all adversities and win. Hence the likelihood of a calm pre-match Captains' chat was as probable as Les Bird catching a pass on the wing.

Manila airport is a transport hub like no other and not really where you want to land, ever. With the experience of a wise old hand, Stitch Hutton had booked us all on Cebu Air and we flew straight into Cebu island itself.

The modern air-conditioned coach took us out of the main town, over a huge bridge to the south which seemed incongruous that there was sufficient cash available to build the structure in the nation after all of Imelda's shoe purchases.

We were heading for a four or five-star international hotel to drop our bags and then head out for some toot and totty on this Friday evening. We never got there.

Well we did eventually, but with the fifty-seater bus full with thirsty scrotes, the driver very sensibly decided that he would comply with the persuasive suggestion from the middle seats, "if you don't stop this fucking bus at the next fanny bar I'm going to piss on the floor."

So, in a most unlikely spot on the side of a mountain, with jungle creepers creating an almost complete canopy over the road, we stopped at a large timber bungalow bar perched on stilts over the valley below.

With family restaurant-style pot plants on the entry veranda and normal mid-afternoon sunshine blazing down, the youth of the tour leapt whooping from the bus, Bevan hobbling with practiced style and the Old Hands more cautiously stretching and blinking in the sunlight seriously considering what we may find inside. This didn't look like a bar dispensing fluff.

How could we have doubted the natives and their ability to please. The room was a large open timber space with a long, clean and efficient-looking bar on the right-hand side decorated with more pot plants, an array of heavy-duty, red bar stools and twinkling fairy lights. Two or three pool tables filled the main area which then opened onto a charming balcony offering delightful views of the jungle-side Philippines.

Perched languidly on pool table edges, lounging on plastic upholstered wall hugging sofas, standing, swatting and wandering was a veritable flange of local bikini-clad fanny. From peering into handheld make-up mirrors and tranquil application of lipsticks, the girls went from a standing start to school-yard 100m sprint mode.

The Sock was already full of Pesos and unlike venues such as Hong Kong or Singapore or Beijing, in this country beers and girly drinks were cheap and there was almost never the possibility of being ripped-off. To be thoroughly assured of that security you also have to put some prudent, minor checks and balances in place, so the cash was placed in the tight-fisted, Scottish, mean, un-releasing, vault-like, secure hands of Andy McRubble.

It was of little surprise to us that our new contingent of curious and creative player youth were able to invent strip-pool and become incredibly successful at it with many of the girls naked before you could blink.

Despite the fact that many of our younger players had been working in Asia for years, they had allowed the euphoria of tour to overcome their common sense and forget that girls spending twenty hours a day next to a pool table rapidly acquire the skill sets of Steve Davis and will in the end be snookering you and your wallet later in the evening, in the nicest, cuddliest least contagious possible way.

With hours of beer drinking and trays of thousands of tequilas donated to the local skirt or more appropriately skirt-less, and with the sun having set some hours before, a shout went out for food.

Jimmy Howard, a long-time Rhino and on this tour must have been sixty years young, had worked in the Philippines for decades as a very successful pest control expert for a massive global company and acquired the homely sobriquet of *Ratcatcher*.

He was also almost unique on the planet in that he had successfully morphed from being a semi-professional football goal-keeper in the English league to playing rugby. A round ball convert to elliptical is unique, not just because the two codes, their teams, rules/laws, spirit and team ethos are so different, but that many soccer boys just don't mix and survive. Jimmy was obviously obstinate and dull and ugly enough to endure. There's nothing wrong with football and apparently quite a few people play it and watch it, but why would you do that when there is rugby?

Rats is convivial friendship personified and despite having knees and hips that stopped functioning properly in about 1925, he takes to the field every year on every tour with more bandage strapping than Boris Karloff and keeps his side of the scrum up with nothing more than conviction and a huge storage of intestinal gas, against almost any opposition.

Jimmy gave the proprietor instructions and somehow from out there in the bush, within minutes, there arrived the largest delivery of Kentucky Fried Chicken family buckets probably ever assembled in Cebu for one destination. There were none of those metro-city-man complaints about trash food and everyone tucked-in and devoured the lot with many a lithe, nimble figure suitably oiled, externally.

The bar owner was no mug and realised he had captured a big spending fish and with all his staff thoroughly enthralled, engaged and full of pop and, soon to be, sperm. There should be no incident that may upset this lucrative apple cart and so, probably much to the chagrin of his local clients, he instigated a "Lock-In – Lock–Out". This suited our mob perfectly and we stayed there for hours and hours.

It was reported, because I cannot personally recall, that after the 'new security policy' was implemented, then the Rhino's band of Jimmy Rats on harmonica could be heard in concert with Jason on the local keyboard and with JK crooning away the old Classics. Such hidden talents rarely exposed in public were legend for, well, for as long as anyone can remember...hic.

*

Long after the Sun had been tucked-up in bed and sung a lullaby, we arrived at our hotel and the check-in process was undiluted chaos with only minimal night staff upon such a very late arrival. We found our beds, some with giggling Uncle Sam-spiced extras and went to sleep.

The Saturday morning, after some customary room calls, reminders and more reminders, found everyone at breakfast and chomping away on a splendid Western buffet and some who preferred boiled Chinese chicken's feet or both.

Mark Turner, an erstwhile Royal Hong Kong Plod, was 6'4" of tall gristle but with what appeared, relative to altitude, a much undersized bald skull with an almost flat to receding brow that supported the notion that he must have one of those modern compact copper's brains, because a normal brain would not have fitted in that sleek cranium.

Mark had arrived at the Coffee Shop on level one unable to use his hands at all because his finger-tips were massively swollen and disfigured. He pleaded ignorance and physical battery on the basis someone must have done this to him when he was asleep.

This increased the mystery further because apart from being one truncheon short of a full armory, Turner was also known to be far too tight of wallet to have purchased one of the Chicken Breasts last evening and must have slept alone…hmmm.

Upon closer inspection it appeared that only the very pads of his digits and thumb were badly burnt. This was not going to be one of Agatha Christie's most complex conundrums, certainly not if Turner was involved.

With croissants and coffee polished off, a delegation of ex-coppers and yours truly trooped up to Mark's room and there all was revealed. Being as pissed as only an ex-law enforcement officer can get when he lets his hair down, Turner had collapsed on his bed with all the lights on in his room. He must have awoken, gone for a piss or just realized he craved darkness and done the deed.

There on the TV table were all of the bedroom, bathroom, bedside-table and entrance lobby light bulbs neatly arranged in a long row, each rocking gently in its own slightly charred varnish niche, all this with the lingering essence of singed fingers.

"Oh yeah, I remember now, I couldn't find the fucking light switches".

Is it any wonder that even Ronny Biggs managed to evade the clutches of Scotland Yard's finest for thirty years.

*

The bus arrived and we all packed in with our kit bags, those that were to play or maybe not play, depending upon Mark's frame of mind and his blisters, and those who would simply be adding colour and gas to the sidelines.

The trip to the ground was unremarkable. I do recall that generally the roads were much as the drive the day before, one of small two-way tarmac roads all set about very closely with vegetation.

It was from this dense, giant, steaming, croaking cabbage patch that the Club gates appeared and the undergrowth melted away to expose a modern flat-roofed, two-storey, brick-rendered clubhouse with a timber balcony all along one side peering over a well-tended, if slightly over-used, rugby pitch. There was a car park and gently sloping grassed banks hemming in the sports arena. The encroaching jungle was actually surprisingly close to the pitch edges and must have been a result of exhausting the supply of machetes or hoofing balls in there didn't matter as these lads had a huge IRB match ball budget.

The game was to kick off at about 2.00pm so there was some ninety minutes to kill and we were milling about like eight-year old new boys at boarding school when Luceri took charge.

"All kit on NOW...with bootlaces tight and the last of you tossers to start running around the outside of that fucking pitch will suffer my boot up his arse." He roared.

With that simple call and on the basis that Luceri is a very threatening individual indeed even when he is smiling, the group sprung into action. Now with twenty plus tourists there were going to be a few who had brought their kit that would be disappointed, because it's fifteen in a team and a few blood-bin options. Even Turner knew better and hadn't moved a muscle other than to light up a fag.

"Mark I was hoping to get a five-minute run today, any chance?" I whimpered.

'Who said that?"

"Behind you....me....JP"

"Why of course old boy whenever you want. You let me know when it suits you to take the field and I'll drag one of those other bums off and you can have a fun little scamper, is that ok?" That's what I thought he said but no, he actually said.

"Naar I doubt it JP, I have loads of young, proven, keen, fit, good-looking, able, skillful chaps here and I can almost state, with a high degree of certainty and in the clear knowledge that I didn't get where I am today, buy swapping one of them with an old useless, burnt-out twat like you?" If Mark had one fault it was not speaking his mind.

Well blow me down, but there was a moment of déjà vu because I am pretty sure the captain on the day said the same thing to me last year, or did he?...or was that to be next year?

So, after a fifteen minute run about around Luceri separated the forwards from the backs and then arranged the fat boys into three groups and started a series of strenuous lineouts and scrums and breakdowns and mauls and other stuff using the non-playing contingent as useful cannon-fodder opposition.

Halfway through this commando exercise Edinburgh's finest public schoolboy Simon Dakers came up next to me gasping on the pitch and asked.

"JP....och what on earth is bloody Luceri on aboot? *Pod* this and *pod* that...what the fuck is a bloody *pod*?"

"DAKERS! Get over here you skulking, blue Scottish git!" shouted the chummy Lumberjack.

And with that he doubled away again for another ruck. See that's the benefit of having a man from Canada teaching new stuff to old dogs.

I fear my memory of the game has faded and there was generally nothing very remarkable about those eighty minutes other than in the second half a most unexpected shout from Mark, who had played the first half on the pitch and then commanded the remaining period from the sideline.

"JP...you're up, five minutes, get out there and make it count."

And with that I proudly took the field and actually ran with the ball in my hands three times and probably the same number of yards. Not bad for a prop and even more valuable was a nod of approval by Luceri when my time was up. Dakers said it was not an appreciative nod but a nervous twitch he had developed years ago as a tree-feller but that was bollocks I told myself and maybe it was also a surprising chink in Mark's armour that showed he was a kind, thoughtful human.

Both teams agreed the game represented an excellent training match opportunity and so rolling subs were agreed and that may have been their undoing as we had five million to their ten spare blokes. They were good and well-practiced and tough and resilient but with our new youth and multiple pod training, everything we did turned to gold and silver and platinum. We won, they were upset but realistic in defeat, and we drank their health innumerable times until the sun went down.

*

Day #3 was AGM day and you may recall such events were always held over water for the Rhinos RFC, and this was to be no exception. As usual, committee members had fixed and clear roles for the formal activities and others like me, had more casual duties in the tour court hearing. One of the impressive things was that many of the established Rhino's always made huge effort by hiring or buying poignant and particular traditional fancy-dress, depending on the nation being visited.

Now on the morning of the AGM, Sunday morning, our solemn and very experienced Rhino leader Bill, awoke to find he was not alone and, conscious of the fact that the breakfast hour was fast approaching, he must get ready and urgently shoo the floosy from the room.

"Come on Phyllis, time to get up…you shower then leave quick-quick chop-chop." Bill said to the recumbent, unmoving figure against the wall.

"bbbrem…nnerm…Suuunday…sleep-in Boss…." said the pile of blankets.

"No, No noooo…now come on Thelma, get up and shower."

That had no effect and Bill decided he should then wash first and then get the tart moving.

(Phyllis or Maude, Thelma or Agatha – amazingly all the young Filipino girls have ancient English WW1 names and not Spanish derivatives - and I have no idea why – answers on a post-card please.).

*

So that is exactly what did happen, with dripping towel around his waist and the bed clothes torn from the slumbering maiden, she sulkily but with good grace, staggered into the bathroom and started her ablutions.

Now Bill dried and donned his hired outfit for the day and just as he smoothed the last wrinkle from his outer garment, so Miss Cebu emerged from the bathroom, looked up and with a sudden hand covering her mouth to stifle the scream, she slumped to the floor with her palms spread flat on the carpet in supplication.

For there in front of her on a Sunday morning was a Bishop!

Bill had gone the whole hog with the long black cassock with Bishop's pink piping, the outer chimere and topped with a formal mitre making him appear nine feet tall. Bill not only rented costumes but also always took time to rehearse his roles and adopted *that persona* for the day, brilliant.

Without relieving her anxiety in anyway, Bill lent down and taking her by the hand, raised her to her trembling, size five tiny feet with a kindly, "Come now my child, time to dress and pop home… ok?"

And so stumbling and mumbling the Lord's Prayer and with downcast eyes, Phyllis took only seconds to dress in her underwear and sequined covered hot pants and matching cropped tank-top and then nodding to the Bishop, she gathered her mini handbag and followed His Eminence from the room.

They were on about level fourteen in the hotel but when in the descending lift, there was a ding and the cab stopped at level nine and a lovely, young, very religious Catholic family of Mum and Dad and a boy and girl of seven or eight years old in their Sunday best, entered the cab. With practiced mischief, Bill had nodded and made the small sign of the cross with an open outward sideways-palm at chest level, then stepped aside to let them in to the rear of the car. He moved back to the front of the lift and with his nose almost touching the door, he bent again and took the tart by the hand.

Happy family whispering behind stopped and there was silence.

At the Coffee Shop first floor landing the doors opened, Bishop Bill bent again and patted the tart on her little round bottom and said, "Same time tonight ok?"

And with that he glanced back at the family, winked and left them and the sequined maiden in a state of continued, stunned silence as the lift door mercifully closed on the episode.

*****

FROGS...OLD ONES

"I like talking to a brick wall, I find that it is the only thing that never contradicts me." Oscar Fingal O'Flahertie Wills Wilde.

It was late in the 1990's when even the British Club and Southerners current First Team members, who had easily exceeded their sell-by-date as youngsters, finally decided enough was enough and, far from retiring, decided to start an Old Boys side.

Old rouges – Trevor Day, Eddie Evans, Minkey with traditional Northern headdress and Rusty Challon still wearing his festive Santa cap in February – always game for a laugh.

Well the stalwarts, led by Johnny Deards, did form an Ancients side and played a few games, notably starting with the World Old Farts competition in Ireland the year before and with a large playing contingent of bandaged Mummies and an even more prolific selection of disabled but keen watchers. They acquitted themselves well but more importantly, they returned with a new vibrant zeal that was to engender life and enthusiasm into many worriedly aging expats staring mournfully at a chess board thinking *'is that all that's left for me'.*

John Deards, Vinno, Hamish, Andy McDowell, Bob

Merrigan, Roddy Kerr, others and I contrived to arrange a clandestine meeting of old minds in the upstairs, darkened, private room of the Wall St Bar on Soi 33 with the New Zealand proprietor Rick and soon to be principle sponsor fussing around us like an old hen.

All of these chaps were captains of industry in their own right and so the agenda, discussions, plans, reviews, ideas, spontaneous ripostes were a veritable feast of ego jousting and by the end of hours of debate fuck-all was decided.

Somehow, through the vagaries of bargaining, high-quality negotiations with some quite spectacular back-stabbing, this protracted, messy and painful labour eventually bore forth the Bangkok Bangers Old Boys RFC.

These mighty champions of the decision-making table were under no illusions that in fact they formed the core of the playing team, with only McDowell spearheading the sideline chanting and G&T quaffing at every juncture. Unlike some others, Mc.D stuck rigidly to his task to almost drink the distilleries of Gordons dry.

Roles and responsibilities allocated, team kit devised, logo approved, and an outline list of possible players over thirty-five years of age (most were actually already in their late forties), the newly-created club looked about for suitable opposition.

We had organised a few distinctly *warm-up* evening training sessions at a gratefully provided nearby international school pitch, the school remaining anonymous in case it affects their future intake quota. From this active start we were able to sort ourselves into possible playing positions. In the end it transpired we had one serviceable centre of any merit, a winger with one arm and nineteen props.

In all our years of playing rugger in the Kingdom there had been a small phalanx of referees prepared to take to the field and soak up the insults. Not the least amongst them was David Viccars, a registered Hong Kong Football Club official referee, with sports-field valour to the merit of a VC and Bar, he was from a renowned cavalry regiment and a tank commander...a prize the City of Angels is blessed with even to this day.

That wasn't our ref...we had Grant Signal.

There are referees and there are referees. They come in all shapes, speeds, sizes and varying degrees of capability ranging generally from 'bloody good chap' to 'fer fuck's sake where did we get this bloke from'...we didn't have any of them...we had Grant Signal.

If it is possible to maintain control over thirty steaming, wily, guileful, devious old rugger players whilst gasping, farting and stumbling about in the tropical sunshine with just enough breath to belch through a whistle then that was the man we could maybe put up with. No, we had Grant Signal.

Somewhere, somehow, someone wrote down the laws of our much respected and revered game. Don't ask the players - they had no idea what the fuck was going on until that time-honoured whistle blew and would be told ..."*to get back you scab...penalty*". Well if you can grasp that concept of ignorance and wring it's neck of all goodness and then multiply that by ten to the power a million...that's Grant Signal...our champion referee, and bloody proud we are of him!

Our chum Mr Signal is 5'5" tall, stout without excess flab, a pointy nose, a small slightly pinched mouth, black hair swept over his head and should he have the intent to grow a small stumpy moustache, he would closely resemble that infamous gent from just south of Poland in the early part of last century. Looking for one word to best describe Grant, look no further than 'ferret'.

By some fluke of timing, or cynical planning by Hamish, it came to pass that a touring French team was in the vicinity and needed a game..."*aach aye, dinni pannikk they'rr all old boys for sure*" he confirmed.

I was a little skeptical on the level of rugby these Foggy blokes may play and after much quaffing of beer with Hamish it turns out that most of the Gauls were ex-rugby league professionals with a smattering of former Foreign Legion court-marshalled scallywags, with the remaining being criminals scoured from the dungeons of erstwhile French North African colonies.

The day arrived and our team gathered in the unequalled luxury of the school changing rooms – we were used to disrobing and donning jock straps behind a tree in a public park – where any form of nudity was a capital offence.

I had been out to greet the arriving team and even I was dismayed as the bus disgorged the most frightful, enormous, ugly, scarred, powerfully-built monsters that emerged…two of them had eye patches!

I returned to our changing room and looked about at our equally hard-looking team members. Unfortunately, here to make these men *look hard* you must don the *glasses of delusion* from Harry Potter and imagine a misty, ephemeral haze in the room – I was actually staring not at a room of huge killers but at retired geography teachers, passed-over bank clerks, bar owners and a large contingent of overweight fat blokes with ruddy complexions and smouldering fags in their mouths.

Old Blinky, a retired bespectacled music teacher from Cardiff secondary modern came up and whispered in a conspiratorial snigger …"well Boyyo what's they like then eh?"

I meant to say, "Taff they are just a bunch of jumped up Froggy twats with permed hair and too much Eau de toilette…no bloody problem mate"….but instead I whimpered …"We're fucked !"

Grant ensured, in that mistaken style of his, that we, the hosts, took the field first to suffer even longer in the blazing sun, a point not lost on the Gauls and they all decided that another long visit to the bog was in order before coming out into the intense daylight.

As we turned to face the opposition at least two of our team yelped, and uttering, *"fuck that for a game a soldiers you twats I'm off,"* fled the field.

At this point and in the firm knowledge that the Bangkok Bangers had no subs bench, Grant came into his own and in broken O-level Frog he told them they had to drop two players so they too would be an equal thirteen.

The colossal Breton captain shrugged saying. "Oh c'est vrai et c'est normale dans la jeu de coup avec pied les roastbeef Monsieur". Roughly translated - "that's ok with us, 15's too many anyway Sir".

And so to the kick off: well there followed a thirty-five minute revisit to Agincourt, Crecy, Malpalquet and some other forgotten hand-to-hand bloodbaths during our conquests of Canadian and other Froggy lands. Suffice to say that within five minutes of the ball in play the Frogs were down to twelve and a man in the showers for biting. Another joined his soapy mate not ten minutes later for eye gouging.

Hope stirred in our loins as we considered that we could, with Grant's mad happy whistle, beat these bloody Gauls if we could get their team down to say, six.

It has to be said that the renowned ignorance for the laws of the game or fair play-on rules utilised by Grant was getting the better of Froggy patience and, as the world knows all too well, that is a fragile thing at the best of times.

Thus came the straw that broke the proverbial Foreign Legion's camel's back – at the next line-out the Breton had leapt in the air and viciously elbowed our jumper in the face who crumpled in a spurting fountain of claret and the long, shrill signal whistle was heard loud and clear like an air raid siren.

As Grant was gasping, gagging for breath and formulating the right French words, to our horror, their hooker knelt down behind Grant's erect frame and as the red card was brandished for the umpteenth time and the words "Off with you!" were uttered, the big bloke pushed Grant in the chest and in a super slow-motion fall he landed flat on his back in the mud.

Without breaking hypothetical verbal stride, Grant, still in the rigid red-card brandishing mode, lowered his right arm to near his starboard buttock and in the still kneeling Frenchman's leering face and said, **"You're off too.... you Froggy bastard!"**

The game was then abandoned.

*****

119

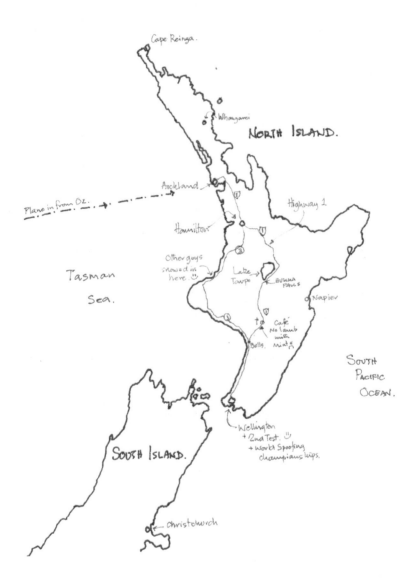

Cape Reinga.

Whangarei

NORTH ISLAND.

Auckland

Plane in from OZ.

Highway 1

Hamilton

Other guys snowed in here. ☺

Tasman

Sea.

Lake Taupo

HUKKA FALLS

Napier

Café No lamb with mint. ☹

Bulls

SOUTH PACIFIC OCEAN.

Wellington
+ 2nd Test. ☺
+ World Spoofing championships.

SOUTH ISLAND.

Christchurch

THE 1993 LIONS

"To regain my youth I would do anything in the world, except get up early, take exercise or become respectable." Oscar Wilde

I had been in the Kingdom of Siam since early 1991 and been on a few memorable rugby tours around Asia to play in the various 15's, 7's and later the emerging enjoyment of the 10's game; a cross between the two existing formats which, although obvious, this fusion of team sizes lent itself more to the *plausible tour*, but I had never been on a 'rugger tour' just to watch others play.

Five of us, and not all current rugby players, had now come together to travel to Wellington, New Zealand and watch the Second British and Irish Lions Test against the All Blacks.

Our team were:

- *Meggo* – aka Dr Paul Meggison; our tall, sinewy, guileful second row and Dr of animal feedstuffs, English, but now calling Wagga Wagga home with an enormous swathe of NSW to call his own; sadly the halfwit called his ranch Ponderosa.
- Jimmy *'Ratcatcher'* Howard: our perennial touring prop and my mentor and roomy to all corners of the Orient. The veritable spine, the glue, the chewed-gum of our group holding sway over disagreements and any decision of consequence.
- *Vinno* – Vincent Swift; founding Father of the *Gentlemen of the East* which eventually morphed into the *Rhinos rugby club*, originally from Liverpool but now of sufficient massive corporate and commercial self-wealth that you did not have to count your fingers after shaking hands. An 82kgs flanker but prepared to lower his standards and supplement as a back as needed.
- *Chris C* – CEO of a massive multi-national corporation and not a rugby team member *per se* but his thickset, 6'4" frame implied a current risk and he was a keen fan

of the Lions and the tours they made. Jovial, witty and capable of huge alcoholic intake.

- *JP* (me): Surrey-born boy having arrived in Thailand in early 1991, current Captain of the British Club's 1ˢᵗ XV, now thoroughly indoctrinated into the bars, beer-swilling and exotic Asian rugby scene and equally as fascinated with this, a first watching tour of our great British home-grown team, and some Shamrock blokes from the Republic.

Our route took us on Qantas from Bangkok to Sydney and then the hop over The Ditch to Auckland on some Kiwi airline, from whence we would hire a car and drive down through North Island to Wellington for both the Second Lion's Test and a night at the Royal Port Nicholas Yacht Club for the World Spoofing championships. And therein lies a tale before we had even landed.

*

Having all our kit made for the British Club RFC over the recent years by Khun Porn of Golden Sports Ltd near the main stadium and Hualamphong train station in Bangkok, we had decided to make a commemorative playing-style shirt. It included a Union Jack on one short sleeve and the Thai flag on the other. White for the body and with two emblems embroidered on the chest, Lions quartered shield on the right and a 'face-on' clenched fist with three gold coins under it and the words:

World Spoofing Championship, Wellington New Zealand. 1993.

For those unfamiliar with Spoofing, almost unimaginable in rugby lads but clearly there were some who don't know what it entailed, I will quickly outline the principles of the pub 'drinking game' noting that our 'school' and those around Asia were considerably more formal than the relaxed pub spoof in the UK.

It can be played by two or more players and, after deciding how many rounds would be considered a suitable sporting challenge, the players would face off and commence.

It was always treated as a polite contest and it was *law* that the loser (who got the correct total of coins in the group) graciously and very graciously would say, *"Thank you gentlemen it has been a pleasure"* and then walk to the bar and order only however many beers or shorts or mixers were needed for yourself and your chums/opposition. No one could miss out on a drink. The eventual 'winner' pays for the round. The cost for one or two players in a game is ok as a round, but you needed a bloody mortgage when the groups got to ten or twelve.

Anyway, briefly;

1. You stand in a group facing inwards, have three matching coins in your pocket (actually they can be any three sizes of coin, other than at a World Spoofing Championship when you MUST hold matching coin denominations.). Or you can actually have no coins and call 'none' and keep fooling the group with no coins at all.

2. You may borrow coins from a playing chum.

3. Incorrect call; you cannot for example call three with only two in your hand or any such combination. This could lead to a group 'raised eyebrow' and a fine.

4. You select your coins from your pocket and then when ready, simultaneously you all hold those chosen coins in your fist, bring it out to arm's length in front of you and 'when the hands are out' the game begins. Always being careful to not let any spare unused coins chink or jingle in your pocket. Such sounds heard when you called three would be deemed an impossible call and close to 'cheating' and you would be fined.

5. The greatest possible, highly-revered call in a large school, is to declare "Spoof" and open your empty hand

there and then and not at the end, for all to see. Which meant that you considered everyone was holding nothing. Rarely a winning call but worth the massive social kudus that your chums gave you with a respectful nod and a muttered '*twat*' under their breath.

6. Whomsoever has been agreed, by the democratic spinning of a toothpick, as the initial starter considers how many coins could be in the various fists, one, two or three or none, adds them up and states his guessed total number for the group clearly.

7. After the first round, the winner of the last, after a suitable period of experiencing that warm glow of success, would call *"when the hands are out"* and a new game would start.

8. All persons must re-assemble in the exact positions in the raggedy circular group they were in for the previous round (excluding any deserters, when it was acceptable to close ranks on an ever-decreasing group). Any errors or loss of memory on your location (no GPS in those days) meant you would be fined a round of beers and your chums would only then assist by reminding you.

9. In the Lore of Spoofing it is essential, nay ungentlemanly, to simply shout out your call without an extended period of intense concentration, staring blankly into space, humming and inspecting your feet, grimacing and slobbering like a bulldog, or whatever you consider makes you look like a thinking man or Isaac Newton straining on a new Theory, but essential.

10. Your call cannot be more than the collective possible total or you are fined a complete round of drinks.

11. When the final guy has called legally, the starter ceremoniously opens his flat hand to the group and exposes his coins. Each does this in turn and the total is tallied and the lucky chap to "win" (actually viewed almost as losing as you have left the chummy pack to sit on your own is the unspoken sentiment) must then leave the group with those traditional kind words and

the first out pops to the bar and orders a complete round of alcoholic drinks.

12. The first out can elect to ask all of the players what they would like (that list is not written down but memory only) or make a concoction of his own for all to drink and no objections.

13. Failing to order before the next player is out is an immediate fine of buying another round of drinks.

14. Failing to order the correct drinks for your chums as requested is…a fine.

15. You must listen intently to all the calls, you cannot ask for a repeat of the call or you are fined a round of drinks.

16. If you inadvertently say the same as a previous call three times (easily done when pished and in a huge group) you are fined a round of drinks.

17. The Lore also strictly controls any form of demonstrative celebration when you 'go out'. It is only human nature that when faced with another or yet another massive costly round of drinks to pay for, you would emit a squeak of joy. NO. Any raised shout, exclamation deemed to be uncouth, any raised fist pumping (*) or even a slowly raised fist above the horizontal (**) would be deemed unacceptable and…you would be fined an immediate round of drinks.

   - (*) It is genetically impossible for any Yanks to play this game without failing at this requirement…fist pumping is obviously a womb-based tic in all developing Septics.

   - (**) To prevent extended and boring argument over what is deemed the definition of horizontal – it is deemed to be 'the height of the door handle on a Citroen Deux Chevaux' when seated in the driving position.

18. If this was not scary enough, the Lore also frowned very heavily on anyone using real numbers to indicate their offer. So you cannot simply shout out those numerical

tones you learnt in school…five…twelve…seven. It had to be done by saying the code word for that number and these are globally acceptable formal terms and must be adhered to. (See Appendix for 'The Calls')

19. As a few examples :
    a. 9 would be 'The German Virgin' (because she always said 'Nein!')
    b. 11 was 'Legs Eleven' or 'The Dead Parrot' or 'any recently deceased celebrity'…Mother Theresa was always a favorite to cause consternation, cos she could have 9 or 11.
    c. 10 was 'The Kiwi' or 'Marine's breakfast' (an egg on a plate with one sausage)
    d. 'Joe Tupai' was the call for One, because it was Kiwi legend that during a lull in the frantic passions of shagging some bird, he had noticed her butt hole was nearby and so he impertinently inserted his 'Dirty Digit'…also an alternative shout for One.

20. This can also lead you to hot water and another fine if the code word you have selected is wrong. Aged thirsty, players have a ghastly and uncanny memory for all calls made by anyone over the last three hours, or is that years?

21. All Calls are in English.

22. No one may eat during Spoofing, unless unanimously agreed on shared tit-bits.

23. No one may consider going to the loo during a round. If you did, you were fined for ungentlemanly pathetic bladder control…round of drinks.

24. New members during their first event may make mistakes but if that new lad was hopelessly delinquent, then the necessary Sponsor who brought him into that School would be fined a round of drinks.

25. You cannot leave the School when you feel like it. No excuses allow you to just flee the scene. Death in the family, "I think I'm pregnant", "oops is that the time,

my wife will kill me"…naar. Again Lore dictates that you may only leave the game when one has clearly stated, once the hands are out, "Gentlemen this will be my final round" before the starter starts. Obviously a guileful starter will quickly shout out his call before the unhappy deserter has finished his sentence – hence inadmissible as a reason for leaving and bound-in for another period of hiccupping and quaffing.

26. No ladies may Spoof unless it is the second Tuesday after the New Year.

So, armed with such information you would enjoy a delightful night's drinking with chums and new acquaintances until the early hours, probably at huge cost and if repeated on a regular basis, divorce usually followed.

*

We had boarded the Qantas flight, had our meal and then gathered in the open side-galley for stand-up beers and a chat. We were in the first main economy class block between bulkheads and must have had some twenty rows of ten seats across in a standard Jumbo and so we were amongst some two hundred returning Aussie families, including some tourists.

A large athletic Aussie bloke sauntered up to us and introduced himself as Bruce and enquired in his Aussie twang what we Poms were up to.

"Look mate, we've all noticed the emblem on yer guernseys (sports jerseys) and see the note about World Spuuffing, can yer's tell us about that?" the last looking over his shoulder at the cabin and releasing a small wheezy snigger.

"Yeah sure Bruce, it's a game we blokes play together and of course it's a drinking game with rules and punishment if you come last."

"Rrrrrriight," he mused, awaiting more explanation, "so how's that work exactly mate"…wheezy snigger… "I mean can the Sheila's play?"

Winking, I said. "Oh no this is strictly a men's game eh."

"Yeaaaah riiiight I bet it is mate," grinned Bruce.

"Well we all stand in a circle to get a bit of privacy and get the hands out."

"Pppprrrt..right on ya' and then what," says Bruce leaning in conspiratorially.

"We spin a toothpick or something pointy to elect who goes first and the game starts."

"Yeeeaah rrrright," Grin getting broader.

"The first guy to get it right goes out and orders the beer," I continued.

"Look Johnno, is there a biscuit or something your gotta hit?" he proffers.

"No Bruce there can be no food or eating during the game....oh... unless unanimously agreed to share at the same time."

"Pppprt...you're kidding right...you'd all share the biscuit between youse?"

"Well not just a biscuit it could be cheese or nacho's or sliced sausages...you know group pick-upon food." I clarified.

At this, Bruce turns and explains to his now attentive a hundred and ninety-four fellow economy class audience all straining over their shoulders to peek at the galley and the weird Poms, "Righto guys, so they do do it on the food and then it's sharezies all round!"

"Chriiist, strewth is that for real"...the whole cabin murmured.

"We are off to the World Championships where everyone comes from all over the world, as it implies, and we all Spoof-off together...this time at the Wellington Yacht Club." I offered.

"Fer Christ sakes' are you serious mate...this is un-ber-bloody-believable...did youse hear that Sheila...at the bloody Yacht Club for Christ's sake!"

Well we couldn't figure out why there was such consternation and almost scathing looks for the cheap seats as we had provided brief but reliable advice on the game and yet there was something afoot.

Well the double-entendre disinformation chat with Bruce went on with even more mismatching understanding and shock from them until I had to ask, "Bruce this is a drinking game we play with coins in our hands and you count in your mind and state your total and the best guess wins – what's the issue here?"

"Oh," said Bruce. "So uuhmm…it's not…uuhmm men just doing it…in a group?"

"Doing what?" I asked, realizing for the first time we really were at cross purposes about this issue.

By now the cabin were mostly up on their knees in the seats peering back at us all…hushed, expectant, poised.

Bruce leaned in and cupping his hand to my ear he whispered, "In Aussie mate, where weeze all come's from, Spuuffin' means wanking."

Stunned at our cultural ignorance I prudishly gasped "Good heavens NO Bruce this is just a game with coins and who loses buys the beer, no none of *that* business!"

Bruce physically deflates with evident relief and turns to all about us and shouts,

"It's ok guys they're not Spuuffin' wankers, it's just a beer drinking game with coins and stuff." And the multitude in one collective sigh let out their trapped breath in a long busting gust and turned to sit in their seats, much relieved that the world was not holding, what they thought, in its collective hand.

*

We transferred at Sydney to Kiwi-Flot Air and waved a fond farewell to Bruce and the cabin with them all wishing us luck in the…errm Spuufing tourney.

The next flight was uneventful and we smoothly transitioned to hire car transport and set off out of Auckland down Highway 1 to Hamilton in Waikato country.

We stayed overnight, as the evenings got dark quickly in the Southern Summer, booking into a large B&B motel-type establishment, ate supper and kipped like the dead.

The Highway to took us to Lake Taupo, our first port of call during the two-day drive tour we planned to reach Wellington.

Here we stopped on the side of the lake at a delightful modern, extremely well-kept bungalow style lodge on the water's edge and all set about with flower beds and indigenous trees.

This was The Fishing Lodge and we leapt at the idea of a couple of small boats and some trout fishing, accompanied with suitably large cooler boxes of Steinlager and some sarnies and crisps.

We spent many hours in our small ship-lapped, wooden row boats with 15 hp outboards and unbelievably we caught three enormous trout. There were celebratory 1993 *hi-fives* (probably a low-key thumbs up in those days) and cracked open more beer and swigged away until we realized we had moved some considerable distance across the vast lake and should return to the Lodge as the evening was rapidly cooling and the light fading.

We made it back just as dusk swallowed the sun and sporting our huge fish, entered the lodge bar and were greeted with loud cheers and hand clapping by the few locals in the bar. Probably genuine clapping after earlier casting bets on *how pathetic these Poms are gonna be at fushin'*…and actually we had disappointed them by catchin' their 'fush', but in the true sporting Kiwi ethos we did get a pat on the back.

We asked about Le Chateau hotel and where it could be found, now unfortunately in the dark. All the staff had come out of the kitchens and the front desk to be near such unusual guests, and they offered at least five different sets of directions, which seemed unlikely as there were only about two tarmaced roads in North Island in total.

We gathered the data and stored it away as there then commenced the most serious practicing game of Spoofing for beers and mixers the Lodge had ever seen. It was vicious and cut throat and unrelenting with flaming Sambuca's and traffic lights and Gorilla-snots being guzzled between gallons of beer.

Not only had the Lodge ever sold so many cocktails, I am certain they had never taken in so much money in one evening. We were massively pished and still had to drive up the volcano and find the hotel.

We staggered from the Lodge again with many farewell wishes and finding our car in the unlit car park, I put the fish down to assist with rearranging the contents of the car as we now had to fit in our local guide who would lead us half way and then get out.

*

Meggo drove well, disgorged the guide and sped on up hairpin bends and blind corners to the very top of the volcano and found our grand Chateau hotel, truly a fine mock Froggy, pointy-roofed edifice, and staggered into the lobby and booked in.

Chris demanded the Chief Chef attend upon us to be guided on the need to prepare and cook our fabulous trout for dinner. It was late but by now we were hungry.

"JP pass the fish over mate," said CEO CC.

"Ugh?"

"The fish you twat…where are the trout?"

And with that we all realized they were back in the dark, dark car park at the Lodge. We dashed for a phone and the front desk called the Lodge. Meggo took the handset and asked, "Can someone help and check the car park for…."

"Naar mate, no Poms been here and no trout in the car park at all…no…none," was the reply before Meggo had even uttered the reason for the call, and the line burred and went dead.

"The scheming bloody bastards!" echoed round the plush, fake Froggy-aristocratic-decoration of the lobby.

Hungry, we went to bed, happy at the day's antics but now wary of the locals and their trustworthiness.

The morning beamed brightly through the curtains and upon flexing stiff trout fishing muscles, I looked out in wonder at the magnificent sight of the giant volcano and hotel grounds now all shrouded in a perfectly-silent blanket of thick snow. This even got my Roomy Ratcatcher out of bed with a huge fart and a matching burp to enjoy the new view.

We all trooped down for breakfast and it was a traditional Olde English-style offering, porridge and golden syrup, Kellogg's corn flakes and milk, steaming kippers, poached egg and whole regiments of crisp toast in their racks. Tea and coffee as refills and even some Gallic croissants and jam to befit the architectural circumstance.

Stuffed and expectant, we paid and left and after a brief squabble in the car park about who was really going to drive in the snow, I declined after being branded *'the worst bloody driver in Asia you bloody arse Prichard'*. Hurtful though it was, I did have concerns about no snow chains and those hairpin bends. A Pyrrhic victory I thought.

6'4" Meggo with attitude climbed behind the wheel and in a swirling, slipping and embarrassing pirouette in the six inches of snow, we headed south out of the car park.

The details are a little misty but before taking the road thru Wanganui and Manawatu, I demanded that we detour to see the Hukka Falls which is the main outfall from Lake Taupo and is the most frightfully powerful waterfall you will ever witness.

Falls, not excessive and majestic width-wise like Niagara, but the fact that the lake's contents fled through a deep and square natural canal to the edge of the rock formation and there, dived-off in a solid long 'cube' of water about fifteen yards wide and the same deep made them a marvel. A massive green, never ending 'Play-dough' spurge of water made all the more magnificent as there was almost no sound other than a very deep bass throbbing where the cascade entered the steamy pond below and must have burrowed miles into the earth's core.

"Fabulous." I shrieked and my mates stared with the vacant eyes of the ignorant and the uncaring buffoons that they were, collectively picked their noses and headed back to the car.

Meggo in fishing gear – apparently quite an
accomplished angler – caught fuck all that day!

It has to be said that I had, much to the shock and surprise of my father, passed my 'A' level in Geography. As the journey unfolded, there, at every turn, in one short space of one country, were the vast collection of real-life morphological wonders of nature laid out before me: Ox-bow lakes, Horst shear fractures, Clints'n Grikes, volcanos – live, dormant and dead, bubbling mud pools and spurting geysers. We almost ran out of tissues by the time we reached the town of Bull on HY1.

Now here there was the first driving dilemma because at this 'Y' junction, there was the option to turn North West and take the HY3 along the northern coast road to Foxton, Levine and thence Wellington or we could break off and head South-ish thru the centre of North Island taking HY1 and I could glory in more landscape features.

There were two other cars full of Poms at this same junction pointing at the signs and gesticulating and like us arguing about which was best and they too had dispute and uproar as their route was discussed.

After the hurtful comments about my driving prowess, I insisted and shouted and may even have shed a tear, but I won and we zoomed off down HY1 following the Manawatu river and more super morphological features.

As a postscript to this fateful route trip decision, we later met those same blokes in a bar in Wellington *after the Test* and they declared mournfully that they had turned off to HY3, reached the coast and then been trapped in their cars for two days by the worst snow blizzard in recorded history and had missed the match entirely.

Geography 1, Ignorant Tossers 0.

*

So, we drove on down towards Wellington and at lunchtime stopped at a rather lonely roadside café - a converted church, which had chalk boards outside advertising *"Lamb like you've never had it"*. We dived in, ordered the standard Steinlagers and looked at the menu.

Now I am a firm and dedicated lamb flesh-eating supporter but with the traditional mint sauce or mint jelly. Well, true to the chalky advert, all lamb at this deconsecrated place of worship, came as we had never imagined, impregnated with garlic, salted exterior, ham and cheese filling, toffee topping and any number of banana options, but no mint. The kindly waitress, almost crying, mumbled that they hadn't cooked with mint for years, no demand. Bugga.

So, after various portions of lamb with apricot gravy or some such nonsense, we returned to the chariot satisfied, if a little gastronomically compromised, and sped off to Wellington.

We arrived in the capital, found our hotel, the name of which escapes us all, but it was posh and modern and known to the All Blacks. We then called and met our host for the weekend, none other than Murray Graham Mexted himself. Must have been stealth, wealth and connections by Vinno to conjure-up such a super star.

Murray held thirty-four consecutive caps for the All Blacks playing at No 8, plus thirty-eight non-tests as Captain between the years 1979 to 1985. He was a published author of his own book *Pieces of Eight* and amongst those non-tests he took part in the Five Nations v World XV in 1985 winning 32-15 at Twicker's and that team included some white South Africans during the Apartheid era, amongst them, Naas Botha.

He also played in the controversial Cavaliers Tour to SA in 1986, where they lost three of the four tests and the Tour Captain Andy Dalton broke his jaw early on and their participation was widely condemned upon their return. All those who went on tour were banned for a few matches and many new young bloods were introduced and the team was then dubbed 'The Baby Blacks' and many of them stayed and the old guard lost out.

Anyway, we had a superstar to lead us about and sup beers over the weekend. Murray was also a dedicated Spoofer and was taking us to the Yacht Club on the Sunday evening.

Friday night was a civilized dinner and wine evening and then after a few beers at the Molly Malone's pub it was off to bed in anticipation of the next day's Test.

*

Saturday dawned grey and chilly. We met Murray in the hotel bar about noon, driving off to the Athletic Park stadium for the game in Murray's estate wagon.

Unlike any of the future Lions Tours, marketing had simply not been a strong point then and there were no red shirts of any merit, no Lions paraphernalia and quite frankly, so far from home, there were no Lions fans. To put this in perspective, after the match there were us five, two or three wandering the pitch and three pissed-up blokes lying on the ground in the dead ball area, and of course those poor fellows in the snow drift. That was it, say twenty.

Four years later in Durban we were sitting amongst 20,000 fans in the East stand of King's Park, all in scarlet and by 2001 in Oz the local paper noted that viewed from the air, Melbourne was '*hemorrhaging with Lions fans walking the streets to the ground*'.

We were, by years of living in Asia, a thin-blooded group of chaps with almost no cold weather wardrobe and so with some cobbled together ski wear and train-spotter anoraks we were poorly prepared for the bitingly cold, freezing wind that shrieked through Wellington on its way from the Antarctic and I hoped it would descend on that *lamb-without-mint* café.

We found our allocated seats in the ancient low-profile stadium some twenty rows back from the pitch edge on the 10 yard line...or was it metres by then? Murray bade adieu for the match and scampered off, I am sure, to a warm box or the heated commentary booth.

The Lions had only lost the first Test to a highly controversial Grant Fox penalty in the dying minutes to lose 18-20, and so we were uber-hyped for a real battle and a comeback by our lads...they didn't disappoint.

I just recall a freezing day in the stands, a small school boy behind me in his playing shorts and blue skin, I mean blue skin and his teeth chattering away like a road grinder removing tarmac, the wingers must have suffered bloody frostbite, oh they are *backs*, who cares.

Well it was a frightfully violent and committed game with collisions clearly heard in row twenty for all tackles made on both sides and that cedar tree Martin Bayfield at 27'9" dominated the line outs. Gavin Hastings was brilliant with the boot and Rob dropped a goal. Wee Rory Underwood scored a try and that was that: 20-7 victory and we had won and levelled the series.

Beer swilling during the match was simply not possible as there were no wandering salesmen with belly-trays available in the stands. It was too cold to have your hands out of your pockets for more than a brief sporting clap as an All Black was felled and we couldn't go to the bar anyway because we were stuck frozen to our plastic seats.

Hence our ecstatic, euphoric celebrations amongst our host nation's mob were a sober, muted 'Hurrah...jolly good...great work" and a longing for a huge mug of hot, steaming cocoa.

After the match we had agreed with Murray that we would stand in the middle of the pitch, as it was completely open to the spectators and no security in those days to tell you when to sneeze or breathe, and he could find us there.

The tall, black haired, powerful frame of MM appeared from the morass and led us out from the stadium to the imagined prospect of a lovely warm pub with a real fire, cocoa and some warm buns. In fact, the Arctic wind now possessed a ghastly, painful, horizontal stinging drizzle and whimpering to a man, our group hurried after the long strides of our host towards the car park.

As we shuffled like stooped, rag clad, war-time Polish refugees against the wind, there were numerous single-storied buildings with delightful warm orange glowing lights coming from their windows and hearth smoke whipping away from their chimneys. Every single one had a sign "Do not enter without a reservation. FULL"

It was Bethlehem all over again, but without a Saviour.

It became evident we were not to find refuge from the elements and Murray shouted above the howling wind., "Bugger this, I have something much better in my car bru'."

With Hope sprinting ahead of Expectation and leaving a reality-check well behind in its wake, we arrived at Murray's car, he opened the boot and there was the largest domestic cooler box, sitting, no lurking, like Pandora's Box.

The man's huge, farming hands threw open the lid to expose Steinlagers by the million, all bedded lovingly in non-melting ice. Popping the tops faster than we could chatter "*oh nice Murray...thanks*" he brandished a bottle to each and then a refill, which you had to hold in your ungloved, non-drinking hand and he proposed many a toast to the victorious Lions.

Well the man was a gem. Despite the fact he went on to be the most cycloptic Kiwi sports commentator ever employed by the media, he laughed, told jokes, splurged forth old tales and All Black dirt laundry for at least an hour and by then even the Antarctic had given up trying to kill us and our torsos had adapted to have a core body temperature of -15 Celsius.

*

Back to the hotel for a shower and a warm-up and then out for more drinks seemed to be the plan. Having completed our ablutions, we returned to the lobby only to find it full of the entire All Black team, bench and management staff in their black, tailored suits and ties.

They were all smart, polite and engaging and completely unruffled or damaged or scarred in anyway, as if they had not done anything more taxing than watching the game on TV. It was amazing that we were standing amongst the superstars of the day like Robin Brook, Michael Jones, Sean Fitzpatrick, John Kirwin, Grant Fox and Zinzan Brooke.

There was little doubt in our minds that the Kiwi's were streaks ahead of GB and Europe on the professional player front, money aside. They displayed healthy, genuine interest in *you* being interested in them and smiling and grouping up for pictures with us…complete unknowns but rugby enthusiasts. It was charming, a sports' marketing success and a great memory to take home.

In all the excitement I needed a pee and set off for the gents. Mid-stream, the urinal beside me was taken by the short, bulky frame of their Captain Sean Fitzpatrick and he said. "You guys were bloody marrrvelous today, simply bloody marrrvelous."

I sputtered, " But…but I was only a fan."

"Naar mate, you's were all bloody marrrvelous and I take my hat off to you guys fer wunnin'."

Back in the lobby, Murray was to go with them for dinner and we could find the Lions down the road at Molly Malone's.

So, we set off with the unlikely expectation of actually finding the Lions Team but if we bumped into a few it would be worth it. We found the pub on the corner and trooped inside to a very dimly-lit open bar with tables and chairs in the centre and small booth-like niches around the exposed-brick walls. The bar was at one end and had stools around its belly bump rail. It was very odd to be that dark and sombre. It really was as if there had been a power cut and we were drinking by candlelight.

And there in the gloom were all our heroes.

A wandering barman immediately brought us a beer and we sat a few tables away from our hallowed players quietly sipping and mumbling and frankly plucking up courage to go over and speak to one of them. They were seriously morose and in no way exhibited the trappings of being the victors over the All Blacks and inflicting the largest score ever handed to an AB team at that time.

Upon closer inspection, as the non-light allowed, they were in casual clothes but team casuals, and sporting the Lions emblems, but they were also all seriously damaged and broken. Arms in slings, bandaged heads, spit eyebrows, evident sticky plastered injuries, taped-up fingers and bruises and red blemishes adorned every face and neck. They were truly buggered.

There in the dark we were once again ultra-close and we were the only civilians near these International players, names that again live in the memory forever: Rob Andrew, Will Carling, Leun Evans, Jerry Guscott, a slim Scott Gibbs, Gavin, Rory, Bayfield, Dooley, Martin Johnson, Jason Leonard, Kenny Milne, Brian Moore, Dean Richards and man mountain Mike Teague and others.

This was such a unique situation that I was sure it would never be possible to approach these guys in the years to come, so I stood and advanced to the bar. From behind a seated player, I looked Peter Winterbottom in the eye (well, the one that wasn't black and temporarily shut for repair), and in the lull of their conversation said some dross like, "Bloody well done guys, we are so proud of you and what you did and we'd like to thank you all, a great, fabulous win…well done…" I trailed off.

Peter nodded in a calm respectful way, but I suggest the slowness of that regal movement was not through well-mannered training but more because all batteries were flat.

The back to my immediate left, swiveled on the stool and that back was actually a Back and Stuart Barnes peered scornfully at me and said, "Who the f#@k are you ?......F#@k off!"

Now I am not good at most instructions but that one I do take exception to and hero or no, this could develop I thought.

"Wooooha!!" said Peter, my nodding life-long mate, "Stu that is no way to speak to our lads …so button it."

Or something maybe a little more agricultural, but he did then get off his stool, slowly, delicately and came around the offending rude twat and putting an arm on my shoulder, he led me back to our table and sat and chatted for about twenty minutes.

He congratulated us on flying in to be *live fans* and genuinely offered us some Lion's chatter but his nature, I am advised, was that of a quiet man of few words but he was the most vocal Lion there in that gloomy Irish room.

We had a few more beers, ate some dinner and then all approached the bar, wished them well for the remaining Test and retreated away from the waving and nodding, exhausted throng.

*

Sunday: World Spoofing Championship's day and there was every possibility that YOU could become THE world champion there and then in Wellington Yacht Club. What a prospect, really it was possible – Global fame.

Now the pub game of Spoofing was a very different affair to the 'Worlds' as they were familiarly known. Apart from those Gestapo-like enforced rules, the whole dinner was a Black Tie function and any who had attended a World's before, had a rainbow coloured, thin striped, deck-chair jacket with a Fist emblem embroidered on the top pocket. The jacket being the absolute peak of Spoofing honours and participation and after you have attended, one could order a bolt of fabric from the formal store in some sweat shop in Hanoi or Saigon and then have yours tailored to fit in your local town.

JP in formal fig and apparently reminding many of that famous film star – Lassie taking a shit!

In the evening we were taken to the venue by Murray and entered the privileged and upper-class toffs Yacht Club to be ushered to the large open function room with, what would be in daytime, a splendid set of veranda windows over-looking the marina and a wide timber balcony.

The interior was all Lloyd-George-esque oak paneling, discreet warm glow wall lights, with green baize card tables and some thirty-or-so high round tables with equally tall stools, poised for the gladiatorial event. The whole was filled with posh gents in black tie and the surprisingly numerous, deck-chair clad chaps giving the formalities some colour.

Pre-dinner drinks and greetings to old chums well met once again, took us to the dining period and wine was liberally dispensed by white-clad, black-button waiters as an array of excellent cuisine with a healthy, local seafood theme was served.

The massive imposing figure of Andy Haden made a speech after dinner, before the finals. Haden was standing centre table, with his back to the magnificent vista of Port Nicholson and Wellington Harbour. Vince Swift and I were sitting exactly opposite him, too far away for us to touch him, but well within the range of his huge arms. As he concluded his speech, he picked up his port glass to make the toast, but was irritated to find it was empty.

"Where's the fucking port?" he bellowed at the terrified waitress.

"It's behind you, you cunt!" shouted the more inebriated of the two British Club Spoofers sitting opposite him. Now credit where credit is due, it must have been 'Swift The Sozzled' because 'Prichard the Pickled' was too pished and stupid to even consider such a clever, poetic and harbour-related riposte.

After the Haden debacle, various old blokes spoke of historic Spoofing battles and the MC announced the use of rules, coin requirements, the draw, the elimination system, the Repacharge, the need to keep drinking and the absolute goal to find the new champion for 1993.

And so, to the various rounds of the group stages where four Spoofers took to each high table and out-thought, bored or simply farted their way through to the next round. The next and the final repacharge of *live-again* players brought us and surprisingly me from our group, to the quarter final round.

Here we were divided into smaller groups of three Spoofers per table and the surviving last player would move to the final finals or some-such organized sub-level as there still seemed to be many players still 'in the game'.

Your mates or others would gather around the playing players to see if any of the surviving wisdom could filter back to their obviously deficient experience.

Amazingly my two opponents were to be Murray and the big man, Colin Meads himself. The sea of onlookers parted and the scourge of all national team lineout jumpers and those with enduring 'accidental' disabilities, stomped to our table. I was surprised that Mr Meads was not taller but his huge Desperate Dan chin and general command of that emphatically dangerous bubble he exhibited, did leave me trembling in awe.

One starts with a few free sparring rounds before the MC calls for the formal start of *that* Round. Now I cannot remember exactly at what stage this happened but it was obviously at a late stage of sudden death and the last round to whittle us down to two.

I had learnt, if nothing else, that either because of a massive influx of early Scottish settlers, or the natural trait of farmers to hoard stuff or because the miserly National Mint couldn't afford to stamp enough coins, but the collective end result was that ALL New Zealand spoofers, all of them, only ever called 'None' or 'One'.

In this last round, Murray started and called 'none'. I was next and I thought gosh I'm through to the finals! I was holding one coin in my outstretched hand.

I called, after sombre, funeral-like reflection, 'One'.

Mr Meads was startled with an involuntary whole-body tic and after a moment of silence said, "Well that's bollocks. I was going to call One."

And taking his frowning visage from the table-top beery spillage, looked me in the eye and said "Well?"

I was non-plussed. The expectant, eager but frightened crowd were silent as lambs and I shook my head and offered,

"I beg your pardon Sir?"

"You damn well know that I wanted to call One, so...so what's to be done?"

Oh, I thought, this is awkward. One of the greatest ever rugby legends is being embarrassed by a lowly useless scrote and expecting me to change my call, which I *KNEW* was the winning call...and sadly so did that smirking Mexted monster beside me.

"Oh well...uumm...if I may gentlemen, I wish to change my call to "two"...if I may please?"

Meads grinned, much as he must have done in those halcyon days of set-piece conquests and grunted, "I call One"

We opened our hands and there for all to see was the solitary, miserable, back-stabbing, bastard one coin in my hand.

Colin's closing dismissive words of affection ring in my ears even now, "Thanks Jon...now FUCK OFF!"

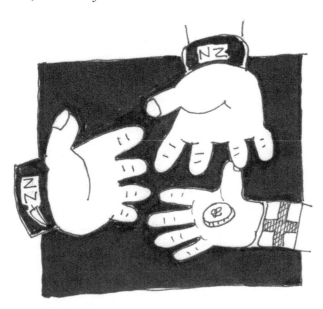

THE LONG DROP

'The real voyage of discovery consists not in seeking new lands but seeing with new eyes.' Marcel Proust

By 1993 I had been on quite a number of local and overseas rugby tours with the Bangkok British Club, which is quite a feat of diplomatic visa acquisition, having only arrived in Thailand in early 1991. These almost impossible to acquire permits to travel were not from the immigration offices of the various sovereign nations I visited, but from the wife.

Now in that autumn of discontent, Jane decided it was only fair that the children, identical twin daughters Holly and Samantha aged five, and my first son Billy ...umm, crawling, snotty and muddy, should see more of their father on a personal one-on-one basis, get to know each other, you know...suffer.

And on this premise she announced that she was going on a tour of her own with seven of her mates. *'NO...there was no stopping her, no don't even try you beggar, I deserve it, you've had your fun, you try and stay here with the three rascals and cope'*...obviously she never said any of those coarse thoughts, it would have been more a peaceful and Nirvanian-like homily....*'it would be good for me and I can find myself, or at least, discover myself.'*

We were living in a delightful four-bedroom private house owned by Thailand's ex-Ambassador to the USA, in Sukhumvit Soi 53 and only three doors down from the-then acting Prime Minister of Thailand, so by lucky happenstance, a very salubrious neighbourhood indeed.

One day, whilst perambulating the very safe and police-patrolled lower end of the Soi, pushing Billy in the buggy and trailing the mischievous twins, Jane had met Mrs Christie Blithering-Hastings-Smythe from No 43. They became friends and after a short time Christie kindly invited us over to their house for dinner.

She was married to Rupert who worked for Reuters (that's not his real surname either but you know those guys from *that* agency always have hyphenated names they just make up to look flash and of a quasi-Prussian-Holstein decent). Rupert was generally overseas a lot and whilst they also had two offspring, Christie opined that she and Jane were in much the same lonely boat of ignored and unappreciated wives and they should get out.

This was not the scheming of dissent and abdication, nor too I think a delicate scream for attention but rather a simple healthy - they can do it, we've never done anything like this so let's prove we can...or something psychologically unbalanced like that.

Anyway that first dinner was held at No 43 and Rupert and I became firm beer-swilling chums, subject of course, to he being in South America, the Congo or St Helena. I was always careful to leave their scary *Psycho*-Bates-like house before dark and whilst sipping drinks in the giant, Indian, rattan Raj chairs in their glazed conservatory, the girls started their planning.

*

Expat life at thirty-two was all new to me and certainly so to my young west country wife Jane and so I would not like to give the impression that my beloved was now homesick away from...well home, oppressed, overworked and with hands hardened by excessive domestic servitude.

The reality was that having met other expats in the first three months before my new family arrived from the UK in 1991, I had already settled the basic requirements of the home and children's education planning (not to mention working). I had also been instructed in the way of Asian Upstairs and Downstairs employment. I might have overdone it a bit.

I had a fabulously loyal company driver called Khun Songwuth, a full-time but off-station gardener called '*Oye*' and a live-in-the-shed alcoholic night security guard called 'That-drunken-old-bastard-has-done-it-again.'

Inside the house we had a senior maid from the North-Eastern Isaan region, Khun Pan, and her daughter Khun M and a junior hard-working maid Khun Goi. So we UK expats were outnumbered almost three to one in the servants-to-toffs ratio. Look, I loved my wife dearly and she deserved all the assistance such domestic help could offer and anyway their combined wages were about the cost of one weekly visit to Sainsbury's.

*

Now of all the credit-card-depleting shopping tours, ultra-luxury Asian health spas, silvery-sandy-beach tropical destinations they could have chosen for their tour, this bunch of eight deranged wives had chosen to trek to Everest's First Base Camp.

Now whilst this was not an SAS do-or-die, eat your dead comrades event in the planning, we collective husbands were aware that this was some considerable challenge and to be frank our homely, reasonably sedate, beautiful wives were a far cry from ready for such a test.

All the girls played or had played sports in their day and in fact, with the regiments of household staff on hand, they were all free most of the day to relax or exert themselves at the British Club to their hearts content.

So they were already quite fit but they knew this was serious and planned a detailed six-month training course to improve walking in big boots, yoga and dance flexibility techniques, carrying packs and improving their stamina levels.

Amazing eh...those wee wifey things that climb into the matrimonial bed can, in almost the blink of an eye, turn from blurry-eyed bundles of cuddly, sexy, warm fun into..."*nope none of that tonight darling, we've got a nine-kilometre hike tomorrow, a four-year swim up the Mekong and anyway my broken clavicle is acting up.*"

Now I could imagine this new, hard working, gritting-of-teeth-in-the-face-of-adversity, west country wife of mine doing this, shockingly new as it was, but Christie?

Christie was the epitome of the product of the English finishing school model, with honours and bar. She was 5'5", petite to the point of Barbie brittle, blonde and always dressed in expensive-looking, haut-couture and really as far from a hard, long mountainous trek as to Clarkson being modest and humble.

Well bugger me, but the whole group set to a weekly regime with enthusiasm and grit that never waned. We were lucky on the kit front, in that Jane and I were already seasoned Alpine skiers so she had all the warm clothing except maybe better trekking trousers and a pair of stout boots to be worn in.

There was one last supper at Antony Hopkins' mum's place, where husbands were for once sitting in the dim shadows of discussion and the room, and the girls were vibrant with excited pre-tour nerves and anticipation. Sadly, there were no modern smart phones to record the happy, expectant faces of the wives nor too the dark and worried expressions of the fathers who faced a solid ten days of stand-alone child care.

The next weekday morning, those husbands that could, took their spouses to Don Muaeng airport and tearfully waved them off to Nepal in the foothills of the Himalayas.

*

I don't recall all of the details of the Route, in fact I wasn't there, so none is the real picture, but from the happy chirpings of my wife and with the aid of Google I can patch in some facts. I have also included altitude estimates in parenthesis for added trekkie authenticity.

They landed in Kashmir (1,300m), where there was, not surprisingly, fighting going on ever since the British had been there in the 1850's or more exactly Alexander The Great had been there before Jesus. They found their agency guide and checked into the last vestige of luxury they were to experience for more than a week.

They then took a local flight up to Luka in the Khumba valley area at 2,800m a.m.s.l. (more trekkie jargon: *above mean sea level*) and it was here that the agency guide introduced them to the team of Sherpas who would lead them up the mountain passes to their destination and hopefully bring them all back safely.

There was one Sherpa shared between two ladies and a couple of spare human mules to carry provisions and mountain-necessary stuff. These were the super-thin-blooded peoples of Nepal renowned as the world's most sturdy climbers with an indomitable will to scale peaks.

Look, the guide probably did go with them too but whatever the final make-up of this intrepid caravan, this was a far cry from the comprehensive and globally fanatically HSE safe treks on offer today. That was it: eight birds from Britain, a probable Nepalese translator and ten blokes in goatskin duvets and some food.

Jane and Christie were to point out that these guys were also the nicest, loveliest blokes you would ever want to meet if you were lost in a -40 degree blizzard, with wolves howling about you and a probable life expectancy of twenty-five seconds, but not, however, blokes to sleep with in a communal dormitory using the same air and without four hundred tonnes of rose petal Potpourri.

With a lifestyle and habitual weather-restricting practice of rarely, if ever, taking off your clothes for any reason, combined with excessive heavy lifting, gargantuan sweat glands, a distinct and ingrained fear of washing, a daily diet of goat fat both ingested and used as a hair tonic, these kind and helpful, hardworking Sherpas smelt more like week-old tropical road kill.

How's that smell you quip? Well, next time when you see old Fido freshly squished and re-squished by heavy traffic on the open roads of Asia, do take the time to get out of your car, stand four feet down-wind and take a really deep breath and the full glory of Edmund Hilary's amazing feat and Tenzing's actual feet will be realised.

They got underway with the first up-hill walk to Phakding (2,650m) and then in the coming days on to Namche Bazaar (3,446m) which is the ethereal capital of the Sherpa, on up to Thyangboche Monestary (3,867m), a glimpse of the sacred lakes of Gokyo (I am not sure they could actually see these from their pathway but it adds some colour to the trail.) and on and on and on to the valley of First Base Camp.

Now somewhere just outside the first pee stop away from Phakding (2,650m + 300mm), poor Agatha gave a whimper, then a squeak and then a shriek and sat down on the path clutching her head.

As everyone knows who does daft hill-walking or trekking or bush wandering, any such walking group gradually settles into a long line of those at the front and those that ain't. Well this bevvy of birds were a Band of Brothers, errm Sisters, who were all for one and one for all, so they duly dashed back down the ankle snapping trail or scampered upwards, depending on how *ain't* they were, to where Agatha lay groaning.

"Bbrruup, brreuuurpt, burrp!" burped Tenzing's distant cousin. This being the first mildly incoherent words any of the tribe had spoken since the start.

"Wot?" said Caroline from Colchester. "Wot did 'e say just then?"

"BBRRUUP…aargha Bbrrupt." came the helpful emphasis from Sherpa Phoostank, his close relative.

"Oh, Golly gosh, deary me, oh what a toodoo," mused the translator. "And so close from the start too."

Colchester was now beside herself with frustration, well actually that was Helen from Hull but no-ones counting. "Wot arr' vey going on abbart?"

"I most sorry to report that Miss Agatha has been stricken with altitude sickness," the guide stated.

There then proceeded one of those twenty-hour group hugs-ins that only girls can do with prissy, fussing, cooing and loving care to eventually encourage poor Agatha back to her feet and with robust metaphorical pats on the backs and actual shoves up the bum, they moved her closer to the sun by about four inches. "Shrieeeeeek."

The Sherpas had all seen this before and after the 5,000[th] case of thick-blooded daft white folk to collapse on the path, they knew a good time to brew up and set to with slow and practiced ease.

"Look, there is nothing for it," said the guide. "This is serious and she will not, absolutely not, be able to climb any higher and we do not have the time to help her acclimatise, even if she can, and so there is no alternative, we must send her back to the hotel with Sherpa Thankfaakferthat."

WOW - went the collective female self-preserving gene. Lose one of us already, actually part company and leave one of our maidens to the completely unknown risks and threats or potential threats of unthinkable abuse from a grunting goatskin duvet?

Well, there were, I am happy to report, no such dangers and Agatha was safely escorted back down the valley and was to enjoy six days of hotel luxury until the group returned.

Now of course, they were in a much more realistic and legendary number and so with a small tear in the eye (note they were training to preserve water wherever possible) they waved goodbye to Agatha and the Magnificent Seven turned their collective psyche to the trail ahead and the vague scent of Sherpa tea in the distance.

*

The daily itinerary, in between indubitably magnificent, nay, majestic mountain views, was reasonably repetitive. Wake, eat pre-packed breakfast of local components, loo and walk up hill. Stop, wee and then eat pre-packed lunch of Nepalese goodies, walk uphill more. Reach the prescribed uphill milestone for the day and then stay overnight in an ancient *lodge*, sleeping only after another delightfully questionable pre-packaged dinner.

Remember the indigenous peoples' relative ignorance of bathroom familiarity? Well these lodge facilities were massively overstated in the degree of amenity and hygiene they offered but again, you ain't here on this trek to immerse yourself only in the culture, the culture was very definitely destined to immerse itself on you.

With the very, very restricted water resources available, what with all that snow about you ask? Well yes, whichever clever dick had built the summer mountain goat shed eight-hundred years before, they had done it with malice aforethought, as far from a crystal stream as the local topography would allow.

So you can imagine the washing facilities boasted hot and cold water taps to each basin but only one of them worked between April and late August and the other was a heart wrenching lie and not connected at all.

The toilets were built of similar local materials but logs cut thin and nailed to a simple rectangular timber frame, because this structure was 'moveable'. The Long Drop trench would be dug, say six to eight feet deep and say seven feet long and the 'shed' placed over the area spanning the trench and with enough room for you to prepare for the event behind an outwards opening rickety, plank-nailed door. When trench was full, move shed - simple.

This is a five star example of a Himalayan WC – even has an outside lock to prevent Yeti use in the off-season.

These long drop toilets come in all shapes and sizes but as one authority on the internet noted '*it is truly the scourge of all Western explorers*'. You will have seen images or pictures of toilets in the bush with a lone porcelain WC, or a shed with a timber floor with extra planks to indicate where your feet would go and then in between the barely trustable planks, the black hole into which you must perform in a thoroughly un-Western squat. Or those community toilets with no partitions but a timber sideboard structure with raised toilet seats. Well this one was not like them, neither a true squatter nor too a loo seat.

This WC shed was made of two compartments with nailed planks to the side and corroded, corrugated metal roof and two outwards opening 'doors' made of more badly-nailed, vertical planks with those long bracket hinges and the gaps between the planks allowed for some ventilation and delightful mountain viewing as you performed but such joyful gaps had to be balanced against the embarrassment possibility that those outside could see through just as well as those inside could see out.

The floor was just hillside made level and about three feet for you to undo, release, pop out of *Onesy* suits, drop trousers and prepare for the seat. Now the seat was actually a period piece of ancient timber, a pole about eight inches in diameter and polished by thousands and thousands of bottoms over the millennia. The hillside ended, as you could imagine, at the lip of the trench and the pole was suspended about two feet off the dirt and about a foot over the pit from the trench edge. So your heels were definitely on the edge of the pit as you wriggled to position the required orifice to have sight of the black hole pit. The trench was about two and half to three feet wide and so there was a certain clarity of mind needed to ensure that you undertook that Nadia Comaneci bar-balancing act without the backward option to dismount to the rear.

*

The ladies and their accompanying male escort were the only humans they met at any of these lodge stops, except for the way down, so they had the remarkable joy of at least four nights of the little-known and oft-forgotten, almost musical, Nepalese Nasal & Anal Ensemble.

In the evening, the girls would initially have the long communal timber log shed room to themselves and after ablutions, using the preciously carried water to clean teeth, rinse face and definitely take that last pee. Then changing into their woollen nighties or fleecy neck-to-toe jim-jams, or onesy suits in the current vernacular, they would bang on the door and the Sherpas would dutifully and in silence, enter, lock the door with the wooden latch and then amble through the ranks and unload themselves on the floor at the far end of the room and sleep until their natural clock awoke them for a brew at 05.00 sharp.

The girls sleeping facilities were low timber-framed cots with threadbare, yak-haired three-inch-thick mattresses but to our intrepid but wholly exhausted team they were a veritable Princess's feather bed.

Shortly after the team's goodnight wishes to each other and fervent hopes the bed bugs didn't, the girls were introduced to the most complex, all-consuming, variety of snoring and farting ever recorded by females on the planet. Each Sherpa unconsciously trying to outdo the massive gaseous expulsion released beside him or emitting guttural sleep apnoea gasps and snores Norris and Ross McWhirter would have been proud to record for *that* Guinness book.

Anyway, half way through the third night of the trip Christie awoke, if fitful nuclear-disturbed sleep can be so considered as sleep, and feeling rumblings in her wee tummy decided to pop to the loo. This was most unusual and certainly against the girls' written taboo rule – no night-time pees alone.

Now remember her training; finishing school, Kent. There was no woolly convent-school shroud for Christie, she was wearing her most incongruous but highly fetching short cut lingerie sheer top with matching brief-to-extremely-brief, briefs. Outside, the warmth of the day had turned to a viciously cold and windy night and was manifesting itself in a spooky low howling under a waxing moon. Once she was outside she was all alone with herself and her delightfully rigid nipples that always appear in such circumstances.

Twenty freezing paces to the bog, open door, shut door, apply safety string loop to the bent nail in the frame in case of Yeti attack and then carefully, very carefully perch on the beam without falling in. Christie got all of these choreographed moves right, all except the last one.

During the final wriggle into position as noted earlier, and with a sleepy old sense of balance, combined with the apprehension brought on by a gurgling belly, with tummy swooping, first parachute jumping sensations she toppled backwards, luckily banged her bonce on the earth pit edge of the trough which righted her head-down descent, and with Mexican cliff high diving precision, entered the liquid below feet first.

Now we have all been to long drops in our time at Cadet camps, scouts or pop music festivals and blinked uncertainly into the dim depths of the chasm, hoping, yet not really hoping, to glimpse what was down there.

Well that would have been one of those healthy-diet long drops and not like this one perched on a Nepalese mountainside full of every tourists' worst deposits of the sub-continents' incontinence. Christie was now chest deep in the most unimaginable cold, wet, aged, lumpy but viscous excretia and being 5'5" tall she was ten inches short of the top of the trench with arms extended.

After the initial shock of finding herself really up shit's creek without a paddle and knowing that no amount of shouting and screaming for help was going to be heard over the Sherpa symphony or the banshee howling of the wind, she metaphorically sat down to think what to do.

In a surprisingly lucid train of thought, she realised she would not have long, as now she was aware of the awful stench and the real possibility of restricted oxygen and she must quickly get out of her own accord.

Well let's all praise Yoga and lithe dance practice now because by hunching shoulders and raising knees and pushing off from the trench sides Christie slowly and inexorably extracted herself with a satisfying audible 'gloop' from the morass and headed upwards to safety.

Hooking an arm over the untrustworthy seat beam, Christie levered herself free of the pit, undid the Yeti security latch and slopped with wet and mucusy strides to the Lodge door.

Imagine this predicament. You are naked, except for a tiny wisp of a tissue of material and you are caked in a slimy concoction of every climber's and Sherpa's worst dribbly, foul-smelling curried diarrhea. You are a walking Petri dish of lumps and dribbling ooze and sticky hard dried smears of turd. It is rancid, semi-fermenting, fetid, worm-infested shit. It's in between your toes, infused into all your lower cracks, on your hands, under your nails, smeared on your face and drying in a lumpy morass on you back. The rank bitter odour of rancid, reeking, putrefying untreated sewerage mixed with gallons and gallons of concentrated eye stinging urine that makes you gag for air and dizzy with the sheer enormity of the awful pong...and it's actually you!

The remaining members of the Magnificent Seven, once they had awoken and overcome their initial gut-lurching nausea, brandished tissues, old and throw-away-able T shirts, water bottles and spit, Channel fragrance by the litre, and tidied up Christie with the same wholesome and loving care they had all bestowed on all their first child's nappy.

The Sherpas, oblivious to both noise and the new odour, slept through the lot. But it is a testament to all of the group's commitment and hardy nostrils that they continued on the trek and completed it successfully.

And on that note I leave you I hope with a vague but bitter imaginary taste in your mouth of the wholly truthful Legend of Everest's Nastiest-ever fall without loss of life.

*****

FOLK LORE

"The best cure for Sea Sickness, is to sit under a tree." Spike Milligan

I had started my tale of the 1993 Lions trip using the expression 'a plausible tour' but that mien is now actually more relevant to this reflection.

Whilst we had played many 10's tournaments in Hong Kong as the precursor to the International 7's event, the lure of the fabled, romantic island resort of Bali and their 10's competition was just what our club needed. Well the players considered it would be good for morale and also a colourful addition to the historic tour records *for* the club, of course. Their considerations had nothing to do with the renowned beauty and buxom dimensions of their native womenfolk, nothing at all.

Now to organise a *plausible tour,* one needs keen chaps able to pay their way and then you need to take enough of those blokes to provide a full team and a few more on the bench for the inevitable injuries or, at our age, exhaustion. So, an overseas XV-a-side tournament meant at least twenty players and support chaps to make it work. This was a tough ask because so many of our regular players were full-time employees and valuable managers and may simply not be available or were called away at the last moment to work.

Seven-a-side, you offer, is much easier to organise then?

Yes but unfortunately in the 1990's and the early new millennium there were stricter rules on work permits in Thailand in particular and so there were distinctly less fit, young, able and speedy chaps available and one had to rely upon the existing larder of more elderly, less spritely, experienced players and these generally, remembering of course that they were *experienced,* just said 'bollocks' to a 7's tournament in the blazing sunshine and humidity of the Orient.

Now the emerging game of 10's, however, allowed for an almost perfect fusion of *able-to-pay* and *able-to-play* blokes keen on some fun in the sun. Not too fast and furious and yet not all the grind and fisticuffs of fifteen-aside. This, with the added bonus, that you could generally muster around ten or eleven playing tourists and then once at the location recruit some flotsam from other competing teams or the disconnected, free range, marauders who, 'got-boots-will-play' just turn up to the various events, hoping for a run.

In reality, this is really why the 10's format is so well accepted.

In 2001 a small group of British Club pathfinders decided amongst themselves that they would form the vanguard to check out the Bali tournament in October and if suitable, then the club could plan and send a full team for 2002.

Roddy Kerr (Scottish-Aussie; scrum-half), Bevin Morrison (New Zealander; Centre) and Khun Prote (Thai; speedy back but not adverse to a little flanking) saved their pennies and heroically set-off on the reconnaissance mission.

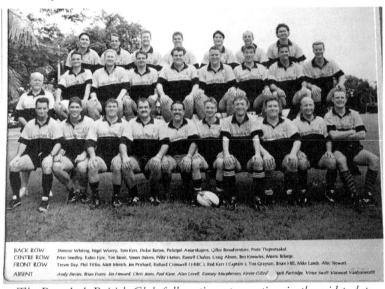

BACK ROW   Dominic Whiting, Nigel Wixrey, Tom Kerr, Dickie Barton, Pichitpol Amarukajorn, Gilles Bonadventure, Prote Thipnetsakul.
CENTRE ROW   Peter Smedley, Robin Eyre, Tim Bacon, Simon Dakers, Peter Hutton, Russell Chalon, Craig Abson, Ben Knowles, Marco Belonje.
FRONT ROW   Trevor Day, Phil Tiffin, Matt Minich, Jon Prichard, Richard Cromwell (HSBC), Rod Kerr (Captain), Tim Grayson, Bruce Hill, Mike Lamb, Alec Stewart.
ABSENT   Andy Davies, Brian Evans, Jim Howard, Chris Jones, Paul Kane, Alan Lovell, Ramsey Macpherson, Kevin O'Reil   Mark Partridge, Vince Swift, Vorawot Vardyawatti

The Bangkok British Club full contingent sometime in the mid to late 90's. Yes that's Richard Cromwell of HSCB in the centre seated – amazingly with his agreement, they were our principle sponsor.

So covert were these pathfinders that at training that next Thursday evening they were called all the cursed names under the sun for not appearing ready for our seriously competitive Thailand League match on the coming Saturday.

This simply evidenced that those that need to know should be told in the first place, but for the sake of the possible tour, weren't.

Well, they returned, sunburnt, missing skin in patches around elbows and knees but thoroughly enthused about the tournament location, facilities and clearly a venue for the standard of rugby like ours. This vital strategic data was served to the committee and after a five nano-second deliberation it was agreed to send a team in 2002.

So with malice aforethought and with the skill and experience of the greatest tour manager ever to come out of Epsom, Bruce Hill set about scheming and booking and planning the tour, all the time mumbling happily about topless Bali native girls balancing fruit on their heads.

Bruce's innate and practiced skill was to list and budget all of the cost centers: flights, transport, accommodation, food, playing kit and of course including the inevitable 'Club funded free beers one evening' (actually paid for by the players in their lump sum). Anyway, it was always sold to us in a Fagan-like manner that "*this is great deal my boyes*" and it always was because almost all of the costs were catered for and only beer kitty payments into the Sock as usual, were needed.

Roddy Kerr (pathfinder) also helped Bruce by collecting the prepaid flight tickets from the agent and then was to hand them out to players at the BC the night before setting off.

Our brilliant tour manager Bruce, for years mentor to many a young scrote, was always a definite for every event, except this tournament was unfortunately not to see Bruce with us as he was called away for work. Now hear this: a quantity surveyor had more pressing work commitments than a rugby tour to Bali? – now that has to be an oxymoron.

Anyway, as it turned out (and probably the real reason for Bruce not coming) some players were so weedy and pathetic and downtrodden they petitioned the committee, days before departure (so must have already bought the extra tickets) that, with the venue being so exotic, romantic and delightful, their wives wanted to come too.

WTF?!...I hear you screech, wives on tour?!

After hours of heated, robust beer-swilling discussion it was agreed they could come, really on no other principle than Andy Talling had just got married to his lovely young bride Beata from Hong Kong, and he was 6'3" and nineteen stone of Cornish granite with attitude.

The briefing was held at the BC and tour kit handed out and copious beers washed away any hard feelings and Bruce turned to Roddy for the flight tickets to give out to each tourist so that they were responsible for not losing them and must attend. But the Plonker-from-Perth (Oz) had left them in his bachelor pad and stated firmly he would bring them the next morning to the airport and hand out at check-in.

This sounds eminently plausible you say, but I fear not, because Roddy had 'previous'. He held many grievous convictions for getting absolutely bugger-fucked drunk in the bars in Soi Cowboy the night before any tour and then not waking in time for the flight. Hence a deep and grumbling, rumbling growl of disapproval from Bruce, but it had to be accepted.

As it turned out Roddy did not let us down and he DID get absolutely bugger-fucked drunk and with about seven tourists all at check-in he did eventually answer his phone in bed at his condo with a groan and then, realisation dawned.

To his credit he was on a motorbike taxi before you could say *twat* and arrived after the flight had left. Luckily there were other airlines with space and Roddy dutifully advised the much-plenty-angry group he would buy replacements and be right back.

He did buy all seven-plus-one replacement tickets with his credit card and, grinning with satisfaction, he handed them out and then with a quizzical expression asked, "You guys gonna' pay me?" As one, the reply echoed around the airport bar, "Faak awf."

Eight tourists you question. Well yes because with other work commitments and many without a wife visa allocation, we couldn't actually raise a full dozen or fourteen players. Neither could the Taipei *Baboons* RFC and our clubs had been in touch with each other by email and agreed to play as a combined side. Bali were so notified.

Uncle Fester was lying down to take the picture. Left from the mustachioed writer: Paul Gill, Roddy Kerr, Trevor Day, Simon Dakers, Tim Greyson, Ramsey McPhearson...and a nose.

We arrived in Denpasar Airport, whizzed through immigration, which in itself was a marvel knowing the usual Indonesian process, grabbed our bags and there was our coach waiting for us.

We were driven to the hotel and sports complex on the Nusa Dua peninsula, checked-in, dumped our bags and then after a brief inspection of the facilities we re-boarded the bus and headed for the bars.

The first night proved to be a relatively light affair as we wanted to present a good showing at this tournament the next day, but we did visit all of the renowned bars and appreciated the local dancing skills. No that was bollocks too. We have never failed to ensure we experienced all of the drinking excesses and the single chaps the attentions and softer comforts of the native females.

*

The next morning found us all booted and kitted and heading away from the hotel buildings passed the array of tennis courts, pools, lawn bowls and outside Tai Chi classes and across acres of grass to the playing field, slightly jaded, but keen players all the way.

There was only one pitch and it did actually have real grass on it and was in quite good nick. It was surrounded with those ubiquitous small, 3m x 3m tents with no side sheets, all selling water, food, beers, memorabilia and even recovery-massage.

Our replacement tour manager had approached the announcer's stand and verified that the draw information provided the night before was still the latest playing plan and we found an unoccupied shady tent or two and plonked down awaiting our time to play.

This was a Ten's tournament, so organised on a ten-minutes-each-way format. Twenty minutes per match plus a wheezing, water-guzzling, farting period at the change-over.

I recall at one kick-off, playing against one of the main Hong Kong clubs, standing near to my Aussie mate and second rower Larry Maley. The ball came towards me out of the clear blue sky, I called and caught it and then looked inside to see Larry shouting for the ball and scampering forwards. The Hong Kong lads were no mugs and ferocious even at this simple level of meeting and I was then amazed to see Larry jinking and sidestepping and sprinting through their screen of tacklers and once through the initial melee there was only their fullback to beat. He was swept aside like an irritating fly and Larry scored, after just twenty seconds.

Wow thought I, this is easy.

The opposition then lined-up in the same fashion, hoofed the ball over planet Jupiter and I called again, caught it brilliantly (I thought) and then looked inside for the steaming Larry.

All I did see to my left was a cringing, stationary, Larry with negative, outstretched open palm hand waving and pursed lips mouthing a silent 'Noooooooo'. I wasn't watching the opposition but looking only at him beside me and he could see the massive tidal wave of angry muscle approaching at speed.

And then with much glee and pent-up embarrassment from the first kick-off, their pack linked shoulders and smashed into me standing in a completely unprotected manner. They drove me back, over the touch line, through the few spectators and then crushed me through a water dispensing tent under 3,000 tons of angry, Colony grunts.

See, even at forty-four you can learn new stuff. Never trust an Aussie.

It was a two-day event and we would have had to play at least another two or three matches in our group on Day 1. It was fun because there is quite a tight-knit group of tour-going chums from each of the principle Asian Clubs and we would have bumped, punched and gouged many of them in the past. ISCI from Jakarta, Singapore CC, Manila Nomads, Hanoi Dragons, Saigon Geckos etc. a real family gathering.

When our last match of the day ended and with some skin still on knees and elbows, thanks groundsman, clumps of players and spectators headed back to the main hotel complex for a shower and a swim.

There were numerous swimming pools each with various given functions: family pool, kiddy's pool and then a large 'L' shaped twin-use pool with a deep end 'laps swimming' arrangement and the short leg shelving to a walkabout-waist-deep pool zone with an in-pool sunken bar.

To give the impression of being vaguely human we showered off the sweat and pitch grime in the changing rooms and then headed for the pool and its integral bar. There were about twenty-five to thirty blokes all standing around the bar area in the pool, some on the fixed underwater stools, some enjoying the overhead bar shade but most in a crescent shape gulping beer and engaged in the usual mindless boy chat.

After about thirty minutes, Andy Talling arrived with his delightful, wife Beata.

Beata was, and is, a close friend of mine and a well-educated, clever Hong Kong national, who had worked in Andy's office and that magic around the photocopier and at the coffee machine, transformed their formal relationship into a binding loving one. And now as a token of that love, Andy had decided she should experience a rugby tour. Personally, I suspect there was a Cantonese threat in there that he couldn't refuse, but let's not judge…much.

Anyway, the cheery, smiling and happy new Mrs Talling threw her towel on a sunbed and entered the pool by the steps some distance from us and said to the ogling throng (Beata was and is, a shapely bird).

"Hi Guys, I won't interfere but I will swim some laps up there and be back soon."

With that, she paddled away and we turned back to discussing whatever we always discuss and had more beers. We were seriously re-hydrating and also because of the delightful setting, probably overdoing the afternoon intake but who cares it was a fabulous Boys Own moment. Our respective kitty masters had brought their Socks and so each round was dutifully paid for with no one needing to leave the pool to get wallets.

So after about three more beers or Beata's twenty or so laps, she returned from the deep zone, found her feet on the shallower area, brushed her hair back in a welter of water and girly-finger-combing and then advanced on our area around the bar.

Andy offered, but Beata declined a beer, then she looked back at the deep end and then back at the bar area and then back at the deep end and finally said.

"Hey Jonny, did you know that the deep end is much colder water than here."

"Really?" I offered.

With more glancing at the deep end and the area she was now standing in and with the full attention of the lads, "Yes…it is distinctly warmer here, I know that's deep water and this is shallow and the sun and everything but, here it's almost hot," she said splashing her tiny Oriental hands in the mystical conundrum.

And then, as no one was proposing a possible thesis on the subject, she looked up into the thirty-odd bovine, relaxed, contented, male faces.

Quite a few silent seconds passed.

"OMG!!…that's   disgusting…simply disgusting…oh…oh…oh!"

Beata paddled out to the steps still fuming, climbed out of the pool and with that look that even a granite Tor cannot refuse, Andy drained his bottle and gave it to me and exited stage left for a massive bollocking in the bedroom.

*

In the evening, Beata was all smiles and cheery and even laughed at the memory. Andy had developed a large red mark on the side his face that I'm pretty sure wasn't there after the last match.

We all went out again that night and visited the main drag of bars which ranged from simple, grass-roofed booths to aluminium-glazed, air-conditioned emporiums with excellent bar staff, smiling happy service, beautiful local maidens and really cheap beer.

Again, the collective Asian rugby club family environment gathered us all into chummy chatting beer-swilling groups and gradually even our BC group dispersed with other club factions and did whatever may supposedly happen on tours. I of course, went straight to bed with a good book.

*

Day 2 arrived and the 08.00 breakfast in the hotel coffee shop/cafeteria saw many a bleary eye and hobbling chap. They all had to come to terms with the fact we had been knocked out of the cup competition by those Hong Kong knobs and so we had an earlier start in the plate competition and needed to get moving.

Russ aka Uncle Fester is the shady character far left. This picture still stands proudly in our sponsor Khun Mint's bar: Long Gun Soi Cowboy, Bangkok.

Whatever happened that day in terms of match winning, losing or end result, I really only remember the match where Uncle Fester came into his own.

In our mixed marriage with the Taipei Baboons RFC, Fester and I were the props and Larry Maley and Andy Talling second rows, alternating with other fit primates as the matches progressed.

Our Russ Coad was the spitting image of the *Addam's Family's* Uncle Fester and that was his given name at our club.

Russ didn't have the dark shadows under his sparkly eyes or the lank stooping frame, but he did have the bald head, sunk deep into broad, massively muscled shoulders, huge arms permanently at thirty-five degrees to his rock-solid torso which gave him a *Terminator* air if nothing else.

He was a huge man and ex-Rugby League from Wigan or Hull KR's or somewhere but also a quiet-spoken northern man. His job was managing a vehicle chassis and sub-frame straightening body-shop for insurance companies after any given road accident. A cheap investment we thought, as he wouldn't need any bloody tools or presses or hydraulic equipment, he'd just do it himself!

How this 5'7"wrecking ball was ever used in the game of fast-moving, quick-thinking League players eluded all of us, but he was an excellent prop in the Union game.

Within moments of kicking-off against some other side, the referee called for a scrum and we formed up with Fester at loose-head prop and I was at tight-head with some Baboon at hooker.

I glanced across and saw Fester smile at his opposite prop, well actually I think it was meant to be an inner smile, but he had forgotten to mask it in public. The lad was about normal height but gangly and most unfortunately, American and with a pony-tail.

It was our 'put-in' and for those not in the know of the simple front row arrangements, that meant that Fester's head was on the outside of the intermeshing heads fitting into the gaps between the two sets of opposing three men from each team. The Yank's head therefore was locked between Fester's huge dome and the Baboon's skull.

This meant that as the ball was fed into the tunnel formed by the arching humans, on the left-hand-side (Fester's) we would have the advantage that our hooker was 'one head' closer to the ball and hence could probably strike his leg quicker to heel the ball back.

We were playing before the new laws had been introduced to formalise each stage of a scrum clearly pronounced by the referee, as in - getting in position, binding onto opposition shirts and then engaging in a calm and controlled manner, supposedly. Anyway, none of these gentlemanly and medically improving, new arrangements were in place in the rank amateur game we played.

As we went down for the first-time engagement, Fester simply tilted his bonce and closed the gap where the Yankee head was going at speed and they clashed heads in a spectacular fashion. California grunted a lot but sucked-it-up and the hooker did what hookers do and the game played on.

Handling errors and knock-ons were a common occurrence at our level of play so there were lots of rest periods for the backs, but bloody hard work periods called scrums to the fat boys, lots.

The next scrum and the same happened. With our surprisingly keen second rows pushing behind our behinds, the contact area was quite fierce but the first head contact was clearly heard with a cracking of skulls and a now a much-hurt yelp of pain from the Septic.

More cock-ups by our backs and another scrum.

Yes…CRACK went the two heads again, this time I suspect with a little frustration from Uncle Fester as his opponent was still alive and kicking.

The pony-tail reared-up, before the ball was put in and screamed, **"Foor Faaarking Faarks sake, that's faarkin' it you douch-bag…stop faaaking doing that!"**

The referee, who had been inspecting the alignment of the backs, a point not missed by Fester's peripheral vision, looked back and demanded silence and get on with the bloody game. I suspect I saw, down the tunnel, a tiny grin creasing our northern man's cherubic face.

Second half and more pathetic mishandling in the tropical sun led to another scrum. This time pre-empted by a pointy finger and a scowl from the now much-lumpy-American's-head.

"Don't even faaakin' think about it you Limey shit." he offered.

Fester raised eyebrows and exuded innocence and ignorance as to what his Colonial mate could be referring to.

DOUBLE, DOUBLE CRASH! and this one had gristle, spinal fluid leaks and, I suggest, some anal discharge by old Yankee raspberry head.

Up he came in a welter of spittle and swinging fists, missing Fester by a practiced mile and nearly walloping the ref.

"Stop THAT this instant or you are off!" the official admonished the now-bleeding Yank. And he turned on the angelic, loveable face of Russ and said, "and we will have no more of that head clashing young man! Stop that immediately!"

Fester was completely confused by being addressed as a *young man* and after a moment of reflection, this huge, huge man gave a shrug of his massive shoulders and squeaked in a really high pitched squeaky, hurt northern squeak, *"Buut it's mee foockin' job!"*

The ten-man scrum, friend and foe, fell about laughing on both sides, except the leaking Yank of course, which may have been an indication of his own popularity in his club. The damaged, claret-drenched chap left the field to be replaced by a seriously scared-to-terrified young prop. He needn't have worried; Fester's job was done for the day and indeed a few minutes later the whistle went and I can recall nothing of the post-match celebrations except that *The Squeak* was now caste in Folk Lore for ever.

*

PS: I must add that the next year's tournament clashed with our annual Rugby Club Dinner Dance date and hotel bookings were blocked solid so we stayed at home and didn't go.

Sadly, you will recall in 2003 there was the atrocious Bali Bombing in those very bars we frequented and amongst all of the holiday-makers and local fatalities and casualties there were some fifteen of our Asian and expat rugby buddies murdered and lost forever.

I cannot describe how we all felt about this loss but it struck home personally and deeply in the rugby fraternity.

A moment's silence to remember them.

*****

THE BUTCHER

"I sometimes think that God, in creating man, rather over estimated His abilities." Oscar Wilde

February 2018. I was at the British Club in Bangkok paying my bill or settling-up for something. I rarely seem to visit this old haunt these days compared with those halcyon years in the 90's and early 2000's and whilst musing over the essentially inexpensive monthly membership fees for such a jewel in the city, muscle memory guided my feet from the accounts office to the Churchill Bar.

A much-modernised room from the original when the bar was moved and redecorated in about 1996, but apart from thicker, embossed, tied-back curtains and the remaining wall space filled with aged pictures of teams gone by, the content was much the same. The bar had the hundred years of visiting clubs sporting shields fixed to the cornice or leaning on small shelves around the room. There is a long high bar with a padded, green-leather, belly-bump rail and a very respectable selection of draught beer taps on display and always the ubiquitous uniformed, gold-buttoned, smiling staff offering an affable and kindly greeting.

The bar was unusually empty and despite the long period of not visiting the BC, the delightful barmaid was already, out of habit and excellent memory, pouring me a pint of Tiger. I like to think that despite their admirable training and lovely Thai temperament, they had a special soft spot for me (indicated maybe by the slightly sneaky, wry smile) as the old Rugby Section Captain and later Chairman. This sense was not only because in those days the rugby section was a massively successful and social machine but also because during many bouts of visiting rugby touring team games, 'Mirror Man' had found me losing and therefore naked in the bar again and again and again. On each occasion of course, hauled before the Main Club Committee the next morning and ironically, given yet another dressing down.

Pint in hand, I wandered the walls glancing at the old sepia team pictures until my circumnavigation brought me to *The Butcher's Board*. This teak and brass plaque including all of its spelling errors, is the Spoofer's Annual record of past Thailand National Champions and donated by myself back in 1997 when I was elevated to that lofty eminence. I can only assume that anyone watching me peering at the plaque must have been reminded of the vacant, staring, probably dribbling, extras in *One Flew over the Cuckoo's Nest* as I was whisked away down memory lane to *that* rugby tour of 1996 when I acquired *that* sobriquet...

*

Pat Cotter, a wily old coyote hailing from Carlisle in the Lake District, had been in Phuket for many years running a successful, safe and essentially cheap Scuba diving company for expats and of course the tourists in the turquoise waters of the Andaman Sea. That was his hobby. His real job was setting up and managing and playing in the local rugby team: the Phuket Vagabonds.

No team has been better named since, and with the dextrous use of word-search, they were all the most fearsome group of vagrants, hobos, drifters and nare-do-wells you would ever not want to meet. They were actually a collection of highly-trained oil rig workers from Australia, New Zealand and UK ranging from platform project managers to geologists to directional drillers and the deep-water inspection divers and munts acting as the prop-forwards who humped the pipes about. When together, their skill sets and native rugby training would have given the All Blacks a run for their money...in the first ten minutes at least. Luckily, they were rarely, if ever, able to field their full complement because work breaks did not coincide.

What a great job we all thought, slaving in the humidity of the Bay of Bangkok or the tranquil waters of Indonesia, six months on and six months off with wages even Saddam and

Gaddafi would have been jealous of and living those six months off, languishing on the silvery sands of Phuket's west coast.

Now Patrick, then about thirty-eight, was a thin, six-foot, stick-like flyhalf with black hair (narcissistically dyed black when the roots start showing), pointy-nosed, with large, almost architectural eyebrows and being the Dive Master he is, a fit and stamina-filled bundle of mischief. His Cumbrian upbringing has also provided Pat with a huge capacity for drinking alcohol of whatsoever he may be presented with, far in excess of the usual weight : volume human ratio, matched only by that annoying habit of also getting up the next morning after any monumental pish-up, fresh as a daisy...the bugger.

The usual tour format arranged by the BC Master of Tours, Bruce Hill, was for our lads to meet at Bangkok's Don Mueang airport on the Friday evening in No1's, smash into early beers at the Bentley's Pub, fly to Phuket, survive the breakneck minibus ride to the tourist capital of Patong, check into the Tara Patong hotel, then get on the lash in the bars along Soi Bangla. That's not true. I forgot that Pat always met us at the airport and ensured there were two cases of uber-cooled beers in an eskie in the bus. It was his kind way of ensuring we were hospitably met and no time to sober up.

The match would be on Saturday, usually at the manicured pitch in the grounds of the International school (hookers and beer banned, but actually both disguised and smuggled in), and then following whatsoever the result - more pish in the bars all that night.

Then on Sunday morning about 11.00am a BC court fines session, which coincidentally involves vast quantities of more alcohol but not now drunk at one's leisure but forced down you by the club's undercover Nazi thugs appointed by Fuhrer Hill. This would be followed by travelling as a pathetic, bedraggled, intoxicated troop of refugees back to the airport in the evening and home.

*

There would be a prearranged meeting bar with Pat on the Friday evening, almost always the U2 Bar (until the Tsunami of course), we would then meet the Vagabonds and dutifully redistribute our wealth amongst the poor, starving, scantily-clad, female masses in the bars.

How many of the Vagabonds may be available to play, and here I mean freed up from their multi-million dollar drilling jobs and on the island, would be established by seeing them in the bar with Pat. This of course would give us a good indication of how tough the opposition was going to be.

Ha! a clever ruse, but in fact the buggers never, ever turned up, well maybe one or two of the old Corps like 'Hot Dog', but most were doing press-ups and getting a good night's sleep before the battle the next day. Never mind because Pat's sole responsibility was to force as much beer and tequila down our throats as possible so we would be hung over and crap the next day. He was very good at his job and drank at least the same as us or he led the contests, just because he could.

Soi Bangla is the Island's equivalent of Patpong in Bangkok, except it ain't, because it's not a seething, seedy collection of pick-pockets, cheap clothing, bric-a-brac and wrist-watch stalls enclosed by dark bar thuggery and populated with generally aging disgruntled Chiang Mai girls, or boys with tits.

Soi Bangla is on a tropical island, perpendicular to the golden beach and festooned with the most fabulous-looking hookers from all reaches of the Kingdom. It is a hundred and fifty yards of neon-illuminated small bars, large bars, discos, pharmacies, ATM machines, burger stands, more pharmacies (see they are a clean lot down there) and a fabulous atmosphere of fun and expectant sex from both the sun-drenched tourists as romantic couples and the professional working girls, all hyped and encouraged by the booming speakers blasting out the latest disco noise. In fact, for those who did like the katoey option (boys with tits) there was always the side-street proudly posted as Soi Eric, I am reliably informed.

And so it came to pass that we congregated again at the U2 Bar, owned by a magnificently friendly, cheerful and surprisingly quiet spoken Yank called Bill Bloggs. (BB and his *wife* incidentally survived being dish-washed around inside his house during the tsunami of 2004 and spat out of an upstairs window and lived only by grabbing onto the fronds of a passing coconut tree or some such serendipitous life-saving structure.) He entertained us with his wonderful stock of ultra-cool beers, sexy staff and brilliantly selected music for our age group.

In the usual way the lads played the standard Thai bar games of 'connect four' or various local takes using rigged dice in individual cups and there was even darts for those seeking a more traditional sport. Remember the girls played this stuff all night, every night and were experts in hood-winking all young lads with early losses and party-fun shrieks of dismay only waiting until the offer of betting on the next game and then miraculously there was a serious fleecing of wallets but with a mindful and clever girly-loss thrown in. It was all fun and hell that's why we were there!

The Old crew exchanged exaggerated past stories with Pat, watched the throng of tanned bodies passing by the bar and generally wiled away the hours with, of course, gallons of drink being dutifully chased down us with Tequila-Titties by Pat.

I should mention here that tour manager Bruce also had pre-arranged the room sharing roster and I was buddied-up with a cheery Aussie bloke, an unusual choice, but there was no protest from me.

Skippy is Australian, in fact he is so definitely Australian that if you were ever to cut open an artery (which we often hoped someone would do), then no blood would flow, only Castlemaine XXXX and behind the dribbling, you would hear the soft lilting theme of *Waltzing Matilda*. He doesn't play rugby but he does take to the field of Aussie Rules when there is a match organised in the Kingdom, but he would be placed at 'Short stop' or 'Rover's Butt end' or whatsoever they call the tiny, hard-working blokes in the side, for Skippy is not the usual 6'6" tall, sinewy-muscled athlete you normally have to contend with on the field or in the bar.

Skippy, in those days, was single and a small athletic, trim, beach-tanned, blond-haired, blue-eyed lad, who was blessed with great humour and oodles of charm that all the expat ladies just fell-for every time. A major marketing advantage over the competition, as he was then working for one of those moving, logistics companies that bring or ship out your goods when you come and go from the country. Any enquiries by a wife to her circle of fellow wives at coffee morning or kiddies-corner or sports events, as to whom they should use for their move, there was no question that wee Skippy would be proposed. This recommendation made with a knowing, smirky, smouldering smile implying that not only the household goods would be in safe hands.

Me and Skippy in the middle, he's got
the beer in his hand – probably stole it!

Skip's most amazing feature for us boys was he had a photographic memory for ALL old and also really ancient and also up-to-date sporting events, scores, player's profiles, manager's and statistics we didn't even know existed. This was a walking-talking Sky Sports hard disc of all sports data before they were even considered as a future invention.

He was also, remember, Australian...and short.

So, to counter his vertically-challenged frame, he had also developed a life-preserving, deplorable habit of being a bloody annoying, anti-Pom, Aussie argumentative, twat. But we treasured him for that trait, as it was genuinely harmless and always amusing.

Well that night after the last ale had been supped and the tequila, salt and lemons had all gone I found that I had acquired a small, light-brown friend and she was to assist me back to the hotel. I had forgotten of course that I was sharing with wee Gobby...oh I mean Skippy.

We arrived at the room to find Skippy already in bed and apparently asleep. There were two beds in the room, each four-foot wide and mine was in the middle of the room and Skippy's against the wall of the bathroom. We reduced lighting and showered and then headed for bed. Now a four-foot bed with a large 105kgs bloke in it allows for not much else but we lay side-by-side balancing and about to begin that most quixotic of events, the touch and feel and hopeful arousal after 55,000 beers.

It was now that Skippy revealed he was awake and with much scrunching and wrapper removal noise, offered, "Hi JP, how's it going mate? want some Kit-Kat, what about yer's Sheila?"

"Sssssh Skips, she's very embarrassed that we are sharing anyway, so you squeaking away isn't helping ok?"

"Sure mate whatever...."

Silence for a brief period and then a further concerto of silver foil wrapper and "Are youse sure you don't want any Kit-Kat?"

"Skippy sssh....Really...shut up."

Eventually my roomy did subside into sleep and things had developed nicely, if a little flaccidly at first, but when my knob finally took on the semblance of a penetrating implement of considerable proportions, I heaved the maiden up on top and we wriggled and squirmed for a time finding the balance and mattress limits and then *'Tally Ho'* we were away with a gusto and intent. I was quite surprised either of us had that much energy left in the tank.

After some moments, I was further surprised that there was considerable squelching sounds and female juices were jetting everywhere in the darkness and my Asian beauty was moaning and cooing with what I assumed was pleasure, and this further stimulated me and we rode and squirmed and slopped about in the bed until eventually the slim maiden gave a great sigh and slumped over my shoulder onto the pillow and lay still.

I hadn't come myself but I was massively impressed with my love making and the reactions such passion had inspired in the bird and feeling chuffed and more than a little enthralled, I whipped off the condom and headed for the bathroom in the darkened room.

Now I was reasonably fit in those days and lean muscle did exist on the torso and as many men would never admit, as I entered the bathroom with the light on, I puffed out my Romeo chest and glanced in the mirror.

I was dumbstruck and then shocked and amazed at the same time because I was covered, not in female love secretions, but gallons of blood! My whole crotch was a crimson lumpy mass of dark congealed blood, where she had ridden the beast so ardently. The blood had shot out sideways smeared across my hips, up my belly and chest in radiating spurts, had hit my chin and gone on to smear my cheeks and catch in lumps in my eyebrows. It was wet and runny and dribbling down my legs, it was a live example of that kid's painting game where you squirt some liquid paint on a high-spinning paper wheel and you get that *Star Wars* hyper-space moment. I was a walking bloody abattoir.

Then in my moment of shock, I mentally whizzed past monthly period blood and recalled her almost expiry-like gasp and the collapsing figure onto the pillow…was she dead?

I dived under the shower and watched the *Psycho* blood swirling down the plughole and then toweled quickly and hopped back to the bedroom. The last thing I needed was for Skippy to awaken or indeed to find a dead hooker in my bed and so I carefully shook the arm of the recumbent girl and then almost leapt for joy when she murmured. I resolved she must go now and I would pay extra for the short time shag, but send her home a.s.a.p.

She was dizzy and keen to stay but I was sure it was for the best (for me) that she should leave and hopefully blood loss of this magnitude was usual for her, but extreme, she would be ok…eh?

I opened the room door, *"Tilac, krap khun krap, le'gorr glap baan leaow leaow na krap…Tilac"* in my best broken romantic Thai, gave her one last peck on the cheek, poked a bundle of Thai purple baht notes in her hand and with a final firm shove off down the corridor, I closed the door and crept to bed guilty of lots of stuff and sad I was such a low-life.

In the morning I woke late but first and was shocked at the mess. A Hollywood special effects department with fifty dead chickens rung of all their life juices could not have lathered my bed sheets in more gore.

So, I quickly made the bed in a rudimentary fashion, covering up the crime scene, wiped the blood from the side table and trailing line to the bathroom, cleaned up the bathroom floor and removed all evidence before The Skip arose.

Skippy was good with sports data but hopeless at keeping any sort of secret and lived for rumour and innuendo – probably one of his lovable traits for the bored expat wives? Anyway, we had a saying; *'Tele-a-fax, Tele-a-phone, Tele-a-Skippy'* and all would be communicated efficiently and bloody quickly to the waiting world, so *Mum* was the word here.

This was the day of the match and so that meant, get up, complete ablutions, get your kit and scrabble down for breakfast and there was no time generally to return to the bedrooms, and thence head out in the late morning and drive to the pitch.

We left our room together and bumped into the two Yankee lads in the corridor from the room next door. They were mates of Trevor's and one played rugby with a sketchy to almost non-existent knowledge of the laws and the other didn't but had joined the club for the *craic*.

Then there was the usual gradual coming together of the team as mates wandered in to the dining area, all looking bedraggled, sore-headed and sleepy, just as Pat had intended.

The Tara Patong Hotel served the same fare as most three-star dives and the buffet-style vista of boiled chicken mini-Frankfurters, thirty congealing cold fried eggs, with small sheets of pale ham drowning in a dish of hot water, was the menu's All American Breakfast and we all tucked in like rabid hungry wolves.

When all was assembled, Bruce shouted for order and announced the bus was ready and all to get their bags and get on board. It was at this stage I checked and realised I had left my playing boots in the bedroom and was therefore probably destined for a fine at the court on Sunday. I whizzed to the room on level three.

Running, I turned the corner and oh!...horror of horrors, there at our bedroom door was the maid's cleaning trolley and our door open. Well there was nothing for it but to bash on and suffer the strife that would surely follow and the cost of new sheets in replacement for the OJ Simpson night of passion.

Well I entered the room and the maid was standing at the foot of my bed having stripped it and was glaring at the dark maroon mess with stern matron hands on hips and then looked with fury at me.

"WTF?!" was obviously in her lips, but with the agility of a cat, I grabbed my boots bag and with an exaggerated shrug, I pointed to Skippy's clean but ruffled, unmade bed and said "That one is mine," and I fled the scene.

This tale is actually not so much about the rugby match, the score, the joys of winning or the misery of losing, nor too the funny antics of the teams and players in the bars but actually it's about the charades that went on in our shared bedroom. So if you wanted game plays and robust tackling you are going to be disappointed.

And so, I shall skip the tour beers and bars and fun fanny stuff you really want to read about and fast forward to the end of Saturday night and take it from there.

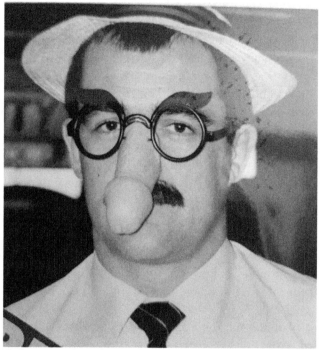

Had to wear these glasses after leaving my kit in the bedroom...

With a belly full of beer mixing nicely with cheap tequilas and gorilla-snot shorts, I had returned from the bars to our room alone, found Skippy very definitely asleep and alone with blankets pulled up to his chin with soft snorting implying '*out for the count*' and I stripped, used the bathroom, extinguished the lights and got into bed.

For anyone not familiar with a gorilla-snot I shall enlighten. Take a large sherry glass and fill half-full with sweet sherry and then add a measure of Bailey's Irish cream. The glob of Bailey's then shrinks like a suddenly-chilled scrotum, apparently sucking up water from the surrounding Portuguese liquor, and congeals into a hanging blob of, well, gorilla snot. This you then down in one and as the sherry lines your gullet you experience the nauseating slide of a giant ball of snot which does not helpfully thin to pass your dangling epiglottis but remains as a ghastly squidgy morass. A successful GS brings an involuntary wretch from all virgins.

Lying there I reflected briefly on the days fun and mischief when I became aware that there was a curious hanging odour in the room. It was familiar but out of place and hard to put your finger on in my deluded and musty boozed-up mind. Stale aftershave, a dead and decaying rat in the ceiling air-con space, hhmmm, nope none of those...oh I know: shit.

Now I had just used the bathroom and recorded it as clean and sanitized so apart from bad pants thrown behind the curtains (who does that?), it had to be emanating from 'the other bed in the room'.

Fearing this to be serious and needing some immediate solutions, I turned on the lights and standing over his bed, I whipped back Skippy's covers and there he lay with his jeans and pants around his knees all thoroughly decorated with filth and a pong that would have made Gollum gag. He lay like the dead, unmoving.

As a planning manager at birth, I realized that *we* needed to plan how to get a drunk, fighting man out of his bed and into the shower without shit literally and actually hitting the fan.

I ran the shower to an acceptable temperature, pulled back and tied up the shower curtain which would surely suffer in the scuffle to come, made sure the plughole was free to run and returned to the cesspit.

In one professional move (I am not, nor have I ever been, a medical carer, so please ignore any errors in my method) I hauled his trousers and pants up, hopefully enclosing most of the rancid smelling poo, grasped him softly behind his head and cooing like a love-struck dove, I pulled him into a sitting position and as he awoke and started the drowning-man-flaying-about I expected, I pulled him upright and marched him to the bathroom.

Well he was only about 65kgs ringing wet, but there then started the most amazing and violent form of human Marlin fishing ever enacted by two men in a bedroom. Wherein he fought, bit, scratched, wriggled, went limp, leapt and fought, all the while putting his filth covered hands on the walls, the furniture, the TV and the bathroom door.

Well, pished as I was, I was bigger and stronger and he ended up in the bath under the spraying water and with further struggle but an element of understanding, his jeans and pants and top came off and I hurled them to the corner of the room and got on with washing my poo-covered mate.

These activities were of course not a silent ballet but carried out with the most amazing collection and repertoire of screaming Aussie cricket foul-mouthed sledging. This was on a scale surpassing the usual sporting Aussie words at the crease and almost, almost as ghastly as Warner and Smith during the Third Test in Cape Town. This hotel bathroom incident, I quickly clarify, did not have any ball tampering!

As we fought and struggled, I suddenly became aware of loud Yankee screaming from the room next door and an evident diplomatic dispute with a tart.

The tart's voice seemed an octave too low and I realized then that the naïve Yanks had mistakenly engaged in contract with a *katoey*. That is nasty and can get very nasty and unpleasant for my lads, as the boy-girls here have a *penchance* for violence later, when you are not looking.

What to do with the cleaner and now offensive and wriggling suitcase mover? I could think of nothing else, so I punched him hard in the chest and lowered him slightly stunned and breathless into the bath, checked his wee heart was still beating and donning my pants, I whipped out into the corridor, carefully putting a shoe in the self-closing door for my return.

Yep the classic Asian – Daft Farang bar-*girl* stand-off was in full swing, "I aint payin' you, you shit stabber. How dare youuu have a cock!" in a wailing Southern drawl.

"You pay me money, you pay one 'tousan baht…pay now," demanded the lady.

'Whay, in all that's holy, should ma' mate pay you's any money you cock-in-hand mother-f#@ker!"

"Pay or you be sorry, you pay now!" she said pointing and stamping a foot.

Well I am sure it was more entertaining than those simple words but the crisis had to stop and their money had to change hands and quickly before 'she' lost interest and walked. So, pushing the two Septics back into their room, I turned to the lad-with-tits and verbally offered five hundred baht as a good settlement and after a last struggle for more, she agreed and put her hand out.

I turned to the lads and asked for the cash. The one with the real girl shrank back and I was left with one combatant and we had another two minutes of wrangling and discount demands and then I shouted and grabbed him by the shirt and the money appeared. Apart from me not usually carrying bank notes in my pants, it had to be *seen* to be their money or Miss Pong could be back for more. A deal done and paid was the only way and she took the money, thanked me and minced off down the corridor and I shut the door on our colonies for the last time that night.

As I turned for my room, content that the dispute was successfully concluded, Skippy peered from around the door frame, squinted in the lamp glow and shouted.

"F@#k youse dick-face Prichard!" and slammed the door.

'Gosh,' I thought. 'Why is everyone so seriously anti-JP and I'm just trying to help.'

I traipsed downstairs to the front desk in just my boxer shorts, got another door key from the completely unfazed hotel night-porter-chap and trudged back still perplexed as to who was hurting whom here?

I opened the door and there sprawled on the floor, not a yard inside the door, was the naked bum in the air figure of my dearest chum Skippy. I picked him up, carried him to his bed, closed the pood-in sheets and lay him on the bed and covered him with the blankets.

I then spent many minutes, with a dampened face towel, wiping down all the areas of hand smeared poo on walls, door handles, the TV, the side table, the writing desk, another wall and my own face.

In the morning the room was witness to a few honest, manly, but subdued, and many unsaid words, the most extensive spoken being Skippy's, "hmmmm…yep that happened…ok…thanks Blu…hhmmmm."

We always got up on the Sunday, packed bags and headed for the breakfast room, because we would then check out and find a bar about 11.00 am, sup some early ales and then hold the tour court for misdemeanors and crimes against the state, severely punished with alcoholic tortures for those found guilty - few if any, ever acquitted and then head for the airport and home.

At the end of breakfast, the Bruce Hill shout went up for the bus and somehow, even as the most experienced tourist there, I glanced and realized I had forgotten my boot bag, again.

Cursing only at the stupidity of one so stupid as to do this twice, I trudged upstairs and around the corner and down the corridor still in a world of reflection. Only looking-up paces from the room with room key in hand, I saw the maid's trolley outside our door...again.

Déjà vu encore une fois ensued, with me entering the room, picking-up my kit bag, glancing briefly at a doubly furious, speechless matron with hands on hips, the full horror of the poo'd-in sheets of *'my bed'* ripped back and exposed and humming like an untended cesspit, nodded and left the room at the trot.

Ironically, whilst I acquired the nickname of *The Butcher of Bangkok*, it was Skippy who suffered the most long term effect with the change of only two consonants...dear, dear **Skiddy**.

*****

BYZANTIUM

"I must point out that my rule of life prescribes as an absolute sacred rite smoking cigars and also the drinking of alcohol before, after and if need be during all meals and in the intervals between them." Winston Churchill

The Rhino's RFC was twenty-five years old in 2010 and it was decided that another far-far-away place, rather than a local Asian tour, would give suitable gravitas to the event. So during the AGM of 2009 various locations were proposed and despite a virulent call for more Asian fanny, the committee in their wisdom chose Byzantium.

In fact, and here I am almost certain that it had escaped their notice, that whilst Istanbul (contemporary name for Constantinople, which was the modern substitute for Byzantium at the time of the final centuries of the Roman empire) was in *the West* and therefore apparently far-far-away from our normal Eastern haunts, our opposition, the Ottoman's RFC were by geographical location over the bridge in *the East*, and therefore technically in Asia-Minor. So the 25th anniversary was therefore strictly speaking enacted on 'home soil' if slightly sandy and much trod by camels.

Tours are always in June for the (Asian) Rhinos but, maybe because of the 25th anniversary, some deity had prescribed that by some perennial, elliptical orbit-rotational nonsense the Earth had, it seemed, been swung much closer to our Sun than usual and the entire tour was spent in a swelter of extra-blazing sunshine and sheets of perspiration, hang-dog open-mouthed expressions and the curse of damp pants and chaffed groins.

Anyway, it all started with a very pleasant surprise in that we all (well those living in proper cities with airports and not cleared scrub in the jungle) travelled by Turkish Airways, who were punctual, professional and supportive of the groups of pished-up old blokes. The airline's fleet was all new craft and despite the Islamic ownership they did supply beer and wines on board, all of which were thoroughly tested by the tourists.

So, after an eight-hour flight we decanted at Al Kannifartinow Airport and were swept into town to our hotel.

This was in the centre of town and at the same time perched right on the very banks of the Bosphorus and so we had a good gawp at the denizens and their architecture as we swept through. Actually, there is a seriously well-heeled middle class in Istanbul to the point where it seemed every citizen drove two cars, at the same time, so to say *swept through* was a little optimistic, aaargh we were back in Bangkok traffic.

Now to provide an outline educated guide to the water passing our hotels' Eastern façade, you should note it is neither a river nor a sea. It is in fact the narrow gap out of the Black Sea between the main landmasses of Europe and Asia Minor that drains all of the colossal southern Russian rivers, the Dnieper, Dniester, Southern Bug, Don, Rioni and of course the Danube into the Sea of Azov and thence to the Black Sea and onward to the eastern end of the Mediterranean Sea. It is almost entirely fresh water and truly is melted snow and it's bloody freezing. The Back Sea is in fact about 18% saline and this is due to the very unusual feature of an underwater salt-water stream flowing *back* from the eastern Med into the Black Sea along the sea bottom as the incoming fresh water displaces the tide-less Med.

The hotel was a newly-opened, modern shell of contemporary minimalist style, but with well-fitted rooms and a fabulous stepped, aluminium sliding door bar that opened its entire vista onto the surging Russian melt-water, with tiers of stone terraces adorned with large sprawling canvas sunshades and gold-buttoned waiters hiding in every nook and cranny to serve you. As your glass contents lowered, so they sprang into action.

As you may imagine, many a Rhino believed that the 25th Anniversary was best served by simply staying put in the bar and getting trousered for five days. Luckily it didn't go to a vote.

Once again, I was sharing with none other than my usual superstar roomy, Jimmy 'Ratcatcher' Howard (by now 105 years old) who always took me under his wing (on this tour, a slightly more sweaty environment than usual owing to that bloody erratic orbit). Ratcatcher mentored me through the ways of Islam, respect for the locals and especially the local law enforcement chaps, no gawping or leering at evidently committed wives, the good food guide and the need to do some essential sightseeing. This city was an epicentre of religious meeting points, a veritable tectonic plate node of beliefs and we *mosque'nt* miss out, he quipped.

We had arrived on the Thursday, found the hotel and then after a few, quite a few expensive beers in the terraced bar, were alerted to the joys of walking *The* shopping street of the city that led down to Taksim Square. This was a must as the named square alone so resembled the name of our past Thailand Prime Minister Mr Taksin, prior to his arrest warrant and subsequent much reported fugitive escape from the Kingdom and continued weekly globe hopping and passport buying antics.

We all piled into a bus so we would stay together like a Boy Scout troop rather than trust to the vagaries of taxi-caravans that never work out; well they do if the point was that you wanted the six separate taxi drivers to spiral out and take everyone to far-flung and in no way related locations to the requested one at the point of origin. The Turk looked particularly adept at that form of deception.

Well there were Rhinos seeking food, Rhinos seeking beer and food, Rhinos seeking that rare and elusive Asian-Euro fanny (that apparently formed horizontally) and those even contemplating buying a little something for the wife back home.

We all disembarked at the head of Taksim pedestrian shopping street and stood there amazed, gobsmacked and buffeted by the shear enormity of the mass of human traffic flowing up and down this street. The avenue (without the trees) was immense at some 50-60 yards wide, lit by festive strings of lights and those civic-minded local authority buffoons who create heraldic shields or dolphins that then adorn the lamp posts. There were the odd sets of benches around oasis of planters but these were completely obscured by the seething mass of humanity. Remember it was only Thursday.

There must have been a hundred, billion, million people all with shopping bags making them five-foot wide at the knees, walking slowly or striding out manfully, tugging kids, eating on-the-go and almost everyone was smoking like an Indian cremation. These were bustling, hurried people heading in both directions with no signs *'Keep Left if going uphill'* or *'Keep Right if you're going the other-way'* and yet there were no collisions, no angry confrontations, no ill-will exhibited anywhere, just happy busy ants buying loads of stuff and heading home, ants who must have been smoking grass.

There were shops and curio bazaars cum bric-a-brac stalls and lots of cafés and restaurants all were packed full with beer-drinking chaps and their birds and at every turn, charmingly, discreet bijou coffee shops with open fronts spilling almost into the stream of humanity whizzing by, serving expresso's by the gazillion, well of course not actual Italian expresso's but the local Turkish Kahve.

All of these people were lavishly dressed in exquisitely tailored clothes or certainly boutique fare of fine clothes, silks and furs and with designer-labelled bags. We looked, in comparison, like evacuees.

We split up informally into the aforementioned groups on the basis of interest and also because there was zero chance of finding a collection of seating for us all in one establishment. I was with the beer and food regiment soon to be sated with both and my clothing and skin so infused with camel-dung fags that most of the wardrobe had to be incinerated and my new-Turkish-cigarette-skin-pong stayed until about August. None of these trivial negatives were evident at the time because the shopping spectacle was so extravagant and unlike Oxford Street scrums or posh parts of gay Paris or elegant Milano.

The foods were quickly and easily served through the cafe throng by trays balanced at arm's length and placed almost reverently in our crowded table space. Rice, eggplants, stuffed dolmas and fish, with arrays of meat-based kebabs, yogurt dips and mild spices – all a fusion of Levantine-Balkan foods. All washed down with the local Bomonti beer. I am no food critique but my precept that Thai food is the best in the world got a serious nudge in the ribs.

After hours of scoffing and hosing it was time to ride that boat down the human rapids to Taksim Square itself and then head home. Well the roller-coaster trip was a giant twenty-minute scrum with no physical contact and we appeared at Taksim Square only to find it 'under construction'. Every turn and byway were filled with JCB's and fluorescent-clad men beavering away at stuff underground or splurging concrete into forms all awash with light from hundreds of floodlights.

This was spoiling the moment, so with the resolve of refugees and the expectation of reaching our destination weak, we grabbed taxis and sped off to the hotel for a final Bomonti and sleep. It had been a great day meeting crowds of new folks and gobbling their cuisine and guzzling their beverages.

*

Friday dawned and some final Rhinos from remote Asian aerodromes appeared, still with some jungle foliage dangling from their baggage and hair. The match was to be on Saturday and so Friday was another touristy day of sight-seeing and food.

I remembered that in fact I had been to Istanbul on a school Easter cruise when I was about twelve, (well a penal boat used by parents to keep their sons away from their screaming daughters, as a parent now I realised this was a great idea by someone: a much-afflicted parent I guess.)

I remember our school trip to the Blue Mosque or, more formally, the Sultan Ahmed Mosque, but in reality those memories were pasty, dim, misty things compared with the stark and lasting reflections of the Bazaar and the purchasing power of the British School boy armed with hundreds of thousands of Monopoly pound notes.

Tourist hookah-pipes, clutches of alabaster eggs, camel-skin rugs, Ottoman stools, brass Kahve pots were all bought by the hundredweight and lugged back to the SS *Navasa* or SS *Uganda* and such conquest spoil all the more rewarding, not for the fact that it was *'free'*, but that the Bazaar swindling Turks had a gleam in their eyes as they had sold four alabaster eggs for One Hundred English pounds. Ha joyous justice I say!

Of course, once Uncle Ahmed had shown Grandpa Mustaffa his bundle of pound notes printed on one side only, the game was up and soon a swarm of Turkish coppers sped up the gangplank and dormitories were ransacked and ships officers walked the decks cussing and shouting but nothing could be done and in the cooling froth of detective zeal: the Turks left our vessel with nowt to show and no redemption for the Bazaar hawkers. Fuck 'em I say...still got my eggs.

*

With maps in hand we set out after breakfast for Sultanahmet Park to take in the massively historical site of the Sophia Mosque or, more correctly, the Hagia Sophia and in an opposing side of the park, the Blue Mosque.

The day was a clear, blue, cloudless sky with blazing sunshine and soon there was a sheen of perspiration and ever-dampening paper maps but our gait was still purposeful and direct.

We did wander the manicured and colourful gardens taking in lesser sites, ancient battlements and crumbling city walls that probably dated from the times of Attila and his desirous gaze.

The park had small drink stalls and ice-cream vendors to keep us alive and soon the red brick walls and minarets of Sophia appeared on the larboard bow and we took arty soft focus, deep depth-of-field pictures with specialist Canon and Olympus kit or simply snapped away with our then hi-tech mobiles.

To go inside, we hired sarongs to clad our exposed legs and flowery shorts and we were suitably impressed and reverently hushed with the size and grandeur of the open interior, the height and splendour of the massive dome and the large, mighty support columns and all about decorated with giant plates of Arabic runes and stained-glass windows. This was originally built in 360 AD and was a Christian Orthodox Church for nigh-on 1,000 years, albeit fifty-seven years within that period it had been a Catholic Cathedral, but during Sultan Mehmed's invasion of 1453 it was converted to be a mosque and now recently it is more a revered museum than a practicing religious centre.

The Blue Mosque or Sultan Ahmed Mosque, takes its informal name from the mainly blue tiles used on the interior; with the outside it is a simple grey stone and roof tiles. It was completed in 1616, long after Sophia Mosque had been converted to Islam and is an active place of worship to this day. It sports six minarets (which only Mecca was permitted and as a consequence the centre of Sunni worship added a 7th Minaret). The four main minarets are fluted and pencil-shaped with their distinctive three balconies, or Serefe's, to call the believers to prayer.

I gave you all that potted history out of guilt, because we were too lazy to even walk over the park to the Blue Wonder and instead headed-off for lunch and a beer. We walked into what looked like a hillside of housing perched one on another to the summit but in fact these were all separate four or five or six-storey buildings built around small roads, veins rather than arteries of transport, wherein only small vehicles or bikes or scooters and pedestrians could venture. Cobbled lanes led up and up with many off-shooting minor branches leading into dusty dim alleys that even the bright sunlight could not penetrate.

This was Ratcatcher's idea and plan and with a healthy appetite and bloodhound's nose for food, he led on up the turning paths.

Many of the buildings whilst six-storey at the base, were only one or two storeys when they met the twisting roads higher up and it was here that another phenomenon was found – the magnificent and much secret roof-top restaurants of Istanbul. Twisting spiral stairs up to the open roof area amplify the marvel and uniqueness of this city and there was your table laid for dining under a pergola festooned with healthy productive vines.

Well the service was fabulous, almost homely, but efficient and served with a humble panache and pride. One dish of the local delicacies come after another and we were fed almost to death until the owner stated we must leave room for his strawberries. A curious call but our group of some eight or ten fat boys could force down a little fruit.

A platter the size of a Hercules shield appeared piled two feet high with the largest, juiciest, tastiest, naturally sweet, strawberries on God's (whichever that may be) Green Earth.

We had been there so long the sun was now setting and a last round or two of Kahve's was enjoyed on the open rooftop balcony before we bade our farewells and burped and farted our way back down the alleys and in darkness trudged back to the hotel.

*

Game day arrived and after breakfast and a few beers and camel fags on the bar's terraces it was noted that the opposition was almost an hour's coach drive away over the huge '15th July Martyr's Bridge' which sported two massive abutments and spanned the 1,560m between Ortakoy and Beylerbeyi over the Bosphorus…that's Europe to Asia in one structural leap.

The matchday bus took us over the bridge and we sped off on a six or eight-lane highway East to the Ottoman's camp. Again, Rhino *research* stretched that word to credulity, as we spent not less than two hours heading eastwards. We arrived at the clubhouse and bleary-eyed, stumbled from the coach into, if possible, even brighter sunshine. It was a small simple bungalow of a clubhouse with a sandy car park and separated from the pitch by more dust and telephone poles strenuously holding up what looked like all the telephone cables from Europe to Asia-Minor.

Like the true athletes we were, it was always customary to walk the pitch before a game. The professionals on TV are doing this and assessing the windage, the grass-blade length, firmness underfoot and therefore choice of stud length or the groundsman's old trick of over-watering, in an effort to gauge what the locals had done to possibly gain an edge.

That's not our goal.

Our flyhalf almost disdainfully squints at the posts on the basis that hoofing an oval ball through that space was as lightly as heaving *that camel thru the eye of a needle*.

The pitch was hard, 22.7% tufty grass covered and 77.3% dust and granular sand. It was smaller than regulation and with an in-goal area the size of a Penny Black. This was why we were inspecting the pitch: to check for the percentage possibility of skin loss during tackles or any contact with the ground, how wide the ground was - to establish how much lung was going to be needed and in the distantly remote chance of getting there, space to score a try. *Stud length* was only ever reviewed in the evening before going on the lash with our mates.

As we ambled back to the car park, so three or four of their young players had arrived and in the true nature of the ever-commercial Turk, they had set up a car boot sale of Ottoman's RFC kit for us to scrutinise and buy.

Those images we all have of the WW1 Dardanelle's cliff-top, dark-skinned, wrinkle-eyed, martial Turk, were so far away from the modern young, almost pale, soft-skinned lads that stood before us speaking the Queen's best, quite stunned us. They were lightly built but looked like whippets and other things that run at speed. Well almost anything runs faster than a Rhino mid-tour in the infernal heat of near-Persia.

"Ooh geepers, you guys are ginormous." Faisal choked out.

"This is our match playing shirt, but ummm…we only have *'large size'*…which…ummm," he said holding up a child-size hankie.

'Sorry but that is not going to fit you guys is it?" the salesman murmured apologetically. "do you have anyone smaller in your team that may be interested?"

Offering no succor at all, our hooker advised with fag in mouth. "Naar, in fact the big blokes arn't about…must be inside."

A strangled whimper squeaked. "There are others bigger than you?"

*

And there, I think, you have it. It was unfortunately to be a game of '*men against boys*', and no amount of scamper in eighty minutes can out-do 20,000 tonnes of fat boy on the hoof.

The game was played in fine spirt, most of it being exhaled in clouds of alcoholic vapor at every scrum, and despite the appalling sunshine, the loss of skin to that ghastly sand and every sinew of speedy Ottoman effort, we overcame Johnny Turk and won the day.

Even by 2010, our old rugby habits or rehydrating after the game on beer came to the fore and we toasted the name of that old diplomat to the Turkish Commission in Moscow: *Mustapha Kunt* a million times and to their credit, the diminutive Ottoman's drank us to exhaustion.

A very generous team, if lacking in fat boys and guile, and on the basis of magnitude or lack of it, few, if any kit items changed hands either way, and we bid our farewells, climbed the steps into the coach and headed back West.

As the coach crawled along a thoroughly choked and congested highway, I reflected again on my Windsor RFC rugby scrum-half buddy Bob McDonald reading *Midnight Express* with his feet up and crossed on the handrail in a Magistrate's Court in UK and thinking…humm. The contents of the book worried me, not the disrespectable tool reading it.

You may recall that Ratcatcher had explicitly reminded me of the local coppers and their renowned lack of a sense of humour, sorry humanity. And so it came to pass: our first brush with the law.

The usual shout went up when we were about a hundred and fifty yards from the clubhouse urinals we had just left. "Stop the bus please…gotta' take a piss."

This was ignored as were the next fifty shouts, but eventually everyone was busting for a whizz and the driver was wholly perplexed as there was nowhere to stop, there were no Services, stops or laybys or highway WC's. So he simply pulled-over to the side of the road and asked in broken Turk-lish if we could all line up along the nearside of the bus so no-one could see us piddling, a most heinous crime in modern day Turkey, apparently.

We all piled off the bus and dutifully ran to our parallel stations and zippers flew, cocks out and a truly representative tide of yellow sea washed dust from the bus and most of the highway.

Now someone, and he remains anonymous, instructed the driver to move forward in the slow-moving traffic, just one coach length as the waters burst and so despite the best laid plans of men, thirty-five urinating, sweating kinsmen were exposed in all their glory to the shocked embarrassment of the passing traffic.

'Oh never mind', I hear you protest, 'they could simply swivel round and remain discrete'. No such luck. With the coach being a stunted thing at best and thirty-five fat blokes all lined up shoulder-to-shoulder there is no room to swivel without piddling on your mate and remember here, we are talking *The Moses re-enactment of the Israelites pissing event*, impossible to stop and as all men know, grabbing and crushing your willy to stop the flow is the most painful thing after childbirth, apparently.

So only once exhausted of waste water were the array of willies tucked back into trousers and shorts and we re-boarded the bus, each cuffing the grinning driver as we stepped past.

The pneumatic doors wheezed shut and we joined the slow-moving traffic again, all relieved and many a Rhino chortling at the stupidity of grown men. Chortle was soon to turn to groaning misery as the in-coach local musical entertainment was gradually drowned out by a squadron of blood curdling copper's sirens.

Clearly, we were the cause of this law enforcement noise and now the driver was visibly trembling as we stopped on the hard-shoulder and uniformed traffic cops rapped on the doors to open. More pneumatic gasping and Johnny Turk in full uniform and even sporting those wide-hipped motor bike jodhpurs, burst up the steps screaming unfriendly official venom.

The driver pissed himself and was hauled outside and shot in the head, well, verbally. He returned with the screaming Chief of Law and was instructed to turn off the engine.

Not so bad we all thought, as they left us in the coach whilst the driver bore the brunt of the hi-tempo copper music. It became obvious that the policeman knew his stuff and we were to sit there in that bus in the blazing heat with no air-con for at least ninety minutes. Not the same I know, but I did further reflect on those poor tourists all those years ago, hi-jacked and stranded at Mogadishu airport for days on the tarmac barbeque, with no AC and overflowing toilets.

Well eventually, and I suspect, only because the sun had lost its passion and it must have been near Prayer time, the rozzers let us go. I am not sure the driver was ever let off and I have visions of the poor bloke '*locked-up…not abroad*'.

I don't recall the arrival back at the hotel in the dark after however many hours of ultra-slow coach trip misery we endured, but as a positive, we were treated to a setting sun of Turkish-Delight notoriety.

*

Sunday, AGM day and yet more beautiful sunshine beamed through the slightly-opened draperies, forcing the shadowy dreams of police cells and vicious truncheons off into the corners of the room.

The committee had, as traditionally required, organized a boat for the AGM and we were to be collected from our very own pier at the hotel.

The vessel arrived and we were all stupefied at the splendour of the craft on hire: at least four decks above the water, counting the lookout cabin on top. Oodles of open deck with deck-chairs and recliners and shade for all. Inside there was a huge prepared banquet of nosh and cooler-boxes of super chilled Bomonti local beer.

As we were to cast off, it was discovered that during roll-call some players were missing. Luckily this was the age of the mobile and data roaming and we soon discovered that we must collect our chairman, Chief Minister for War and El Presidente some two nautical miles upstream.

As remarked before, many a Rhino player was game to hire, design-n-sow or obtain by stealth, costumes of the local inhabitants and El Presidente was the walking-talking epitome of this brand of tourist.

A two-mile boat trip against the 'tide' can be thirsty work and we smashed into the Bomonti like heat crazed Dervishes, all of which adds a certain early pissed state of mind to those on board.

As we swept into the small bay in the Bosphorus to collect our dignitaries in their finery, so it turned out that our rugby playing Aussie Boxer XXXX (let's use that name *Forecks*) had also donned his costume on board, which was a simple, bright scarlet *morph suit*, and he was keen to show the locals. A morph suit, for those not familiar, is an elasticated very-stretchy material, one-piece costume with integral head, feet and gloves and zipped discretely up the back. So elastic that it clings exactly to the shape inside.

As we bumped into the pier's used tyres, so Forecks sprang ashore, sped up the pier and danced and cavorted around the local stalls selling food stuffs and tosh. Now this apish behaviour would be all fine and good if it were not for the prudish nature of the Islamite and more specifically, what he feels his wife(ves) should see at the market.

Now Forecks was an excellent specimen of finely-muscled man: flat of belly, biceps bulging and thighs like a race horse, cropped hair and a fine pointy nose to show how exactly a morph suit can outline the body and ALL it's morphology.

Remember that the morph suit is the only garment actually worn. Well it was a sunny but outwardly still chilly morning and XXXX's ball bag and equally pointy trouser sausage were perfectly captured in red elastic cling-film wrap and on full display to the Burka'd ladies and dusty children. Clad but I fear *not-clad* in the eyes of Johnny Turk or even a broad-minded German sauna user.

The road adjoining the water at this point followed the rocky outcrops and meandered in and out of view, as indeed did the strains of the screeching sirens of the law, once again approaching our group. Clearly Musaffah had called the Rozzers.

It was another thirty minutes of the committee and our second police negotiation; fine paying and white man promises never to bring a red man ashore again in that attire. All the while the boat passengers were curfewed to the boat to prevent any further social disorder with the yokels.

With the authorities suitably salved, the President swept on board as an 8ft tall Sultan. Bedecked in the wide full-length robes of many colours, with twisty golden rope belts and sporting a massive round turban he condemned XXXX to death by beer drinking and to assist him on his way we all set too in a similar endeavour of empathetic suicide.

Hours passed and food was gobbled and committee regulations reiterated in the background on procedures and itineraries along with a strict and very clear announcement that the vessel had only been hired to us on the even stricter instruction that no-one was to jump overboard into the Bosphorus.

And so, before you could say *'stupid-new-zealand-mother-fucking-arsehole'* (which is, I grant you, a mouthful in an emergency), Jimmy Parfit whipped off his shirt and ran to the side of the ship and flailing like a deranged monkey leapt over the side and hit the water.

No sooner had the extraordinarily loud noise of his belly hitting water reverberated over the still chugging engines, than our old chums the police sirens sonorously sounded over the lapping waves as our ship's captain called for 'full stop' and we wallowed to a wobbling halt.

The offending criminal Parfit had swum through the strong freezing current around to the blind side of our boat from the Water Police and climbed aboard the diving deck at the rear and with arms raised akimbo shouted some beer-sotted Maori chant.

The cops mega-phone hailed Our Sultan from their vessel and the Laws of Turkish Water were made clear and if **that** ever happened again, everyone was to be arrested and imprisoned for ever.

And even before that final translation was fully grasped, a thoroughly pished-up Jimmy again sprinted across the deck and launched himself skyward and downward. Even the cops were aghast and speechless as the Kiwi twat swam-limped back to the dive deck and lay there sprawled and exhausted. In a final mega-phone burp of warning they sped off and left us to the AGM.

The official business of the meeting was conducted first: any new proposed players (some), recent loss on the committee warranting replacement (never), next year's possible tour venues proposed voted for and ignored by the committee. Then to the court.

All touring clubs do this and have similar formats with an appointed judge to pronounce sentence, a vibrant, gobby and court savvy prosecution and a hopelessly, toothless and irrelevant but historically necessary defense council. This year, as prosecution counsel I had arranged a 25ᵗʰ Anniversary silky-material Mat of Guilt with all past and present Rhinos listed by country or residence. This was now produced and laid upon the deck before the bar and each and every tourist eventually ended-up in the kneeing, bent, prone supplicating posture of the Islamist at prayer. This pose represented the offending guilt, mimicking the local customs but we were essentially in private, naughty but nice.

Offenses were read out offering a long range of accurate, highly-incriminating behaviour on tour. Beer drinking or ghastly local brews were the fines which, after due deliberation by the judge and of course time for the defense to utter some spluttering mitigation, which was totally ignored, sentences duly issued.

Well if we weren't pissed as skunks before, we certainly were by the time late dusk came around and we approached the hotel pier.

If nothing else this tour would be fondly remembered for its fabulous historical nature, sites, the unique intercontinental match, the smells and cuisine of Istanbul and most notably the eerie echoes of the various police squads chasing rhino in Asia-Minor.

*****

CAMBODIA 40TH

"The key to being a good manager is keeping the people who hate me away from those who are still undecided." Casey Stengel

Larry Maley, now there's a name that rings a bell - both in terms of memory and me being on the end of the hardest, nastiest, gum-shield removing *tackle* I have ever suffered in all my puff, and that was me doing the tackling.

Larry was a *jobbing* golf-course engineer and had been land sculpturing and coaxing the Bermuda grasses into life on numerous golf courses throughout Thailand before he eventually aligned his old rugby skills and the British Club needs into one.

By jobbing I mean he was the archetypal, completely relaxed Aussie who must one day have turned to his mates in the pub in Wagga Wagga or family gathering over Christmas dinner or just to his bird-in-hand and muttered those inimitable Aussie words,

"Daarlin' Oye think a'am gonna go walk-abbaart".

And with that he must have promptly grabbed an available plastic shopping bag, packed the extra wife beater (string vest), a spare flip-flop in case he lost one and a toothbrush and simply set off overseas.

Larry was about 42 years young, 6'2" tall, 95kgs of lean muscle, a shock of firmly-curled, strawberry-blond hair (notice I didn't say copper-top), fair-skinned, except for the eight million freckles, and the calm demeanour of a koala. His smile was forever on show and sported a whole graveyard of brilliant white teeth and annoyingly they even had one of those Tony Curtis sparkles when he partnered Roger Moore in that UK crime fighting duo *The Persuaders*.

Around this time, say October 2005, my closest mate, Bruce Hill, had at last reached the ripe old age of forty and decided that we should all partake and go on tour to celebrate such an accomplishment, which I hasten to add, had quite pleasantly shocked both his parents that he would even survive that long.

Larry had upped sticks in Thailand and, fed-up with lawn grass growing by the hectare, had moved to Phnom Phenh, opened a small bijou hotel and started growing some alternative grass. Well that's a shocking summary of a life decision of that magnitude but what it did do was remind Bruce that Larry was now our Man-in-Havana (well you know, PP.) With a man on the ground in such a fleshpot the world is your oyster and we were planning to buy large in seafood.

Me, Birthday Boy 40th Bruce Hill and that rogue Cornish Tor Andy Talling in No1's– and for those of you viewing in black and white – Andy was sporting pink hair at the time.

Not content that our British Club rugby team would always travel on tour in No1's (club pink and black-striped silk blazer, white shirt, silk club tie and grey slacks) Bruce had taken to theming the tours to add some spice and this also allowed the Sock to be regularly replenished with cash by team offenders forgetting one or other of a multitude of daft kit parts.

At the time we all thought his chosen theme was a bit risqué and probably unacceptable to almost everyone on the globe at that time, little did we know it was a pre-cursor to the Jimmy Saville and Rolf Harris revelations.

Anyway we were going on tour as "The Gary Glitter Band" complete with that tour title on the playing shirts.

You may recall Gary (not Larry), had just been done up like a kipper for having his hands in various underage pants and was extradited from Cambodia to the UK …hmm…a very dodgy theme indeed.

Anyway, *the kit* consisted of the usual upper club formal attire but with shocking star-shaped spangly, silvery sun-glasses and a sarong. Sarong, you say, not so bad, except this was a diaphanous bluey-mauve-silky-shiny material that was both almost impossible to tie and keep-up and was at least 87% transparent. Not so bad you say again, except *our under pants* were banned on tour so in effect one was wandering the international airports and streets of fair cities with all your valuables on show if one were to peer vaguely in that area.

It just so happened that that year, Phnom Phenh had also decided to hold a rugby tournament in the main old city stadium and invite young and old club teams from around the region and any that wanted to travel from further afield. Remember this was once part of French Indo-China so there were doubtless going to be the odd Froggy teams flying in from Gaul.

A brief contact with Larry ensured that we were enrolled into the tournament and we also fully booked his hotel for the long weekend.

*

Well the day arrived and we all headed to Bangkok's old Don Mueang airport in a fine state of tour fever.

You know the drill:

- Arrive at the airport on time at the appointed hour or be fined.
- Have all your kit on or be fined.
- Check and double check your tour buddy was also on time or be fined.
- Look happy and carefree or be fined.
- Drop your sarong…an award…a fresh beer and fined.

Amazing how Bruce was able to immediately fill the Sock with more hard currency than the Ugandan national debt.

Bentley's Bar appeared on the starboard quarter and beers were ordered in gay abandon and here the gossamer sarong did for the gay bit. The flight to Cambodia was on Bangkok Air, a reasonably diligent outfit, but delays on arriving and then departing flights was always part of the travel tapestry so more gay abandon at the bar for all, but that was ok because the Sock was already flush, as indeed were many of our group.

A moment of singular joy occurred when our dear Italian golfing buddy Fabrizio Mazzocchi, who had agreed to come on his first ever rugby tour, bumped into half a dozen of his daughter's teachers from her international school. They were off on some Asian Teachers Group Hug scheme but could now travel onwards warmed with the colourful memory of 'that nice sensible Italian man's see-through sarong'.

Somehow, the tour managers or blokes with slightly more maturity than a toddler, did succeed in getting the entire group out of the Land of Smiles and into the Land of Oysters without any legal proceedings or lock-ups abroad.

Rather than follow any sensible plan to first locate Larry's Billabong Hotel and drop off the bags and playing kit, Larry confirmed that we should head straight for Ping-Pong alley and he would meet us there. Brilliant was the chorus from the band and so we lurched for the strip.

Now almost to a man, we were, it has to be said, experienced Asian tourists and knew bars and their contents and smells like the back of, well, a dog.

And so picture this, at approximately 4.30pm on a Friday's balmy oriental evening, a large bawdy group of testosterone wielding, see-thru-sarong-clad expats staggering up the delightfully quaint ex-Froggy colonial street shop-house bars glancing and leering and gesticulating at themselves in the glass reflections and some youngster from the front shouted. "This bar…in here!".

Now at this time I was *returning from being away*, that's got to be West country speak eh. Whilst there were many old hands with whom I had played and toured, there were a lot of new guys that I didn't know and they didn't know me, other than by infamy, but as a senior toddler on this tour I was happy to follow their lead in this unknown town.

This chosen bar followed the usual structural format of a shop front approximately three to four yards wide and then like Mary Poppins' carpet bag, they were 200 miles deep with a bog arrangement at the far end and a bar down most of one side and more mirrors than Brighton Pier on both walls and ceilings.

They are usually painted in dark colours and there are flickering fairy lights, an aging spot light playing on a disco mirror ball that had lost more *teeth* than Henry Cooper, but the bars were usually vaguely clean.

Here that similarity ended.

In this bar, despite the early hour, the cleaner had not visited since after the Khmer Rouge exit and the floor was littered with old fag ends, take-away food bags, discarded clothing and as you walked you stuck to the floor with that ghastly squeaky tearing sound, which could, we assumed, only come from…coming.

None of this mattered because you were wholly concentrating on why there was no oxygen or even breathable air in the bar, which had been completely taken over by the bar owner's annoying habit of throwing 3cwt of mothballs into every urinal and toilet and basin in the erroneous belief that made everything hygienic and scented.

The only person in the place was an unmoving, glassy-eyed old bird behind the bar who came as a matching set with the pub decor and I could only speculate that she too wore *eau de naphthalene*. Anyway, even the youngsters knew a shit-hole when they were in one and turning like a millipede, the leader led us back outside to the fresh air.

"OK…into this one you tossers," The young intrepid explorer announced.

Sadly, and without even the chance of a beer, this must have recurred five or six times in two different streets and all the bars were seriously found wanting. The leading youngster had been hung twice, and then some arsehole said, "Hey JP's here, he would know which bar to go to, he would never fail…quick get that old cunt up here."

This was a hideous position to be in because my street cred had survived over the years to such an extent that even these nippers had heard of my unfailing shite, and yet in this veritable forlorn desert of a Strip, there simply were no bars of any repute and I was to be cast to the lions as were our earlier pathfinders.

Pushed forwards with chummy pats on the back and ill-informed shouts of *'good old Jon'* I was exposed at the front.

I hummed and arr'd and tried to look suitably Henry Stanley-like as I considered our new route through the jungle of unfound fanny and beer. Glancing down a side alley, I pointed to the Star Bar in the corner and pronounced that was our Oasis of Destiny.

Only a few times in one's sporting life are we truly blessed with a moment of sheer luck and this was one of those serendipitous times, because I marched with purpose and stateliness and pushed open the bar door with my eyes closed and holding my breath, as indeed I am sure the throng behind me did the same.

The room was silent, but I sensed this was different and I opened my peepers and there in front of me was a completely naked young local girl with one leg up on the bar, her head bent over and she was furiously strumming away completely oblivious to anyone else and certainly our leering faces.

Our attention was taken away from the perspiring, industrious young maiden as there was a shriek of joy and twenty thousand scantily-clad girls raced down the bar and grabbed whichever male they could and screamed for beer and music. The DJ started with that classic *'One night in Bangkok'* at 4 billion decibels which was mildly ironic…as for once, we weren't.

Even Birthday Boy Bruce was in awe, and he can't even spell that, patted me on the back for old time's sake and passed me an Anchor.

Eventually we did meet up with Larry and in a shocking state of excessive consumption, we all headed to the Billabong to drop off our gear and then it was out for a proper pish up.

Before departing the Billabong, Larry presented Bruce with his Sergeant Major's Staff, a six-foot long solid timber rod with a quasi-formal bulbous head and steel toe for him to officiate at all required functions, amusing really as Bruce was now hoisted by his own petard and would be fined if the official rod was lost, stolen, hidden or forgotten. Anything can happen on tour.

*

Now Bruce's tour was originally conceived as an Old Boys Team (over 35 years old) that would take part in the full tournament, get thrashed by youth and exuberance but enjoy it all the same.

The tour was unusual, in that by the nature of being Bruce's mates, not all of the guests were players of rugby and some hadn't partaken of anything more industrious or aggressive than a two hour Thai massage in thirty years. There were also new guys coming who were mates of mates but vetted and guaranteed as good blokes by the original mate.

Mates' mates coming on tour was not new and we did have a tradition that the unknown bloke's real name was never uttered and he would be known simply as 'Dean's mate' or 'Dickie's mate'. In the case of *Dean's mate* some years before, he went on to play for us in Thailand's league matches for years and later the Bangkok Bangers and even later to referee and in all those years he was simply but proudly forever 'Dean's mate'. His beloved wife wasn't quite so chuffed to only be addressed throughout those tumultuous years as 'Dean's mate's Wife'.

One such stalwart, non-playing, certified AA attendee was our chum Keith Cronshaw, MD of a specialist telecoms contractor who not only generously sponsored the team but supported in presence and with more cash and paid for most of the pish-ups enjoyed by the membership. Anyway, Keith was always first to pay up his ticket for the tour and had done so nano-seconds after being advised of the cost by Bruce. Now it transpires he was committed at work and sadly could not come.

Refunds of any meaningful percentage from Bruce's tour kitty were, and remain, as rare as rocking-horse shit and so it was mutually agreed that the funds could now sponsor two penniless young New Zealand lads, proposed by Eddie Evans, who co-incidentally were outstandingly good players. Eddie decided he too should be on tour to take care of them and let his hair down. Funds were also allocated to bring some young speeding Thai lads in our home team who also were baht-less and needed some cash assistance. Our Welsh wizard Nigel Wixcey at fly half, having moved overseas some years before, was also miraculously available and paid up.

The old decrepit team. Imagine super-slow-mo and the Armageddon *movie – they actually got that inspired picture of slow-moving astronauts from this bunch of sloths,*

Without naming every last player, the decrepit old boy's contingent had now been bolstered, buttressed and engendered with youth and enthusiasm, speed, skills and a better grasp of the laws than Bruce had ever imagined.

All the while, Jimmy '*Ratcatcher*' Howard, (prop, 98kgs) and Keith '*Faak-that-lettuce-diet*' Rowley (club treasurer, 118kgs), would be sitting in the stands doing a fine and very attentive security job amongst out kit bags and equipment to prevent the lovely, cheery, dirt-encrusted battalions of local kids from borrowing and then selling our possessions.

Bob Merrigan was to be chief assistant coach and water boy. He was also our replacement advisor and rolling subs shouter. Once old Ratcatcher had seen people flagging or temporarily damaged during the conflict, he would advise Bob who would be galvanised into action. Many a time confusion reigned when the injured bloke was removed and incorrectly replaced with an unskilled-in-the-arts replacement until Rats could clarify without moving from his position as security bag attendant.

The tournament, whilst full of colourful and far-travelled teams, was only planned as a one-day event, with the usual starting pool groups eventually sending winners into the Cup and losers into Plates, Bowls or to wooden spoon oblivion.

Much to the surprise and shock of all concerned, our patchwork quilt of old fat blokes, Kiwi skills and that really, really fast Thai bloke on our right wing, we cut through the hypothetical butter of every team like a burning dildo and reached the final against the Manila Nomads.

Our rousing pre-kick-off team talk in the middle of the pitch went something like this, "Come on guys, one last game…it's only that mad bunch from Manila and I saw they had more of those Happy Herb Pizzas an hour ago, so we have gotta' win."

"Come on let's do it for Bruce…let's win the Cup!" accompanied by a few weedy cheers.

"Fuck that cunt…he nicked my bird in the bar last night and said I could have her back when she was full," said Mr Christian.

"What a greedy twat…he nicked mine too for twenty minutes and said the same thing. Fuck him," said Captain Bligh's chief steward.

"Come on now pull together…this is a team game and it's Bruce's Birthday and he's our mate." The last with in a Welsh accent as Nigel Wixey offered his voice.

"That cunt ain't my mate." Mutineer 1.

"Who?" Mutineer 2.

"That cunt." Mutineer 1.

"Look the ref's coming and stop that bickering." Wixey.

"He can faak awf an' all...cunt!" Mutineer 1 and now treasonist.

And so the final kicked-off and our indomitable, resolute, friendly, homogeneous Band of Bastards did indeed overcome the Nasty Nomads and shockingly won a Cup for Bruce in the process.

*

The usual evening Awards Ceremony by the hosts was arranged after all teams had cleaned up, showered and donned their evening attire in a fairly utilitarian public community hall. Twenty seat tables and chairs allowed whole team contingents to be together and were on the main wooden floor of the hall and there was a top table for the toffs just under the raised school play stage structure.

The food was buffet-style with the usual Thai/Cambodian hot plates of rice, various fish, chicken and unknown curry-based local treats. Stir-fried vegetables and watermelon for pud. Perfectly adequate and generous for all.

Beers were the local Anchor breweries best and it was flowing well.

Big Bruce, I have witnessed, is capable of drinking almost anyone or anything under the table of an evening. It starts with beers and he moves on to Scotch by the gallon. There is clearly a limit that only he knows when the beer locker is full and he doesn't want any more. Tonight was to be different.

I took it upon myself to visit every table and therefore every team and asked that at least five or six of their players should absentmindedly and without creating either a queue or a hiatus, amble over to our table and wish Bruce a beery toast for his 40th, every player to bring a filled glass of beer and individually toast Bruce with those wee Aussie schooner-sized vessels that were on the tables.

We had of course prepared a veritable South China Sea of beer refills for Bruce to toast these well-meaning chaps under our table and you know, those kind souls from every team did him proud and even my basic arithmetic made that something like 6 x 20 x 200 ml beer shots, not bad as a warm up.

During this period of relative inertia in the hall, someone, probably with strawberry-blond hair, had brought in two or three of those local, magic mushroom pizzas and put them on our table.

While we were busy getting Bruce to hoover beers, our two old mates Dr Paul Meggison (second row, 110kgs) and our ferreting, punchy, noisy, argumentative Trevor Day (centre, 82kgs) had, between expletives, guzzled mouthfuls of the happy pizza and gradually sat back to ruminate and eventually vegetate into a state of complete inactivity and, surprisingly, silence.

Being the caring and aware tour managers that we were, when Trevor eventually slid off his chair and lay in a puddle of stale excess beer with fag-end accoutrements, we deemed that was the safest place for him and kindly pushed him under the trestle table, for his own protection of course.

Meggison, being a doctor, but completely unaware of any narcotic content in the pizzas, suspected that he was having the start of heart palpitations and a possible arrest. He had prided himself on never being arrested on tour (?!), and he skulked, unannounced from the hall and fled to the Billabong hotel.

The MC for the evening then announced that there would a Drinking Race and the key team captains, including our birthday boy Bruce, would be the competitors. At that stage it was about six or seven blokes.

Anyway, the race consisted of each contestant downing a shot of the cheapest available Tequila with the usual salt and lemon, a bottle of well-found Thai Singha beer (which incidentally, Bruce despises) and then the contestants must insert a raw egg into their mouths, break the egg, swallow the mucus mess and eject the shell without anything else being exhausted.

The first to be open-mouthed at the end and be inspected by the MC, wins.

Well knowing my buddy's limit on beer, utter disgust at having to drink yet another cheap tequila and topped with a Singha beer from Hell, I was certain all of that was going to revisit the hall and so set off in search of a suitable receptacle.

Despite team loyalty and various national pride levels in the room, everyone, and here, I mean everyone, wanted Bruce to win and chants went up around the hall before the MC's arm fell. In truth I am sure, like F1 viewing, we are all watching to see the crashes and refuelling cock-ups and here was a bulging Bruce, already full to the brim with gassy beer and there was almost certainly going to be a Hindenburg-like event, except wet rather than fiery.

The arm fell, the tequilas were quaffed, beers chugged and then the egg. Well that broke half the contestants there and then, a huge size-5 egg in your mouth actually restricts your breathing and there were massive geysers of frothing beer and exploding half bitten-through chicken embryos sprayed over top table and the stage.

Luckily Bruce is a QS and can breathe through his arse and so whilst there were detonating humans all around him, Bruce crushed his shell, swallowed the ectoplasm and then very delicately conveyed the spent shell parts into his hand and opened his maw. He had genuinely won.

Now I was in awe, because I had 15/1 on him chucking after the tequila and doubled it on the Singha beer...bastard.

The hall erupted but Bruce didn't. Blowing only a kiss to his audience he carefully descended the stage steps and meandered over to our table sat next to me and murmured, "it's all coming up mate." Conspiratorially I whispered, "It's ok buddy I got you this..."

From under the table I handed him an old A4 paper supply box with the lid off ready for the thunderous chunda. I can still see his cheery little eyes looking sideways at me with real love and affection and after that merest of moments, he put the box on his lap and set about the exhausting process of dispensing all of that unwanted belly mixture at high velocity.

At this point I moved aside and away, because as you all know, those A4 boxes have a large hole in the bottom and all the liquid exhaust was channeled straight to his groin. Without stopping or raising his head he screamed "YOU CAAAAANT".

*

After a wipe down of our messy chief toddler's crotch and gathering the chaps and sweeping Trevor out from under the table, we set off for The Heart of Darkness...again. Well the night went off much as the one the night before, and without repeating the shenanigans and embarrassing episodes of our semi-educated expats trying to converse with the local girls using only Swahili or some lost Polish dialect, I am sure they were suitably fleeced of their dollars and one or two sperms must have been used during proceedings.

I delight in the fact that, for once, Bob Merrigan and I were able to put Bruce, pished as a twat, on the back of a motor-bike taxi boy where, after specific directions and threats of death if he failed to deliver the bundle, he sped off into the unlit back street with Bruce's Sergeant Major's oversized rod dragging on the road and leaving a shower of festive sparks behind the departing behind.

*

Sunday started very slowly indeed with everyone wandering about like zombies, not the hyperactive man-eating ones the Yanks have invented, but slow to almost stationary zombies, unable to communicate and with no discernible fixed goals.

It was planned that there would be a lunch time party around the Billabong pool and everyone was invited to the Birthday Boy's cake cutting and munching.

From their first evening's US$2.00 purchase of a family bag of grass, James, our converted English rugby league centre and Dean's Mate were oft seen snuggled in a corner rolling spliffs like the days of their youth and they clearly hadn't lost any of their skillsets and having acquired such a large family bag, they were generously giving smokes away to anyone who could still breathe.

Well noon came around and the pool was heaving with totty, provided by Dean's Mate in his official capacity of totty master, and happy beer-swilling survivors and more were arriving at the gate by the minute.

Larry brought out the Billabong Brownie Birthday cake resplendent with symbolic candles, couldn't put on forty candles, not because they didn't have that many in Cambodia, but Larry only had twenty digits to count on and doing it twice was quite beyond his pay grade.

Now I do beers and stupid chaser drinks and tequila-titties and all manner of pathetic drinking stuff but I am not really a smoker of recreational extras. Not a goodie-goodie but just not a smoker and never have been interested in the light drug brigade, ok yes a goodie-goodie. Anyway, the brownie cake was a masterpiece of cookery and the product of Larry's months of careful herbivorous cultivation. There was plenty of cake to go around as it was about the size of an ancient Abyssinian shield.

Scantily clad birds handed round the culinary marvel and after piece number two I found a sofa in the shade under the balcony and sat down and then quite involuntarily rolled on my side and lay there unmoving for four hours with concerned visitors prodding me and laughing...the twats. Well there were lots of these dead fish lying about in varying states of unconsciousness and I suppose it was no loss to conversation because no one was capable of chatting anyway before the cake.

Hong Kong's Pot Bellied Pigs team had arrived and as was always their generous MO brought vast stores of booze and beer with them. The Pigs also tucked into the Brownie cake and we were later to hear, much to our amusement, that three of them had to be medi-vac'd back from their temple trekking trip because they thought they were having heart palpitations.

None of us can remember what happened in the traditional fines court. There must have been one and people must have suffered and drunk ghastly concoctions and puked and farted and puked again but I cannot find a surviving soul who can furnish me any memories on this matter to all.

The tour did end and it was generally held to be true that everyone involved was pleased that Bruce would only ever be forty once.

THE RIDDLE

"It is a riddle wrapped in a mystery inside an enigma."
Winston Churchill 1874 –1965

It must have been about 1994 and a Sunday. We were around at our British Club chairman's little oasis in Bangkok: Joe and Bea Grunwell's home with other couples on the Sunday afternoon for a cool down BBQ and general family time. I think only the Grunwell's and our babies were about at that time, everyone else was so much younger…or late to sprog I like to think.

After the splashing and fighting with the kids, the truly exhausted parents collapsed into poolside chairs and loungers before attacking the usual huge array of BBQ food. The men had stood in a protective lager around the furnace, drunk beers and offered their advice on the turning of sausages and steaks, whilst the ladies formed their own grouping of sun-loungers and gossiped (ladies don't chat, they definitely gossip) about the latest expat news.

After the BBQ and more chilled beer and wine, our twin girls, Holly and Sam and our host's daughter Nicole and the two younger boys, my Billy and their James, were sent off to wreck the house while the parents retired hurt and dog-tired inside to the quadrangle of deep soft, comfy sofas.

With the echoing stamp of tiny feet up the stairs and various screams from one bedroom of another, the parents lounged around the large Chiang Mai *sample* teak coffee table (made to order by our wives' Thai Products Corp).

Afternoon beers were now being tempered and massaged by Joe's brandies and whisky's, while the girls guzzled champagne and Bailey's by the bucket, they were of course tasteful enough not to mix the two in one glass.

There was the usual crowd of about five couples but in there was a new pairing of Alan Black and his wife…Mrs Black. Alan was an Irishman and a flanker and great fun to have about, as indeed are all the Paddies I have ever known. Alan was no spring chicken but sinewy and tough and with groomed curly black hair, some history of acne leaving its usual story in his complexion. He had a beard and a scrawny moustache and the most enormous red strawberry birthmark all down the left side of his face. It was a large slightly protruding ruddy birthmark and ran from above his left eye down past his ear covering his whole cheek and did a reverse Cape Horn around his chin.

I had got the usual uncomfortable, self-conscious issue of the birthmark out of the way years ago by uttering some embarrassed expletive and then it was briefly discussed with Alan and understood by all and simply forgotten. Now it was about to be top of the bill.

Andy Davies and Alan Black.

After some particularly shrill screaming from above, the young boys crashed down the stairs, appeared and rushed through the house but my Billy, a lovely four or five-year old blond, bundle of fun and mischief but with the face of an angel and nothing like his aggressive and diabolical twin sisters, stopped running near us and caught his breath.

He stood at the corner of the table and looked at us all as we chatted and then said.

"I have a riddle that I bet none of you can get, doyouwannahearit?"

"Pardon Bill, what did you say?"

The Riddle

"I said, I've got a riddle and I bet you can't get it …doyouwannahearit?" This uttered with that slightly tired and frustrated repeated question tone used by his parents all the time.

"If you do…you will have to listen carefully," he cautioned.

The last being delivered whilst wagging a small pink finger around the circle. This of course again being almost exactly how parents speak to their kids and so he waited for everyone's attention and said.

"Why is Uncle Alan's face different to everyone else's in the room?" and with that he said he'd be back for the answer and disappeared into the garden.

Now despite my bombastic blurt when we had been males together bonding and pointing at the huge facial scar, this somehow was wholly different and I felt mortified. There was a sharp intake of breath from everyone.

"Look Alan, I am so sorry about that he doesn't mean any offense…he's a very polite boy…he's…."

"Oh Be Jeeezuz, Johnno its nutthin' at all and indeed, how can you miss it?"

Which you'd have thought took all the insult and embarrassed focus away and we could all relax, but it hadn't and we all sat up now, I was on the edge of my seat with dread at the final answer.

Minutes later Billy whizzed back past shouting, "Well have you got it yet...have you?" and scampered away.

On the next passing of the Comet Billy I hauled him in by a flailing arm and asked him to calm down and take a rest.

"OK Dad…but have you got the answer?" Stunned adult silence.

Then to the assembled parents he said, "Boy you guys are thicko's…HE'S THE ONLY ONE WITH A BEARD."

*****

Lions Tour 1997

"Everybody is a genius. But if you judge a fish by its ability to climb a tree, it will live it's life believing that it is stupid." Albert Einstein

Eight of us had travelled to New Zealand in 1993, watched only one Test, which we had won in Wellington and it was agreed, in the modern day vernacular as being the most awesome trip and to be repeated every four years without fail.

So here we were now in 1997 in Durban, Natal, South Africa with a larger group of mainly Bangkok British Club players and only a couple of the original tribe, all charged up with excitement at the prospect of a Test series win as we had already won the First Test in Newlands 25-16 and had a fabulous team with Martin Johnson leading the Lions.

It was also the first B&I Lions tour after the apartheid era and the first with players getting used to their new professional status. Remember the Springboks were current World Champions having beaten the All Blacks even with Jona Lomu in 1995 and whilst apparently in some decline they were still a fearsome prospect.

Apparently, the South African *Sports Illustrated* had noted:

.... The British Lions arrived in South Africa rated by its own media, SA media and their supporters as nothing more than rank underdogs. A nice bunch of blokes who were making a bit of history and, in so doing, winning friends rather than matches'.

Cheeky wankers.

There had been no flights cheap enough directly from Bangkok to Jo'burg so we had flown Malaysian Airways to the new and gleaming KLIA airport and wandered the spanking new departure areas, monopolising the circular lifts and generally being mischievous.

When our flight was called we had to queue in a holding area that overlooked a long ramped stair-core and in the base of this stairwell was a dear, ancient old Chinese lady with one of those soft bristled, wide headed, hand held brushes in one gloved mit and a long-handled dust pan in the other. She was sweeping up, slowly, really slowly like working on the very last electrons in a tired old battery.

There now proceeds a brief interlude of which I am not proud.

Delving into my pocket I recovered one of those conference room red laser pointers and aimed the dot in front of old Mrs Wang. The change was startlingly vivid. From the mundane acres of airport fluff she saw everyday, here was her Holy Grail of light and sparkling real garbage.

With this new irresistible lure, she leapt forward and swept it up. But oh no it was still there…dancing along the floor and she staggered forward on her woven cloth slippers chasing the dot. It leapt and bounded and flew and disappeared and reappeared and climbed walls and windows all the while to pathetic childish sniggering from above. She swept and swept and lunged and parried but the dot was a never-to-be-caught sprite of unwholesome mischief. A pang of guilt overcame me and the spot flashed no more and Mrs Wang cast about for the wee shimmering dot, saw nothing and with a shrug, went back to her more relaxed diet of fluff and cobwebs. I will burn in Hell for that alone.

Pretty much the year of '97 formal Team picture in the front of the BC. Most of this bunch were in Durban for the Win!!

Now this was also a first for our club to be going on a long-distance tour without actually playing rugby. After landing in

Jo'burg we caught the domestic connection to Durban. Once we had checked-in to our hotel in the mid-Durban area we all noticed a thirst coming on. The hotel was right on the waterfront with a fabulous vista of the pea green Indian ocean, set under a brilliant, pale blue African sky and enhanced with the twinkling golden sands of the promenade beach. We trooped out of the front door, 'ooohed and aaahrd' at the magnificent view, a few picked noses and scratched arses and then we turned right and fifty yards away found a bar on the corner and sat there for three days drinking pish.

I am sure our parents and families were agog awaiting stories of the wild animals we faced, the game reserves we had visited, the indigenous people's trinkets we had bought but they were all to be very sadly disappointed because we did none of that. We simply sat in that bar on that corner and apart from the odd wander - not too far away- we stuck avidly to our task of drinking Castle. Only the termites sensed the miniscule tremblings of David Livingstone and Henry Stanley wriggling and squirming in their graves at the sheer laziness, un-adventurousness and idle nature of our band.

We had popped back to the hotel on that first day for the buffet lunch because it was highly recommended and coincidentally extremely cheap. And we were pleasantly surprised at the high quality of the food on offer. An immense spread of beautifully-coloured, cooked and carved vegetables piled so high we could only just see the top of the little Bantu lady's head over the sweet peppers. The meat section was a disgrace. It seemed like the kitchen staff had simply moved the whole fucking abattoir there and shoveled in a few game carcasses and a score of plump chickens and the carvery chef proceeded to overload your 22" plates as if you were there on your own to collect for a family of twelve.

Needless to say, after that orgy of meat and spuds and stuff it was amazing we were even able to move but, being the heroes we were, we girded our loins and huge swollen bellies, staggered to the hotel entrance, turned right and returned to our reserved seats under the stripy canopy and drank more beer. More disturbed termites noted rumblings from a humble grave in deepest Congo.

So much ale was being drunk that many of us needed to get more money and needed an ATM. Stopping a local passer-by, a rather large black lady with her hair all tied up in a rainbow of material, probably the national flag, we asked where there was an ATM and she smiled and pointed up the six-lane road beside the bar and waved saying, "Up dare maann, 'bout hundred meeta's". She waved a small hand in goodbye and then with a swinging, flirtatious, quivering bustle she padded off northwards.

As about five of us got up to leave, our skinny little Indian waiter Mr Adun whispered with much frantic shaking of the head and quasi-religious hand movement, "Oh my golly gosh Saahib you don't, really, really don't want to be going up 'dare. Not now… not at this time."

For heaven's sake we said, it's a wide road with broad sweeping sidewalks and perpendicular to the beach front, smack in the middle of Durban, what could possibly go wrong?

"Don't Saahib…just don't." and with those last words of mysterious warning, he scuttled away into the shadows of the bar wringing his hands in trepidation and possible concern that if we didn't return, he would not get a tip.

Five and half big sweaty rugby players (well five and a fly-half) set off up the sunlit street with white-painted buildings, clean and level footpaths, central reservations that broke into elegant royal palm trees and multi-coloured shrubbery. We poked our noses into two or three sex shops along the covered arcade-style avenue (curious to have such hardware stores in that location) and repeating our query again the last cashier pointed to a large whitewashed building in the centre of the broad parkland, indicating that was the bank with an ATM.

As we crossed the road, we all noticed in a subliminal sort of way, that there seemed to be a new curious silence, no cars moving, no birds chirping, no one else on the road or in sight. Then, all too quickly for us to even react, from three or four side streets black clad, crouching, small stepping figures of the local police S.W.A.T team poured out all clasping their ghastly snub-nosed automatic pistols with double-taped magazines, balaclavas and attitude. A team went passed us and their leader whispered through his cloth balaclava, **"Fuck off outta here you stupid fucking twats…NOW!! …Faaaak aaawf or I'll shoot you!!"**

Only Adun, and these blokes, knew it was pay-day and the regular bank robbery was underway, apparently like clockwork every week. We fled back to the safety of our beer canopy…not to venture out again until evensong.

*

Day two dawned and after breakfast and about an hour under our canopy we asked Adun to kindly save our table and we ventured forth in our board shorts and T shirts to check the pier, the sea and possibly gather-up enough energy for a dip.

We ambled along the nearest nearby wooden slats of the wide, uncovered, seventy-metre long pier which bisected the delightful slightly curving beach, took in the local colourful stalls along either side of the central boardwalk and assumed there was no one in the water because it was cold. Pah we thought, that's not going stop us we bragged and peering over the edge of the structure, we considered it was easily deep enough to jump without breaking a leg and started to disrobe.

"Jew doant waantabee yumpin in dare man," said Adun's equally pessimistic African brother manning the stall immediately beside our gathering pile of discarded clothes.

After a squabbling period of testosterone-enhanced blathering we managed a sneering query, "Oh…and why not my good man?"

"Cos a whitee got hesself bit in two by dee shark yestidee!!" He answered, smiling all the while and no doubt a little frustrated with himself that he had opened his mouth too soon and now there was no late morning entertainment. Even the stall-man beside him tutted at his helpfulness and loss of viewing.

With the rapidity only associated with an adulterous man in another man's bedroom discovering the actual husband arriving home, we donned all our beach-ware, thanked our much-blessed African pier chum and fled once again like headless chickens back to our canopy, vowing never to venture out again...ever.

Well Friday night came around and we had been invited to the Durban Sharks clubhouse for a Braai and beers and to watch a local game under the floodlights. (Actually this was probably the clubhouse of the Collegians RFC according to my Durban native chum Angus McKernan).

Their facilities were established on a great swathe of open grass outside the main King's Park stadium with countless pitches around a delightful modern timber clubhouse building with never-ending bars manned by hugely proficient and efficient staff and an equally magnificent balcony overlooking pitch #1 with the King's stadium behind.

We arrived about halfway through the match in the balmy evening ruddiness as the sun set and amazingly I could identify Stephan Terblanche as an active player. Remember in those days the Currie Cup and the other more modern Southern Hemisphere tournaments were years away from being televised or even invented, so to spot at least one known player was a feather in my cap.

After the match the floodlights were dimmed and discrete exterior lighting created a warm and homely glow and the washed and showered players and fans mingled on the pitch and along the side-lines under the balcony. We were no fools, the best bar was on the first floor and only yards from the cool and breezy balcony, so we set up camp there and continued hosing.

Well as all things must go around that come around, that cheeky sprite once again placed that laser in my hand and with chuckles aforethought and my mate's encouragement, I leaned over the balcony handrail and zapped the laser right on Stephan's forehead.

In praise of the South African military training (of which we had completely forgotten as the Castles had mounted up), there as an instantaneous reaction and with a cry from the huge monster in front of Terblanche.

"*FOK!!!...val plat manne ons moet hier fokken uitkom, die fokkers wil ons skiet!!!*", he pushed him hard in the chest, all their beers went flying and they all dived to the ground and leopard-crawled for cover under the balcony.

Well FUCK thought I, and quickly slid the laser in a mate's pocket as this herd of furious, roaring buffaloes careered up the stairs and burst onto the balcony and surrounded us heaving for breath and purple of face, they screamed.

"Who was the Doos who did that??"

Now whilst the obvious and ingrained reaction on any tour, by any tourist anywhere, at any time is deny, deny and deny, I thought of old Mrs Wang at KLIA airport and decided someone had to die for this and fearing I couldn't speak properly I simply put my hand up, "Me," I squeaked.

A ghastly silence ensued with only snorting, heavy breathing from gigantic men around me and then surprisingly from just that one word the biggest Yarpie there asked, "Are you guys from Engeland?"

I nodded and after another period of silence, he said, "Look that was a very stupid thing to do, especially here in South Africa, but buy us all a replacement beer, no, make that two each and we won't kill you…eh?"

Funnily enough, that little episode broke the ice and not my nose and we proceeded to get pissed with them for hours. The Rand was in the toilet so for us the price of club beer was almost nothing and we kept paying all night. Well, apart from the laser, I also held The Sock.

*

Match day arrived and we were fizzing with excitement. Trevor Day recounts, like a religious text, that I had shouted at them all to '*bloody well remember every bloody minute of this day and the tour for such events only come once in a lifetime!'*. Sage words no doubt…until the next tour.

After a suitable period of beer drinking at young Adun's bar with our host scampering about between us all distributing Castles, we boldly decided to walk to the ground taking roadies with us, which we were to refresh as we went with plenty of time before kick-off. Well it was a beautiful sunny day with no breeze and we almost skipped gaily along the footpaths unaware that we were probably miles from the stadium (I having seen it from our hotel room window, in the far distance).

Anyway, Durban isn't that big a town and we were in a euphoric and confident state of mind and soon found our way to the beach side of King's Park and were astonished at the change.

We passed through the ubiquitous match day gates and ticket checks on the perimeter but then we had to stride through the tens of thousands of Yarpie cars all parked on the training and playing pitches of the *Sharks' grounds* to even get to the ramps and steps of the East Stand where our seats were all allocated.

This was no ordinary car park, this was an international Braai out-the-back-of-your-Baakie challenge that only the South Africans can do to this magnificent degree. Yes, I know you are going to say Twickenham has a similar Range Rover Club with gallons of Pimms and mummy's best sandwiches with the crusts cut off, but this is definitely quite different.

Only the Persian Empire at it's height under Xerxes at Thermopylae could possibly have erected that many tents, tarpaulin-covered emporiums, podiums, cooking stoves and gigantic flaming cooking ranges overnight! There were mini generators chugging away discretely behind pick-ups, with full-sized, glass-fronted drinks fridges, tables, chairs, Grandpa's recliners, benches and bean bags, overhead cables and lighting for later, dog kennels and allocated toilet areas, rainbow National flags, bunting hanging from every conceivable car aerial or caravan roof.

All this impermanent, momentary, blissful village was then massively populated with grinning, laughing, cheering, singing, huge males, mostly white, but many enormously-muscled black figures, and all topped with the most beautiful array of blonde-haired ladies in summer frocks of spectral colours with sparkling teeth set in wide genuinely happy, cheery faces.

Then we appeared.

We were all dressed in our jeans or shorts and sporting our fabulous scarlet B&I Lions touring shirts with the whole of the back of our specially-tailored shirts covered with the SA Rainbow flag.

As we walked up to the various beer palaces and smoking meat carcasses, there was a change in party atmosphere from gaiety to a general calm, maybe not silence, but an absence of noise.

But as we passed by, the derisive snorting and usual National team bantering started and we enjoyed the to and fro of insults, giving as well as we got and this lasted for the hundred metres or so to the stands. This throng of locals was not abusive at all and probably unlike their more traditional Boer-rooted chums in Pretoria, these Natal natives really were of more British stock and did have a light-hearted sense of humour. Nevertheless, on this day, and in this place, they were our foe.

Not giving the return journey a single thought, we grabbed more beers in plastic pint cups, guzzled and guzzled until it was time to take our seats for the anthems and the kick-off. Our tickets were right up in the upper East Stand and if you have ever been there you know that the steps and gangways and seats of King's Park are precipitous almost to the point of bloody vertical. A normal experienced mountaineer with crampons would take a couple of deep breaths and then nod manfully and set off on the challenge.

For us sun-soaked alcoholics it was almost impossible and there ensued a pathetic hand-to-hand struggle of support, arse-shoving and dragging our group up to our almost celestial seats. Collapsing in our seats, I turned to a fellow Lion's supporter bedecked in scarlet and said, "Sorry that was a bit pathetic."

"No way mate, we all wondered how you had done it so quickly, we took twenty minutes and one of our group is at the first aid station after a nose plant on the step edge."

I admit I am not a regular stadium attendee, but King's Park is magnificent and certainly on this day because, unlike 1993 in Wellington when there were eight of us supporters in mufti, now there were 20,000 all in British and Irish Lions scarlet shirts, all standing and cheering and hosing beers and shouting at mates in a state of some considerable ecstasy at the prospect of the show that was coming. This was all the more exciting because there was a very real possibility that Britain may be able, really able, to win a Test Series in South Africa against the most fearsome Yarrpies.

So for every Ying there must be a Yang, and that Yang was in the West Stand opposite us and it was an equal 20,000 thousand khaki clad *Van de Merver's* actually sitting quietly, sipping brandy's, holding furled flags and I am certain they were sullenly and probably rightly, contemplating that very same thought of victory but this time the horrific possibility ...victory to the bloody Poms.

*

The game was the usual massive battle despite the SA *Sports Illustrated* funeral dirge on our prospects. Joost van der Westhuizen (now very sadly deceased. RIP), Percy Montgomery and Andre Joubert each scored tries but their goal kicking was truly, woefully lacking and they landed no penalties or conversions.

On the other boot, our less than Hollywood-good-looking, wee Welsh God, Neil Jenkins, kicked five penalties and the score was locked at 15-15.

Then came the one of the greatest drop goal moments (other than Johnny's in 2003) I have witnessed live in all my puff. Jerry Guscott, never renowned as a kicker and I believe even a self-confessed non-kicker, collected the ball and as casually as a Sunday pub game, slotted THE drop goal of 1997 and the tour.

Well the noise from that exploded around Natal, and I was assured later that my girly screeching was heard all the way back at my old rugby club in Windsor. It is folk lore that the Springboks attacked and attacked and only ferocious defense and a certain heroic try-preventing tackle by Lawrence Dallaglio kept the bastards out.

Well Didier Mene blew the whistle and the celebrating started, well it did if you were wearing scarlet and you were to continue jumping up and down and hugging unknown but equally ecstatic British and Irish twats for at least another thirty minutes.

I remember looking across the park and seeing absolutely no one, no one in the other stand, apart from the team of cleaners and the odd security uniform. All, all of the 20,000 Yarpies had gone and we were still vibrating like epileptic soccer fans.

This was a magnificent result and it was only the third touring side ever to have won a series in South Africa apart from the B&I Lions in 1974 and the All Blacks in 1996. In hindsight, it was beckoning as we had won all the provincial games except against Northern Transvaal where we only lost 35-30. However improbable it seemed as we walked to the ground, it *had* happened and become a reality and we had been there live to watch it.

But then, realisation dawned - the dreaded walk back thru the Yarpie car park.

Well the local's behaviour on the walk back could not have been further from my dread expectations. Not only were they generous in beer, wine and Braai meat and stuff but they were quite glorious in their smiles, genuine congratulations and unequalled in my memory anywhere on the planet for their love of rugby played and the best team winning on the day, even if it was the bloody Poms. Remember these are proud and rightfully arrogant rugby players and supporters who have a pre-eminent pedigree and an historic grudge against their old British colonial rivals.

Maybe it was the Natal influence and we may have met a different reaction at Ellis Park, who knows, but that day was a magnificent pat on the back to rugby fraternity friendship.

None of that loser resentment was anywhere on display through that car park and we took hours and hours and hours to creep our way through the throng from one party to the next and eventually, pished as parrots and full of steak and Boerewors we staggered back to our hotel.

The next day, Sunday was tea and biscuits at some fancy hotel at Umllanga Rocks and then packing and the Long Trek homeward.

I love Durban and I love them Yarpies and I love the rugby they play in the Currie Cup and their Super XV games. I will definitely save up and go again, actually I have already done that in 2009, but I will do it *again* in 2021 now that The B&I Lions have drawn in 2017 with the All Blacks in their back yard!

THE WISH

A touring side appeared in Bangkok from Staines in the UK and it was 1994. Well I am pretty sure it was a side from Staines and pretty sure it was 1994. I also remembered that we used to play them when I was an active lad at Windsor RFC in the late '70s.

On a recent visit back to England and driving along the banks at Runnymede I saw a sign for "Staines-upon-Thames". Obviously, the local council were fed up with the ribald jokes that must niggle their everyday operations, hence the upgrade to a three-word, hyphenated title. Flashy.

Anyway, they arrived and were an Anglo-Saxon touring side with so much more allure than yet another expat-Asian visiting mob. We were actually grateful for anyone coming on tour but for some reason a '*home*' touring team was a new feel. It also had the added spice of introducing them to the joys and pitfalls of Patpong later in the evening(s).

It must have been late summer as they had come at the time of the 'wet season' and in Thailand you can have wet, very wet, or very, very wet and then full-on monsoon. We were already moving through v.v. wet.

In 1994 we had choked-up and stagnant canals and even old waterways simply severed by new developments and a disaster waiting to happen. Luckily the authorities did get onto this issue and started the clean-up of the canals.

We played Staines in the rain and the result was immaterial but I'm pretty sure Noah won. The elegiac irony here was that the match was finished through the torrential rains of Bangkok's monsoon and yet I recall the match between Staines and Windsor back in 1977 was abandoned mid-way, because of heavy English drizzle.

The British Club was, and is, a fabulous edifice to colonial architecture and to improve on the enjoyment of the facilities, our committee even allocated funds to entertain visiting teams and so combined with our own Rugby Section flushed coffers, after the match we got fed and smashed in the Churchill Bar with the tourists.

After the formal club proceedings in the Churchill Bar, it was customary, nay mandatory, to then take any such team to Patpong, which in those days really was in its heyday. All the time we had spent in the club it had still been raining cats and dogs and elephants.

Sadly, one of their former players, let's call him Jim, was in fact crippled from an earlier spinal accident in the UK and had lost the use of his legs and was wheelchair bound. But none of that handicap affected his ability to drink outrageously, swear and tell jokes and his mates loved him and carried the bugger everywhere. A very touching and bonding experience for all of us and almost a *sobering moment*, but that didn't happen, so pished as parrots, we set off for the girly bars.

The floodwaters were lapping at the entrance doors of the BC, as my wee Aussie mate Skippy and I mounted their hired Toyota mini-bus with Jim and his chair. The rest piled into their cars or, knowing the conditions, wandered off to get taxis leading Staines tourists to the Goldfinger Bar. It is only a short haul from the BC up Silom Road to *The Pong* but the whole area was flooded and as we pulled into the lower-in-level, main Silom road the water came in thru the sliding door seals and soon we were all sloshing about in the bus.

Obviously, the usual chaos of drop off and arrival at the entrance to Patpong was massively increased with the choked traffic and flooding making things forty-million times worse.

The police were there up to their waists in water, directing traffic, which actually was about as effective as herding cats. Our bus driver could only stop some 100-150 metres up the road and we had to jump out and walk back. In the normal course of events this would be fun and not an issue but Jim of course would be neck deep in water.

All of the streets along Silom Road, and many other major thoroughfares, were lined on the pavements with stalls selling food or the usual tourist stuff and they clogged the footpaths to such a degree that their huge umbrellas and the design of the street shop house over-hangs, gave very real shelter to the masses trudging and using the paths. So, whilst jostling in the crowds you were protected from the rain, but an open and easy target for pick-pockets. Bangkok multi-tasking.

I had pre-warned the driver to not get too close to the side of the road because earlier in the day I had seen many of the massively heavy, cast-iron hinged manhole covers, had been blown open and geysers of water were coming OUT of the drains!

As the sliding door slid open, the final joy of the deep water poured into the bus and I stepped out and was immersed to my waist. No way would the wheel-chair work and Jim couldn't hold his breath for fifteen minutes, so we needed a plan.

I was really quite strong, even at thirty-seven years old, and combined with the confidence ten pints of Heineken can give you, I said, "Jim come here, I'll carry you." Of course, this was addressed at Jim's mates because he couldn't just jump lovingly into my arms.

It was about now that my small Aussie mate Skippy started his usual incessant chattering, complaining, personal sledging and general friendly banter.

Skippy was actually two personalities in one small compact body: he was the greatest known human sports data repository and also a moaning Aussie. The first part was truly remarkable for, as you may recall from an earlier chapter, Skippy knew the latest scores and results from almost any sport on the planet with of course any Aussie sport first in line, especially if it had been playing the English. So we were all enraptured when asking him about the latest results from the NFL, or Canadian ice hockey, or the third division football results in Serbia, or Davis Cup scores between Liechtenstein and Sri Lanka. He knew them all and this was before anyone knew about the Internet. He was never, ever wrong.

But the other side of this *data coin* was the true nature of any happy Aussie shining through which involved extensive whining and moaning and bickering. They call us English 'whinging POMs', never has that description been so incorrectly placed by the very people guilty of that ghastly and unsporting trait.

It was like vitriolic, old fisher-women babbling away in the background but in close quarter times like this we were squeezed together and so his chirping was right in my ear. Really the Gestapo and certainly more recently MI6, should hire Skippy because just two hours of this peevish bickering and they would learn all from their captured enemy agents, simply everything, and I understood he was quite cheap on an hourly basis.

So, I steadied myself in the flowing water and Staines RFC

delivered Jim into my waiting arms. I had decided to carry him in my arms and not on my back as it wasn't that far to go. What a mistake. Do you have any idea how hard it is to carry a full-grown rugby male in your arms, in a moving flood? The movies are bullshit, when the hero carries his injured mate all the way over the Sahara, they must have a crane.

To my amazement the waist deep streaming waters were NOT flowing *down* Silom road to the river and the sea, but back *up* Silom to God knows where, and with some degree of urgency.

The covered passage way of the footpath was a no-no for my burden and me, so we trudged along the road next to the stalls in pouring rain and Jim and I hugged in mutual effort to push through the torrents, all the while both of us subjected to the constant barrage of Aussie backbiting and spite from wee Skippy.

It was incessant, irritating, irksome like an old kettle whistling away unattended on the stove. Even a hundred-year sentence of sitting beside a pneumatic concrete breaker would seem peaceful in comparison. No that's noise, real noise, this was far worse, it was a continuous, insidious leaking of verbal pestilence.

The hundred-yard-walk I had contemplated seemed now like an unachievable goal and my arms were screaming in pain and I was gradually losing my grip, physically and mentally. The usual white noise of Bangkok traffic and mayhem was almost totally overwhelmed by Skippy's chatter and I thought, **'For faak's sake Skips, faak off!!'**

And no sooner had the thought left my mind, then silence reigned.

"WTF?" I thought, stopped, and looked around. There was no noise and no Skippy, gone. Even Jim's sigh of relief was audible, sweet silence.

And then I realised, Skippy had gone down one of the open storm-drain manholes and was very probably now being sucked along one of the ghastly drains to a watery grave. OMG and that is exactly what I had been wishing for.

I had mischievously, mentally murdered my mate - a fine piece of alliteration if I say so myself.

No such luck.

Like a whale breaching, but on a smaller scale, Skippy burst up from the road with a massive intake of breath and a truly life-threatened look of shock and terror on his tiny lovable face. God only knows what is down there in the form of scratchy, spiky, steel bars, grease, road filth and infection. Luckily the natural drainage functions were on '*confused mode*' and so Skippy had not been sucked away but merely given a rat's eye view of the true Bangkok Underworld. Another tidy old cliché, if ever I've heard one.

We made it to Goldfinger's Bar and toasted the challenge well beaten, Jim sat on the bar, I appeared to have arms that were at least ten inches longer and we all got even more massively pished. Skippy overcame his immersion test and was now bickering *happily* with other mates.

And so, another well-known old adage comes to mind:

"Be careful what you wish for."

FORTUNA

"For my part, I consider that it will be found much better by all parties to leave the past to history, especially as I propose to write that history myself."
Winston Churchill 1874 – 1965

It seems a little bit like The Commentator's Curse for this collection of memories and I may be pushing my luck, but it has been suggested I list the close to very close brushes I have had with the Grim Reaper.

If you too reflect on your past, there could well be moments that could have gone a very different way and where would you be today…worm food or an airborne puff of ashes?

I am not suggesting examples like when the priest asked you: *"Do you take Helen Agatha to be your…?"* That's the colour and good-fortune or otherwise in your life.

I am talking about possible terminal events that you have just very luckily missed or experienced and survived. I am also not belittling any people who have survived ghastly events like cancer, but that too was a brush with The Reaper and you survived. Mine is a slightly more light-hearted summary, but they are real and I could definitely have croaked but for Fortuna, or Lady Luck and sometimes a cool head.

Serendipity. Here we go:

One

My parents had a great house and also built a new swimming pool in the garden. That's a concrete rectangular shell with an inner liner of HD plastic in the ground, so a real pool not a temporary summer paddling pool.

There were all the pumps and filters located discretely away in an old greenhouse and also an inline boiler for the start of the year's chilly months. Because the boiler was an expensive gas guzzler so too the bills reflected the value of the-then-expensively heated water. Backwashing and filter cleaning were a delicate balance between doing just enough waste water or too much and activating the very acute hearing of my Father, whereupon there would be screeches of *"Are you trying to bloody ruin me son, turn the bloody thing off."*

To further protect the liquid asset, Dad bought a giant sheet of what we all know now as 'bubble wrap' but slightly heavier duty and it covered the whole 5m x 10m surface. (later to be cut in half for easier handling.)

I was up early one morning, and spring had arrived warm and sunny and so it was almost time to remove the cover completely for the summer.

I was about nineteen years old, fit, strong, a great swimmer but a little dozy and stupid. Not much has changed to this day, except the fitness may have dropped off a bit.

I stood alone in the garden, on the side of the pool in the early morning mist, a feature of a heated pool with not a breath of wind. I contemplated what I had wanted to do for ages and did it.

I stood square to the side of the pool in the deep-end and with arms extended I simply fell flat on my face on the nice, soft, crimpily, bubble duvet. Luckily, I had taken a big, deep breath and I could generally hold my breath for about a week so I was stupidly over-confident.

Well this was no Slumberland mattress with a Swedish feather, cotton cover, this was an insidious, enveloping, constricting straight jacket of terror. No sooner had I passed through the surface level of the water than the plastic wrapped around me like a giant two-dimensional python. I was immediately scared witless.

Fortuna (Roman Goddess of good luck, for the non-Classical reader) was also *'fortuna-tely'* up early that morning and quickly nudged Minerva (Goddess of wisdom) to get my brain functioning properly.

I immediately realised that I MUST NOT resist and start fighting the plastic sheet but I must, against all instincts, lie still, float back to the surface, aided by the natural buoyancy of the bubble-wrap. Then gulp air if balance permitted, and then shimmy on my belly using tiny hand swiping motions with the water now a film on the plastic surface to the FAR side of the pool.

That was the longest eight feet of my life.

There is no doubt in my tiny brain THAT event could have most definitely gone the other way and there would have been the local newspaper headlines "Weird fetishist swimmer dies mysteriously in garden pool". Phew.

Two

I had started work in construction and by the age of twenty-six morphed from contracting into project management and design and build and now had to visit our architects in London, from the office building under construction in Guildford on the A3 in Surrey.

Obviously, having been to London on the train many times, I was familiar with the Tube and it was only a short haul from Waterloo to Embankment or some such posh place that architects liked to have on their letterhead.

I was a little weighed-down with a roll of drawings and a heavy, extra-wide, document briefcase. Glancing at the Underground map to ensure I didn't by mistake end up in Dusseldorf, I skipped down the escalator (young knees in those days) which took our tunnel route under the Thames.

I turned for the 'northwards' platform along with what seemed like 40,000 other passengers all going to my architect's office, bustled my way to the front of the platform in the centre of the station, arranged my toes on the yellow line, put down my heavy bag and waited for the train.

The 4" bright yellow line was a new-ish thing that helped maybe aged or partially-sighted folk clearly see the edge. It also gave a reminder to the daft twats like me that there was a hazardous space beyond this line.

You all know the feeling of the coming train down the alimentary canal of underground transport, the slight vibration, the wheeze of air through a thousand old construction holes and then the comforting buffet of warm wind ahead of the train as it burst forth into the station's larger bowel.

I bent down to pick-up my briefcase, not with the practiced and known weight-lifting bending of the knees, maybe because I still had the roll of drawings in my right hand, but with a full body hinge at the hips.

Unbeknownst to me this put my head clearly over the platform edge, and as I straightened up just enough, so the front leading edge of the red painted tube train actually touched and brushed-past my nose and ruffled my merry fringe. I do not have a big nose. The train was not yet hissing to a stop and the massive pile driving shape was still travelling very fast.

There is no doubt in my mind that that headache would not have been treated with a few paracetamol. I suggest a spade and six feet of dirt would have done it.

Three

Again, and almost unbelievably, but here I claim mitigating circumstances of utter frustration dealing with the weasely and time-wasting nature of architects, I may have been slightly distracted, I did exactly the same thing on the return journey. Today, I travel by taxi.

Four

Earlier than the Tube incidents, on a construction site at Maiden Lane, north of King's Cross station, I was the new most junior, spit-upon engineer on site and whilst the other construction managers had to build the fabulous, modern apartment buildings in the complex, I had their drainage pit.

The area allocated to me was the development's future Sports Centre and as space was at a premium on the site, the experienced wily, old coyotes had dug a huge pit where my building was to go and then funneled all of the large site drainage there as a massive settlement pond of sludge before it was then syphoned off to the formal drains of the London Borough of Camden.

We managed to pump out the cesspit that was to be my workplace for the next eighteen months; well my keen and loyal Indian work gang had done that, and as with all things Indian, I have no idea how they did it or where it went.

The other thing my 'fellow manager mates' had done, was allocated to me a carpenter-chippy for the formwork needed for my building structure. He had a shaved head, tattoos, scars where he must have been mauled by a tiger and he was also the Leading Shop Steward for the Worker's Union.

This labour union was a particularly virulent and fanatically, idle bunch and could and did regularly freeze the site for almost no-known reason, drawing construction to a stop and the project-end-date lurched further into the time allocated for the end of the Universe.

Unbelievably 'Bev-the-Knife' and I, a public-school toff, being opposite ends of the social scale met on site, sized each other up, worked hard for a morning and then by end of day, shook hands and became best of mates.

The Indian eight-man crew that had been allocated to me were actually Sikhs and huge men with gruff, bearded faces made all the taller by their turbans. 'Bless-him-Bev' had advised me that tomorrow was such-and-such a Punjab religious festival and I should buy them some sweets, apparently a very friendly and timely spiritual gift.

Paddington station had some lemon bon-bons in a paper packet, so the next morning I bought about four bags and presented these politely to Head Man Mr. Singh (Singh actually means Lion in Punjabi and that's why most Sikh's choose that as a middle name, being the martial race that they are.).

The giant's eyes opened with delight, not at the rather cheap and bitter sweets on offer but that some Britisher had even known to offer such a present. Bev, take a pat on the back mate.

The team were thereafter my most loyal and trusting squad, invisibly escorting me to the train station and standing outside the 'Muscular Arms Pub' when we went in for a pint after work, just in case of any trouble. My personal minders.

Anyway, one day, as my squash-court base slab preparations awaited the liquid concrete placement by the overhead crane, I thought I would climb to the top of the adjacent new block of apartments and watch from the roof.

The outside of the building had received its last coats of paint and snagging touch-ups and the scaffolding was being taken down.

I reached the roof at the far end from my future building and carefully negotiated the piles of detritus and building equipment still strewn about the flat-roof and nearing the small, one-foot high parapet wall, I tripped on a bit of tying-wire and dived off the roof some eight stories up.

'Pike-us Maximus', the ancient Roman God of Diving, saved me by an involuntary throwing-out-of-the-arms and somehow my left arm caught and elbow-wrapped around the only remaining vertical scaffold pole on that entire elevation of the building. In a squealing pirouette of airborne fat bloke, I spun in the air and then hugged the pole until I slid, ignominiously down to the level of boards below me.

I might have had a small to medium-sized damp patch on the front of my trousers by the time I reached terra firma but I did take the time to glance sky-wards to thank the Gods, and that sacred scaffold pole.

Five

In the mid 1970's I had been surfing in a very British sense on small European waves and nothing Hawaiian and I thought I was capable enough to wobble my way back into the beach. Over the years I even learnt to run 'along' the wave not just grip board, raise arse in the air and pray the wave would help me directly back to the beach where the pretty girls were all waiting for us 'Jocks'.

In 1977 I travelled around USA with my two mates Barney and Paul, who didn't surf, and while they smoked stuff in the car park, I had a great time surfing on Huntington Beach in LA doing my thing until someone said, 'Let's go to Malibu'.

I leapt at the chance to visit such a mystical place and off we sped along the grandly-named Pacific Coast Highway in someone's pick-up with boards thrown in the back and cooler boxes of beers, but with handy small paper bags in case of drinking in public and alerting the cops.

I really cannot recall the beach name but I remember there being a headland or point that today is noted as Point Dume (well there's a pointer eh: Doom.) and sandy areas for my mates to lie down, whilst I followed a pod of Waterworld-men, tanned-fish-people on their boards out to sea.

As usual you have to paddle out through the incoming waves, the scale of these, by English standards, were life threatening tsunami walls of water or broken seething masses of foaming death.

You paddled furiously and then just before the unbroken wave or the avalanche of crashing broken water, you leant forward and depressed the nose of your board and miraculously you and the board simply dipped effortlessly under the wave and popped out the other side to then paddle again and repeat five thousand times whenever you wanted to enjoy a thirty-second ride back in. Magic fun and you developed Herculean shoulders and dark skin, real quick.

Every board has three key components:

The Board itself. Today there are numerous styles, lengths and trick type shapes but in those days it was a short pointy board or a Malibu board, which was about two kilometres long.

Then there was *the Skeg* which is the small rigidly-fixed plastic fin under the rear of the board. You could have one, two or three skegs.

Lastly there was *the Lanyard*, that was fixed to an embedded eyelet at the rear skeg end and the two-metre flexible elasticated cord had a Velcro strap around your ankle. If you fell off your board you simply grabbed the cord from your foot and got back on board. There were many lads who didn't invest in this simple strap and if they tipped off then they had to recover their boards from the beach miles away.

I was a very relaxed ocean swimmer and completely at ease with these benign seas and seaweed covered rocks and salt water in my eyes and I followed the experienced Californian lads out past the breakers and then one sits waiting for the next 'set of waves'. Curiously Neptune invariably sends them in threes, three waves together varying in size but generally by the third one, it had learnt how the beach shelved and grew to enormous proportions.

The pro's chose their wave and expertly whizzed off with only light paddling to gain speed and then hop up on their boards and away. One turned to me and said, "Hey Guy, you are new here, remember that when riding the wave there ain't much water over the rocks below, so don't fall off eh....byyyyyeeeee."

'WTF?!' thought I and dipped my head under the water and had a blurry look about. What was the problem? There were mossy type seaweeds covering boulders everywhere below but some twelve feet below the surface.

Anyway, my turn came and I selected my wave and my sort of area of conquest where I expected to surf and paddled away and yes, caught my ever-increasing mound of wave as we headed for the beach.

I do no pretend to understand the molecular, hydraulic, oceanic, rhythmic cycle of wave creation as it nears the shallows and starts to rise up out of the water to form that majestic, vertical arc of water and then tips forward before a mighty display of power. Providing for that singular moment the subject for those beautiful breaking wave profiles so well captured by Japanese master artists.

But what I do now appreciate, is that to form that mighty, swelling, pregnant mountain and then the arc, the volume of water has not come from behind the growing wave but this new wave has sucked in the water from in front using the dying carcass of the last wave and this meant that all the sea in front of me had now literally disappeared and I was on a wave and beneath me now were all the exposed, deadly-looking, barnacle clad, sea-weedy boulders covered with as much water as a healthy spit. Should one fall off here and the wave break, well there would be more than one breakage for sure.

Overcoming the initial rigid shock of a violent and painful falling death, I rode the wave well, skipping along at the base of the clean blue curve and then amazingly stayed vertical through the breaking surf and made it to shore. Falling off in the final metres near the sand, I undid my lanyard and strode manfully up the beach, plonked myself beside my mates and grabbed a beer. No more bloody surfing of that terrifying boulder strewn runway everyone raved about in Malibu.

*

The next summer 1978 I was back in Bude on the north Cornish coast at our family summer house and had been out alone as my mates didn't do this stuff either. I had started in the surf in the northern-most cove of Crooklet's Beach, a nasty, tight rocky cove but great waves as they were bunched in by the projecting rock formations. When I was tired and the tide turned and was going out, I paddled back towards our house, passed Middle Beach and then caught my last few waves on the main Summerlease Beach which was a huge sweeping, open shallow beach with the river Neet or Strat (The only river I know with two names) and the man-made canal both linking and running out to sea on the left side of the beach near our home.

This river estuary area was a dangerous spot for swimmers and apparently two adults had been drowned by the rip or severe under-current caused by the river eddies and the returning waves from the main beach. The two unfortunate paddler/swimmers had apparently actually been dragged under and their bodies only resurfaced some many hundreds of yards out to sea. We have a very good, active and observant Life Guard system during the tourist seasons and they are forever vigilant but one head suddenly disappearing was very hard to spot. The Guards were mostly Aussies, but lots of local lads were also being trained.

I stayed in the deeper water after my last ride and was crossing the end of the river-cum-sea rip zone as it passed the stone mole protecting Bude Haven from the Atlantic, so probably upon reflection, the worst possible spot to be, as a supposedly proficient sea user.

I was relaxed and happy floating vertically in the water but thoroughly exhausted with my arms lazily wrapped over my board and legs dangling below. Then suddenly and without any faint warning, the swirling waters below grabbed, yes literally grabbed, my legs and pulled me forcefully off the board and down into the depths. I had barely time to gulp air and was now rushing headlong in sandy murky water bouncing along the seabed with no possible way of breaking out by swimming. I really, really couldn't fight this swirling water and I remind you, I was very proud of my swimming power and skills. Well they didn't help here and I was a gonner.

Now California came into perspective, as I thought what a pathetic way to die after all the exotic truly dangerous places I had swum and surfed especially that boulder strewn faaking cove in Malibu, but no it was to be here in a calm, balmy English coastal resort.

Then old Minerva (Goddess of Brainy Stuff remember) tweaked my synapses and I recalled my lanyard. I bent down as I was still being dragged along the bottom, reached the strap around my ankle and then with all my remaining strength, hand over hand, crawled back up my rope to the mightily buoyant surfboard skimming along the surface. It probably only lasted seconds but it did truly seem like a lifetime (well technically it was to have been the end of that one) and that simple tie cord saved my life for sure.

So, when you hire a board remember the two key extra parts: Skeg and LANYARD.

Six

I was driving northwards in my company car along the A3 road in Surrey heading for a business meeting in Cobham. The-then very successful and well-known British car manufacturer Vauxhall had designed and now sold the Astra. It was a great five-door, light but well powered unit (no references here to *Top Gear's* analysis, just my own inferior assessment) and I liked it very much. There was only one issue and that was the colour, a dark, rich, chocolate brown.

I'm pretty sure this was one of the last test-dummy cars used in a crash simulation warehouse, but tests completed, this car remained unused and someone had kindly thought, send this one to the dealer and some twat will buy it. It's the only one I had even seen on the roads then, or since. I couldn't complain, it was a Company car and so free.

Anyway, I was a little late for my meeting but nothing drastic and I was driving in the middle of the three-lane road, sort of day-dreaming as you do, but of course still completely in control and aware of my surroundings.

I was alongside a large, fully-laden mega-truck with those green canvas sides and securing straps as we got to the first of the roadside signs with three dashes indicating 300m to the turn-off, when I realised this was my exit. I accelerated and quickly overtook the truck and crossed into his lane and then off for the exit at maybe dash-marker one or just after it. Cheeky, but nothing dangerous or even faintly hazardous I thought.

The turn-off was in a shallow valley and so the exit was a down ramp and there was a roundabout at the bottom, with a bridge structure on one's right and you *had* to stop at the line on the brink of the roundabout.

I slowed and stopped as required and then checked to the right, but before I could even do that, my eyes were drawn to my rear-view mirror. I hadn't even given my last manoeuvre any second thought as it had been a nothing move, in my opinion.

Anyway, my rear-view mirror was now filled with the massive speeding radiator of the offended truck and it was, in my opinion (again, just my opinion) speeding up not slowing down and intended to enter the roundabout without stopping and collecting my Astra as a squashed-fly trophy on the front.

I quickly took my foot off the brake and braced myself in my seat with my head on the head restraint and there was an almighty smash and I was propelled forwards in a screaming welter of distressed steel, shattering glass and screeching tyres, over the curved road and then driven over the high concrete curb on the inner roundabout line and a further twenty yards into the grassy embankment of the roundabout itself.

As I sat there in my steaming wreck, the obviously piqued truck driver reversed and sped off, I can only presume to Calais or some equally exotic, almost untouchable jurisdiction.

I crept out of my car shaking like a Victorian virgin on her wedding night and a small crowd had kindly stopped to ogle and help of course. There were impressive deep tyre gouge marks in the lush green grass, sparkly, toughened-glass shards everywhere and I glanced back at my car to see what damage had been done.

There must have been a Mercedes design engineer in the now swelling crowd, because there was my Astra completely redesigned as the Smart Car you know today.

There was no rear to my car, in fact there were no back seats, there was just a giant crumpled bar of Cadbury's chocolate stuffed up behind my driver's seat.

I was probably in shock as I actually thought this was quite funny until realisation dawned that my brand new bloody golf clubs were in the boot. The rear door was of course concave and mangled and now slightly ajar. I gripped the lip of the hatchback door and gingerly raised it squeaking against the deformed hinges.

I was nervous of discovering some poor stowaway in with my clubs, but there was only my golf bag and it was lying in the crumpled smashed-to-bits-boot of my destroyed chariot, completely unscathed.

As it turned out, maybe not a terminal event but it could have been if there had been another truck coming around the roundabout, so I guess a bit of a limp tale but an early indication of the 'road rage' phenomenon about to hit the UK.

Seven

We return to the ocean and surfing. This time on the East African coast of Kenya at the most picturesque, hidden-away gem of Malindi. This was north of the main town of Mombasa on the coast and you got there by an aged tarmac road snaking through acacia trees and low scrub until you reached the ferry at Kalifi. This was a steep-sided river gully set about with dense, dappled greenery in an otherwise parched landscape of sepia growth.

Here again was a massively romantic exercise of old world charm and bloody hard work. There was a floating platform about thirty metres long and fifteen wide, with steel handrails down both sides and only slightly pitched entry and exit ramps at front and back. The ferry power unit was a large 3" hemp rope at waist height passed through steel eyelets down the upstream side of the craft and anchored at either end on each bank.

You paid a few Kenya shillings for the joy of hauling yourself and any other trucks or cars or cattle that needed to cross, by all the drivers and passengers enjoying a healthy early morning work-out. The river was fast flowing and definitely the most energetic thing I had seen in the past day or so.

It was quite a struggle but once everyone was in place, Mr. Entembe, the pilot, deck crew manager, stowage operative and captain all-in-one, started up a swaying rhythmic body movement with an accompanying deep bass chant. We were all mesmerized into a matching and beguiling team of bare foot Olympic tug-of-war experts in moments.

Sadly, it's probably gone today and replaced with a much more practical and functional concrete bridge, what a loss to Africa and her visitors I say.

Malindi was a sleepy small town of un-rendered and unpainted two-storey buildings with a forlorn and empty dusty market square as we passed through to get to the small beach and the Driftwood Club.

The coast road out of Malindi to the club was at the very back of the sun-bleached white sandy beach and lived under a long, long line of lush trees on both sides of the road and under this natural parasol, the locals set up the usual roadside stalls selling all of their indigenous handicrafts and fabrics. None of the modern day ghastly tat copied and replicated in plastic, then everything was made from local native materials except, of course, the bright, shiny copper bracelets.

These entwined and braided copper wrist loops, both closed and open-ended with comfort bulbs at the open ends, were fashioned from the same wire. This wire was courtesy of the GPO or Telephone Organisation of Kenya and went a long way to explaining the regular and mysterious loss of communications between Nairobi and Mombasa each and almost every month. Normally about three hundred metres of 'lost communication'.

I was only ever in Kenya because I had met the most beautiful girl in the world when I was about fourteen at our tennis club in the UK: Sara de Glanville. She is the eldest of three strikingly-beautiful daughters of Hugh de Glanville (and ex-wife Audrey) who at that time was an active Flying Doctor based in Nairobi. Sara was a tall, athletic, sporty blonde girl, had Hollywood looks and a fabulously honed and well-developed body. We were known by all our mates as 'Beauty and the Beast', a bit harsh on her I thought. We were to *go out* together for some eight or nine years and I would visit Kenya at every opportunity.

On arrival we would always stop at these stalls and buy our holiday needs for the beach, day wear and evening dress. These were the fabulously multicolored, woven cotton sarongs that in Africa were called *Kikoys* for the boys and a lighter, almost sheer material making the *Kangas* for the girls.

They came in long rolls of woven material where at the end of each say six-foot strip of finished cross-woven material, there would be a six-inch strip of only the longitudinal threads and this is where the units would be cut into individual 'sarongs'. Then, as non-smoking hippies, we would sit cross-legged in the shade of a tree and gather small bunches of the cut threads to plait and knot them to close off the 'open ends '- a knotted fringe at each end.

Unlike a Burmese or other SE Asian sarong, these were not hoops of material you stepped into, but worn like a towel wrapped around the man's hips and then scrunched up and bunched as a fold-over buckle. The girls generally looped theirs over their chests or hung them as halter-necks. And that's all from the Guru of Tribal Fashion but this is about all we ever wore but for T shirts or trunks for weeks and weeks.

The Driftwood Club was a simple, brick-based shell of an office and restaurant and bar area with the whole of the upper structure made from driftwood. Sections of corrugated metal sheeting and old tarpaulins were hidden in the tree bough rafters and there were always quaint, rustic leaks everywhere when it rained.

On the odd occasion there would be an impromptu sing-song around a carefully managed fire-pit on the beach, sitting cross-legged and then some annoyingly good-looking bloke would start strumming on his Spanish guitar and sing ballads and other stuff. The girls would swoon and coo and he would be their centre of the universe. Bloody annoying for old uglies like me who absolutely cannot sing and have no ear for music at all and who can only play one musical instrument: the radio.

Anyway, at one of these accursed strumming meets, there was a bloke with a surfboard jammed in the sand. Let's call him Roy and he was 6'2", bronzed and healthy and a good boke who drank cold White Cap beer at the same rate I did. We struck up and became mates. I asked where he was surfing because at our beach the tide couldn't even be bothered to come in-and-out, let alone force a ripple, even on a windy day.

He noted there was a small beach just north of Malindi with a river estuary at one end and a pronounced headland and these features, along with some sea currents, produced reasonable waves. There was no one there and no shacks or human facilities, so we must take our own water and some food.

The girls didn't want to come and so Roy and I declared the East African Surfing Championships open and off we set the next day giving directions about where we would be, in case anyone missed us, which I'm sure they didn't.

The beach was a deep crescent of silver sand running all the way back to some high ground, but only the very edge of the beach at the shoreline was exposed with the rest all covered in wind-blown scrub and bushes and the odd coconut tree. An idyllic setting is a limp description for our monumental challenge of sporting history but it would do.

Roy and I dumped our bags, kikoys and water at the top of the beach, ignored such things as suntan cream and took to the water like dolphins. There were sets of waves as I described earlier and it all looked very promising.

Roy had a massive Malibu board and we both had to carry it to the sea. I had a very short undersized board I had borrowed that day and it only showed a two-inch tip above the water as I sat astride it. Roy was an accomplished surfer to say the least and I did try out his board but it was like lying on the flight deck of USS *Midway*, as water came over the bow and took about five minutes before splashing me in the face. No, Malibu boards were not for me.

We surfed and surfed and burnt and burnt as we sat in the water. The sets of waves were dying away and the sun was heading for a rest in another couple of hours. We were prune fingered and almost cold but *just one more* was our mantra.

We were sitting looking at the shore and chatting about something when I just had that feeling we were being watched and not from the beach. In a spooky sort of way, I turned to look behind me. The horizon had disappeared completely. Actually, I was wrong, it hadn't disappeared, it just wasn't where it was the last time I looked. Now it was about thirty feet above our heads and coming on very quickly. It was a monster rogue wave of truly frightening proportions and nowhere for us to go.

There was no chance of even thinking of riding the ghastly thing.

Roy squealed and I'm sure I would have done the same, but I think I was venting from the other end at the time.

Unlike my earlier advice to you about lanyards on your boards, we didn't have them and thank heavens for that. I shouted at Roy that we needed to ditch the boards and then swim to the very bottom of the bay which wasn't too deep, maybe twenty feet and lie as flat on our chests as possible and stay there until the wave had passed. This was vital as even in those seconds we knew the wave would crest and break right on us. If we were caught in that massive washing-machine it would spin us for a long, long time and almost certainly knock the wind out of us before we reached the beach.

We swam urgently down to the sand and flippering our hands and expelling vital air so we didn't start floating, the water exploded around us and everything was white and gritty and thunderously noisy.

The booming rolled away and we surfaced, checked there wasn't another beast behind and then spluttering we had a nervous laugh and swam to shore. Whatever was on the shore line had gone. It had been swept and hoovered clear of all footprints, leaves, small shrubs, grubs and any windblown stuff. The larger scrub and coconut trees had been thoroughly cleaned and sprung back to shape. Our towels and bags were about seventy yards inland. A frighteningly powerful event.

Again you may say, a bit limp as a story of potential death but if we hadn't swum to the seabed, we would still be in the Heavenly rinse cycle to this day.

That trip also gave me the distinct benefit of being able to brag forever and a day after that I had come second in the East African Surfing Championships. No need to mention there was a limited entry list.

*****

Old Boys reunion Nov 2018…those in the East and still alive.
The Back Row: Bevan Morrison, Guy Hollis, Stuart Dugard,
Roddy Kerr, Gordon Ellard, Marco Belonge, Khun Prote,
Simon Davies, Marvyn Lewis, Stitch Hutton, Me, Bruce Hill,
Ben, Julian Olds, Jack Dunford (BC Chairman).
Front Row: Jimmy Ratchatcher Howard, Andy McDowell,
Colin Hastings, Vinno.

A FLOGGING

"In this world there are only two tragedies; one is not getting what one wants, the other is getting it." Oscar Wilde 1854 – 1900

'Bugs' is a tall, upright, blond-to-mousey-haired Aussie mate, say forty-two years young, who had, in an earlier existence, been a highly respected senior international executive. Anyway, we didn't know that high-flying executive bloke, we knew the Bugs-the-Bar-Owner and raconteur extraordinaire.

Bugs had taken his winnings, sorry, redundancy package, or golden handshake, and invested in a bar, refurbished it with an efficient drinks area, clever seating with tables or higher stand-up elbow shelving, huge sports TV's, an educated and well-trained staff and called it *Blu Bar-b-Que*.

He invested also in a very pretty, to extremely pretty, Thai wife. We shall call her Khun Nid, for the sake of argument, and to allow me adequate time to get to the airport should she ever get her hands on a copy of this dross, put two and seven together and recollect me as the author.

There are three main *areas of bars* that expatriate and visiting tourist or Asian-based businessmen (and equally hard-working lady folk) frequent in Bangkok.

These being, in the first instance, the multifarious bars along the two streets of Patpong on Silom Road, with the seething pathways between the stalls of cheap watches, silk jim-jams and knock-off handbags. These are generally the downstairs beer-swilling, pole-dancing emporiums with real girls and also cute blokes with tits, to tickle your fancy.

(You must immediately now don your Eye-phone or Singsung earplugs and play "One Night in Bangkok" to get the vibrations and the sensations of what I am haltingly trying to write about.)

The upstairs bars have extreme sex shows or personal services (I am reliably informed) and generally also have private armies of thugs who present you with a bill for four beers after, say twenty-five minutes, that easily equals the Brexit exit fee. Pay or be prepared to receive a thorough bashing and a poke in the goolies for good measure. Don't go up there, even as a Third Dan.

Now take that scenario and downgrade it by a level of some two million sleaze points and you have Nana Plaza on Sukhumvit Road. This piss-pit of bars has today leaked out of the Plaza itself and oozed new bars along the street with seating and handrails facing the road and there is a brigade of sad, pished-up old blokes in almost constant residence at all hours of the day and night. Probably my retirement home too.

The Nana Plaza bars themselves are on four or five levels and contained, as implied by the name, within a square of say thirty by forty metres and offer the almost full range of tastes from simple semi-clad girly pole dancing, to naked girls diving for coins in a warm, giant fish tank (I built that one) to the 100% katoey bars nearer the back or on level 3 (I am reliably informed).

Then there is the third area and real jewel in the crown: Soi Cowboy. Again on Sukhumvit Road, but a bit further east of Nana, this single street of four-hundred megawatt neon signage is a delightful collection of far less offensive bar content (this statement would clearly not be accepted by most bloke's wives, but there we go.). These bars were all served by the equally far more calm, smiling and less professional ladies from the north-eastern farming communities of Isaan, and not the historically Chiang Mai reservoir of hard-hearted tarts employed in the two earlier zones.

So those are the three main shady bar districts in the City of Angels and then there is the street of 'after work' hostess bars along Sukhumvit Soi 33. These are simple beer and G&T hostess lounges that are almost all named after eminent painters; Renoir, Van Gough, Rembrandt, Degas, Gauguin, Monet and then Christie's (auction house) and a semi-related Napoleon's at the far end.

A Flogging

This side-street (or soi in Thailand) is where we all went for early networking after work beers and possibly even earlier drowning of sorrows if we hadn't won *that* tender.

*

Now having clarified the drinking hole geography of the town, we return to Blu Bar-b-Que. As briefly mentioned above, this was a great drinking spot and, as titled, it did have a large open-grilled BBQ and served the most fabulously juicy beef burgers with the unique-to-Thailand Aussie idea of a large slice of beetroot on the pattie.

After a successful year and a half of operation Bugs moved *up* in the world of Thai bar owning and with his clever and witty mind opened *Lookie Lookie* in the same side street, off the main side street of 33.

The interior of Lookie was entirely painted out in matt black with shaded, hanging 2.5 watt lighting, these lights being slightly dimmer than a firefly's arse in a deep dank cave in Borneo. There was a well-stocked bar on the left as you came in, a pool table in the rear of the shophouse and all about were high tables with stools. The entire space also populated with stunningly pretty and vivacious Isaan girls wearing only men's long-sleeved business shirts, minimal make-up and no perfume. Not quite in the vein of a family BBQ establishment.

There were sports TV's and an area outside for the filthy smokers in compliance with some new or about to be new, public space clean air ordinance. A house rule which was vehemently ignored by our band of inhalers, much to the chagrin of the government. Generally, one can say that the TV's were effectively redundant, as football was a sad and distant viewing pleasure compared to the Armani shirts and whatever wriggled therein.

Whilst in this bar, I would also reflect and recall a tragic moment when I must have lost control. I had been in Lookie Lookie Bar with all my chums and they and Bugs and all of the very comely, bar-employed, erstwhile maidens, had kindly celebrated my 45th Birthday with gargantuan and fierce pool games, all mounted on the back of two billion beers and maybe the odd spliff.

I am a massive hater of gratuitous graffiti. Some well-conceived and clearly artistic 'paintings' on old derelict stretches of ancient gable-end walls to houses in Lisbon or Hamburg or wherever, are actually welcome. But the dark and messy New York underground or bridge abutment scrawl with aerosols is not my bag and I loathe the dregs that undertake such defacing of public and private spaces.

A week or so after my party, I popped into the LL bar after work and, to clear some bladder space for the planned intake, I quickly visited the immaculately clean and hygienically hoovered toilets at the rear. When, as I re-entered the bar pushing open the clean and gloss painted bog door, I couldn't miss the well-written but scrawled message in large black indelible marker pen at eye level.

"45th Birthday celebrations were bloody marvellous, thanks a lot Bugs. Cheers Jon P. x"

Well I was mortified. I had no memory of such a disgusting mess and immediately apologized to Bugs who laughed and said it was fine and a great memory of a great night. In fact, for years after, chums would meet me in the street or another bar and remark on having just been in LL and going for a pee and been reminded of the scribble and had had a quiet giggle themselves. In the nature of these things, that foul etching is probably there in perpetuity.

*

Anyway, I must now recall a third-hand story, as I was not actually present on this occasion, but it certainly merits inclusion in a tome of this nature.

Apparently, (there's the legal get out word, I hope), Bugs had sidled up to my best mates (now also I had better use their nicknames to protect those purported characters), 'Tits & Arse' aka T&A (smoker) and 'Tart' (part-time cadger of mate's free fags) and in the miasma of smoke and the gloom of the lamp, he speculated, "Hi Guys, I understand that Da Vinci's Bar has changed hands and it is now Demonia. Shall we, uumm, pop in and see what it's like?"

Now T&A may only be a quantity surveyor by name, but he has certainly received some sort of training by Mossad or MI5 because, nuffin' and I do mean not nuffin' goes on in 33 without his notice. So, after the girl opposite cleaned herself of his spray of Tiger beer, T&A replied, "Wot the bloody S&M joint opposite Napoleon?...You saucy old dog Bugs, I didn't know you were into all that."

"Wooowaha, really, is it?...wow...I didn't know that...so maybe not then...eh... I guess not then...maybe?" said the innocent Gold Coast lad.

Without further debate, they all drank up and headed for Demonia for a brief recce.

At about 8.30pm exactly they barged open the quasi-Mediaeval, bolt-headed panel door of Demonia and entered a small vestibule, painted matt black, with some comfortable seats near a small round table. The walls were adorned with old fake shields, crossed swords, spiked maces, locally-made highly-imaginative chastity belts, whips, more ingenious tongs and stuff they had never even imagined.

On the right was a dark high desk with a male dressed in a dark suit. There was an open archway to a room next door with a bar and at that bar stood a high-heeled *nurse* in an ultra-short, frilly, lacey shirt with, let's essentially go with...her tits out. Our Tart is no longer the athlete he once was, but faster than Usain Bolt, he hurdled the two steps up to the bar and with none of the long-term love and attention of Bernardo's Home, adopted the lass and ordered himself a cold beer and hand on her warm bum.

T&A and Bugs resembled the Old Bull on the hill.

In the height of Spring with flowers blooming, bees buzzing and the sun beaming down, a young, impetuous, frisky bull coincidentally called Tart, cantered up to the olde Bull on the hill and urgently nodding his head in the direction of the valley below, where there roamed hundreds of cows in heat he said.

"Hey, hey why don't we dash down there Pops and shag one of them?" Tart said.

"Humpff" said T&A , "Why don't we amble down there and shag 'em all!"

So, the man from the high desk got off his seat and disappeared, only to reappear around the side of the desk as a Mini-me. The vertically challenged manager then produced a couple of thick menus from behind his tiny frame and passing them to the now seated rangy, old Bulls and asked, "A drink gentlemen?"

"Two Heinekens please," said Bugs.

Tyrion Lannister's double retired to the other room saying, "Please read the various options and make a choice on your preferred punishment and we can get started."

I cannot provide you with the whole menu so all I can do is advise that they chose for themselves and the selfish Tart next door a 'thirty-minute wall hanging with a whip to paddle massage' treatment at Baht 1,500 each. Apparently, this was definitely one of the tamer options on offer.

So, it was some surprise to T&A and Tart, but surprisingly not to Bugs, that his ex-mamasan from Lookie Lookie then appeared around the corner, took the olde bulls by the hand and led them into the backroom, with our Tart reluctantly being dragged there by another tart.

There were various darkened doorways and 'treatment rooms' down a corridor made to look like a dungeon passageway and the lads, opting to share a room, were ushered into a dimly-lit cell and asked to sit. This room was painted and made out in faux, rough stone walling and there was a small sofa and a chair on the door side and a slightly raised dias on the opposite wall, with shiny hand and ankle cuffs bolted to the wall in the flayed-man alphabetic 'X' of House Boulton.

They sipped their drinks and squabbled over who would be first. A pointy stick was produced and spun and condemned our Tart to the first thrashing. Now here the lithe athlete Tart, of sprint-to-partially-naked-nurse-fame, adopted the shape of a semi-crippled, arthritic old geezer and bemoaned the fact that he had a bad back and please go easily on him.

Tart was carefully and loving stripped naked and front first chained up to the wall. A new maid appeared in dark provocative lingerie, with a covered tray of what looked like very utilitarian garden implements and placed them on the small table against the remaining wall.

I will not bore you with the gradual *upgrading* of the torture implements but our Tart was robustly and with some force subjected to a flogging with a bendy, floppy piece of hot-water-pipe lagging, then a feather duster, then a slippery short whip with stingy end parts, then a reasonably firm stick, then a thicker brand and finally with a sort of butter churn paddle with protruding steel studs. The sissy was almost weeping by the end and the old Bulls were visible perspiring in the close atmosphere of the cell.

T&A was up next, and in the way of all track-n-field sportsmen, the red-arsed Tart was able to recover enough strength to gasp out and utter, "Thrash that cunt to death, it's his fucking fault I'm here in the first place…the cunt!" and after that tirade our Tart donned his Y fronts and sat down very, very slowly on the cushioned sofa.

T&A is absolutely not a coward and will take his punishment like a man, if there is no last-minute Cpt. Jack Sparrow handy exit. But now he was visibly sweating and had a pale, waxen look to his huge face.

It was at this moment, that Bugs lent forward and whispered conspiratorially to the stripping T&A, "Actually Blu, we're here cos it's my birthday and I thought this could be fun, the bill's on me…do yer's think it really hurts or is that Tart just a woofta?"

The condemned man looked back with a fixed stare and spat.

"Well birthday Twat, let's see shall we!" and advanced to be manacled to the wall.

Well after a further twenty-five minute period of slightly more vigorous whipping and paddling, even the executioner was damp with effort and T&A had a rigid and unhappy air. His bum was like a ripe, red Massachusetts apple, well two of them, and at the final whistle he remained silent, was unchained and with whatever dignity was left he tip-toed back to his pants and again slowly lowered himself to sit beside our Tart.

As Bugs now stepped forward, the beaten slaves remained quiet until he was firmly and securely restrained. Then after a brief mumble together, they both, in unison advised the warm whip lady, **"It's that twat's bloody birthday, so we will give you a large extra tip to thrash the twat to within an inch of his bloody shite Australian life!"**

And assuming she didn't fully understand the sentiment expressed, T&A brandished two baht 1,000 notes and gave them to her now wide and appreciative eyes, saying in his kindergarten Thai, "Awhaw!..de'aw nee, hi jip maark maark tee toot phewan…jip naar…jip maark maark NA!"

Armed with the such a virulent and instructive demand, Khun Wack set about Bugs's butt like a girl possessed. For T&A and our Tart the twenty or so minutes passed far too quickly and were quite stunned when in a gasp of exertion, she stopped and viewed the almost bleeding Australian arse. His actual bum I mean, not the whole of Bugs.

And with the nod of a professional job well done, she bent dripping on the floor and then raised herself to undo the handcuffs and Bugs visibly shrank on his feet and stumbled and uncaring about his nakedness or his pants, flopped with nerveless abandon into the spare chair.

Give him his due, Bugs had been silent throughout the flogging but now looked visibly shaken and quite at sorts about the sexy fun he expected for his birthday.

They dressed slowly, Bugs settled-up with the short guy and the Three Musketeers, waddling like they had defecated in their trousers back to where their drivers were parked and waving a silent wave of goodbye to each other, went home to cry in the privacy of their own bathrooms.

The next week they ventured out and met at Lookie Lookie and immediately upon arrival and while their whiskeys were being prepared, Bugs nodded for them to follow him to the bog.

In that room, our Tart exposed his pink and slightly red bot, T&A undid and dropped his khecks and the boys admired his firm, but thoroughly red-turning-to-orange-aged- bruised buttocks.

Then Bugs gingerly exposed his posterior. His two buns were black and I mean black with that almost metallic Ethiopian blue tinge, and there were stretch-like marks in the skin which was obviously forever damaged. There were some slightly weeping red spots with dribbling lymph, the whole a sorry and obviously painful mess, a poor to very poor birthday gift to himself.

Demonia Bar shut shortly thereafter, probably having inadvertently thrashed a senior local official by mistake and lost their licence and so I never actually ventured through the doors and I submit that loss seems like another serendipitous moment of happy fate.

*****

APPENDIX

A brief summary of The Calls in Gentleman's Spoof:

0. 'Spoof'
1. 'Joe Toupai' or 'The dirty digit'
2. 'Endacott 2' or 'Absent friends' or 'Balls two'
3. 'Flowers 3' – always available or 'Big Mac' or the Straight Bat
4. 'Skins' or Jewish Hospital
5. 'Titanic' 'Belgrano' or any capital ship that sank (cinq) or 'Funf' in a very loud voice
6. Six or 'Axis' (reversed)
7. 'Mission (from Heaven)' or 'Neves' (reversed) or James Bond (007)
8. 'Harry (Tate)' Harry never pays
9. 'German virgin' – she always says Nien!
10. 'Kiwi Tin' or 'Marine's breakfast'
11. 'Legs' or 'Dead African Parrot' or any recently deceased celebrity
12. 'The Imperial' (dozen)
13. 'The Baker's' (dozen)
14. 'Panties' or 'Drawers' – Quatorze
15. 'Film Festival' – Cannes – Quinze
16. 'Neil Sedaka' – sweet sixteen
17. 'Beatles' – she was just seventeen
18. 'Two thirds' (Nelson) – see 27
19. 'Vietnam' – n,n,n,n… Nineteen
20. 'Score'
21. 'Key to the door'
22. 'Ducks' (two little)
23. 'St George' – 23rd April (St. George's Day)
24. 'Tulsa' (Twenty-four hours from) or Gene Pitney
25. 'Quarter' (quarter century)
26. 'Boxing Day' – 26th December
27. 'Full Nelson' – 27 years in captivity

There are some slight local Thai – Asian embellishments for Six with some piquancy:

6. "Horton Six" calling first in a school of 3 and showing that you are holding 3.
6. "Douche Bag Six" calling first in a school of 4 and showing that you are holding 3.

Printed in Great Britain
by Amazon

49200725R00159